Understanding Digital Games

Edited by
Jason Rutter and Jo Bryce

SAGE Publications

London • Thousand Oaks • New Delhi

First published 2006

SAGE Publications Ltd
1 Oliver's Yard
55 City Road
London EC1Y 1SP

SAGE Publications Inc.
2455 Teller Road
Thousand Oaks, California 91320

SAGE Publications India Pvt Ltd
B-42, Panchsheel Enclave
Post Box 4109
New Delhi 110 017

British Library Cataloguing in Publication data

A catalogue record for this book is available
from the British Library

ISBN-10 1-4129-0033-6   ISBN-13 978-1-4129-0033-1
ISBN-10 1-4129-0034-4 (pbk)   ISBN-13 978-1-4129-0034-8

Library of Congress Control Number available

Typeset by C&M Digitals (P) Ltd., Chennai, India
Printed in Great Britain by The Alden Press, Oxford
Printed on paper from sustainable resources

Contents ● ● ●

Contributors ● ● ●

Alberto Alvisi has taught Web Economy at the University of Ferrara since 2001. He held a fellowship at the University of Naples Parthenope in relation to a two-year research project regarding knowledge transfer between small- and medium-sized firms. His research, in addition to digital gaming and competition between systemic products, focuses primarily on new product development as a strategic tool, organizational change, and on the debate between relational and resource-based views of firms.

Jo Bryce is a senior lecturer in Psychology at the University of Central Lancashire. She has extensive research experience on the psychological and social aspects of information communications technologies (ICTs), including mobile devices, the Internet and computer gaming. This research falls into three broad categories: the consequences of ICT use; access constraints to ICTs with a specific focus on gender; and the development of regulatory policies. Her recent work has included editing special editions on digital gaming for *Game Studies* (2003) and *Information, Communication and Society* (2003) and research projects including work on mobile entertainment (European Commission) and counterfeiting (Northern Ireland Office).

Garry Crawford is a senior lecturer in Sociology at Sheffield Hallam University. His research focuses primarily on media audiences and fan cultures. In particular, he has published on sport fan culture, including the book *Consuming Sport* (Routledge, 2004) and, more recently, digital gaming patterns. He is the former editor of the British Sociological Association newsletter 'Network' and is an editorial board member for *Sociological Research Online*.

Tim Dumbleton works for the British Educational Communications and Technology Agency (Becta), the UK Government's lead agency for the use of ICT in education. He manages Becta's advice services aimed at educational content developers. As part of this work, he is responsible for monitoring research and practice related to the use of digital games in educational settings, providing advice to developers about using aspects of games in educational resources and for maintaining dialogue with the games industry. Tim was also involved in setting up Becta's Computer Games in Education Project (2001–2). The Project's reports along with more recent publications are available from the Research section of the Becta website http://www. becta.org.uk/research

Seth Giddings teaches in the School of Cultural Studies at the University of the West of England. He researches the relationships between technology and culture, most recently video games and video game play as everyday techno-culture. He has written on popular film, animation and new media, and also teaches digital media production, with particular interests in the theory and practice of interactive media and the digital moving image.

Martin Hand is an assistant professor in the Department of Sociology at Queen's University, Ontario. His principal areas of research and publication are digital cultural practices, Internet discourse and politics, domestic cultures of technology and consumption. His current research develops theoretical frameworks for analysing aspects of digital photography in Canadian society.

Helen W. Kennedy is a senior lecturer at the University of West England and chair of the Play Research Group. Her areas of research include the body, cyberculture, gender and technology, computer games and play as well as the relationships between bodies, machines and techno-culture. Recent publications have included *Game Cultures* with Jon Dovey (Open University Press, 2006) and several chapters and journal articles on games, gender and culture.

Aphra Kerr is a lecturer at the National University of Ireland at Maynooth, in the Republic of Ireland. She is author of *The Business and Culture of Digital Games: Gamework/Gameplay* (Sage, 2006) and a number of journal articles and book chapters exploring globalization and digital games production, the social construction of gender and player pleasures and digital games. Aphra is a founding member of the Digital Games Research Association (DiGRA) and is a committee member of Women in Games. She is an academic member of the International Game Development Association (IGDA) committee in Ireland and runs the online resource www.gamedevelopers.ie

Geoff King is co-author of *Tomb Raiders and Space Invaders: Videogame Forms and Contexts* (IB Tauris, 2006) and co-editor of *ScreenPlay: Cinema/Videogames/Interfaces* (Wallflower Press, 2002). His has also written a number of books about cinema including *American Independent Cinema* (IB Tauris, 2005), *New Hollywood Cinema: An Introduction* (IB Tauris, 2002), *Film Comedy* (Wallflower Press, 2002) and *Spectacular Narratives: Hollywood in the Age of the Blockbuster* (IB Tauris, 2000). He is a reader in Film and TV Studies at Brunel University, London.

John Kirriemuir is a consultant specializing in the use of computer and video games in the education sector. He has surveyed the use of such games in schools, uncovering and analysing many cases where purely commercial games have been used in curriculum-related classroom scenarios. He has written over 20 papers and articles on this issue, and presented at a number of international conferences.

Tanya Krzywinska is a reader in Film and TV Studies at Brunel University. She is the author of *A Skin For Dancing In: Possession, Witchcraft and Voodoo in Film* (Flicks Books, 2000), *Sex and the Cinema* (Wallflower Press, forthcoming), co-author of *Science Fiction Cinema* (Wallflower Press, 2000), *Tomb Raiders and Space Invaders: Videogame Forms and Contexts* (IB Tauris, 2006) and co-editor of *ScreenPlay: Cinema/Videogames/Interfaces* (Wallflower Press, 2002). She has recently begun work on *Imaginary Worlds: A Cross-media Study of the Aesthetic, Formal and Interpolative Strategies of Virtual Worlds in Popular Media*.

Julian Kücklich is a PhD student at the Centre for Media Research, University of Ulster, Coleraine, where he is working on a dissertation on The Politics of Play in the New Media Industry. He holds an MA in German and American Literature from Ludwigs-Maximilians

University, Munich. He has published several papers on the semiotics, aesthetics and textuality of digital games, and blogs at http://particlestream.motime.com.

Karenza Moore works at the Information Systems Institute at the University of Salford as a research associate on the 'Women in IT' project (WINIT). Previously she was a research associate at the ESRC Centre for Research on Innovation and Competition (CRIC) based at the University of Manchester. Her PhD, undertaken while at the University of Surrey, looked at corporate and consumer versions of the future in relation to mobile communication technologies. Her other long-term principal research interest is in UK club culture and related substance use. She also co-runs 'Out of the Blue', an up-and-coming trance night in Manchester.

Jason Rutter is a research fellow at the ESRC Centre for Research on Innovation and Competition at the University of Manchester. His research and publication interests centre on social aspects of the use of leisure technologies – especially digital gaming, consumption and counterfeits – online communities and computer-mediated interaction. He has edited several collections on digital gaming including *Digital Games Industries* (Ashgate, forthcoming), chaired a number of international conferences and sat on the Executive Board for the Digital Games Research Association (DiGRA).

Cath Sullivan is a senior lecturer in Psychology at the University of Central Lancashire. Her research interests include gender, telework, work and family roles, and the gendering of technology. Cath has published mainly in the areas of telework, gender and the work–family interface, is on the Editorial Board of *Community, Work and Family*, is a judge on the annual Rosabeth Kanter Award for Excellence in Work–Family Research and is a Member of the Steering Group of the European Social Fund WINIT (Women in IT) project at Salford University.

Jonathan Sykes is one of Scotland's leading digital game academics. He currently heads the eMotion Laboratory, a premier facility based at Glasgow Caledonian University used to measure emotional engagement with game-based technologies. The laboratory provides both academics and outside organizations with the tools to capture subtle palettes of human emotion without intrusion upon the user experience. He is a regular contributor to both academic and lay debate on video game technology, having appeared on a number of television programmes including the BBC's *Child of Our Time* and *Tomorrow's World*.

Preface and Acknowledgements

This book is about 'digital games'. This we have chosen as an umbrella term for our object of study and we use it to include everything from the earliest experimental games running in research laboratories to contemporary cutting edge games.

The focus in this collection is on commercially available games rather than those developed primarily for training or therapeutic objectives. However, this does give us the opportunity to explore the ways in which a series of interrelated sectors have evolved to make what we now recognize as the digital games industry. It allows us to see how what was once the province of enthusiasts and bedroom coders has now become a large international industry where licences, development and publishing costs exceed millions of dollars. This is an industry that draws on a highly skilled labour force and which, like other developed parts of the cultural industries, has had to develop an awareness of intellectual property protection, branding and contract negotiation, as well as an imperative to produce quality games which attract both hardcore and more casual games in order to survive.

Digital games are remarkable in the way they are built with, and onto, ever-changing technologies that have increasingly become part of our households. Further, whether we are gamers or not, these games are now part of our broader mediascape as we pass digital games machines in shopping arcades, watch films based upon game narratives, and see game characters advertising products from broadband to soft drinks.

Having been part of a growing industry since the 1970s, digital games are increasingly part of our popular culture too. Television shows such as *The Simpsons* often reference digital games. This intertextuality also runs the other way as *The Simpsons* licence has been used in over twenty digital games running from *The Simpsons Pinball* in 1990 to *The Simpsons Hit and Run* in 2003. While we do not want to generalize too radically from a single example, that such references are written into a programme as successful as *The Simpsons* suggests that there is a sizable audience culturally sensitive enough to understand them.

Similarly, developments in the computer generated imagery (CGI) used in Hollywood films have often grown in a similar direction to the imagery used in digital games: films such as *Tron* (1982) drew heavily on game style imagery, the potential of scenes included in *Star Wars: Episode 1 – The Phantom Menace* (1999), such as the pod race or those featuring Trade Federation battle droids, to be translated into digital games by Lucas Arts was apparent, and films such as the *Toy Story* series or *The Matrix* trilogy appeared to consciously blur texts and imagery used in both game and film.

However, this is by no means an indication that digital games have become part of modern culture in an uncontested manner. Debates continue over evidence and opinion about the impacts of digital gaming. The social consequences of gaming, whether they relate to education, antisocial behaviour, gender or exposure of minors to harmful content, continue to be the site of much interest for academics, policy makers and game developers.

As such, even if one does not engage with digital games, it is difficult not to be aware of their importance as a contemporary cultural phenomenon. The manner in which digital games stand at a node of such a wide range of cultural, technological, political, aesthetic and economic forces is one reason why they have increasingly been the focus of academic research and analysis.

At their best, digital games have shown the potential for new ways of developing and telling stories and worked towards joining the engagement we have with media such as television, film and music with the sense of interaction found in face-to-face communication. They have become a focus for new enthusiasms, expertise and communities that share game playing tips, strategies and opinions. While it remains to be seen whether these potentials are realized as significantly transformative, it is already apparent that digital games sit at the centre of a significant combination of cultural, industrial, technological and social phenomena.

Understanding Digital Games provides a broad collection of work across the different areas of digital games research. Together, the chapters in this book detail a range of possible theoretical and practical approaches to examining digital games and offers a wide variety of resources and tools. After the Introduction, this book is divided into three parts each with a slightly different focus on understanding digital games: 'History and production', 'Theories and approaches' and 'Key debates'.

● History and production

This first part of the book outlines four approaches to understanding the historical, economic and design contexts of digital game production and how these shape the nature of the games we see for sale and the way we buy them. John Kirriemuir provides a thumbnail history of the development of digital game technologies. He details innovations from experiments in early computer technologies to the innovative platforms of today and the emergence of mobile gaming and massively multiplayer online games. He highlights the ways in which the evolution of games has been profoundly linked to the development of gaming technologies and provides detailed examples of key milestones and technologies from the history of digital games.

In Chapter 3, Aphra Kerr explores the 'business' of producing digital games in a contemporary, international market. She draws on a variety of resources to indicate the economic worth of the digital games industry and looks at how this consumer spend is distributed across different technology platforms. She details the relationship between the various sectors of the digital games industry from pre-development to retail and provides a view of how a game moves between these sectors and how revenue generated by sales is distributed across the various agencies involved. Through this she offers a systematic understanding of how these 'key segments' are organized.

Complementing this, Alberto Alvisi's chapter provides a clear exposition of how the basic concepts of economics can inform our understanding of the digital games industry. By introducing key concepts such as 'economies of scale', 'tie ratio' and 'market structures', Alvisi provides an understanding of why digital games and their associated platforms are priced in the way they are. He explores both the production (industry) and demand (consumer) side of the digital games market drawing from current and previous generations of digital games. He persuasively argues that the current landscape of the digital games industry is not merely an artefact of chance but the consequence of issues such as time of entry into new markets, branding, technological innovation and network effects.

While also looking at the production side of digital games, Jon Sykes takes a different viewpoint. His chapter takes a more practitioner-orientated position by looking at the various stages of digital games design. He offers a set of conceptual tools that both those designing games and those wishing to understand the design process can use.

Sykes argues for the importance of developing and maintaining a clear picture of a game's target player within the development process. This, he suggests, is possible by examining the demographics of digital game players and by developing various 'persona' who act as archetypical players of the finished game. He argues that by considering types of gameplay, game themes, methods of learning, user feedback and balance of challenge in a game, and relating these to the player, it is possible to be reflexive about the range of choices open to the game designer.

Theories and approaches

Part Two of this book more clearly concentrates on individual academic disciplines. Each of the chapters outlines key perspectives, theorists and literatures in a specific academic field to demonstrate their relevance to, and use in, approaching the study of digital games and investigating their specific qualities and traits. Drawing upon these, each chapter highlights both the strengths and some of the potential limitations of associated theoretical and methodological approaches.

Julian Kücklich takes the literary aspects of digital games as his object of focus and highlights those elements of games most closely linked to other forms of fiction and narrative texts. He questions how applicable literary theory is to a range of digital games and suggests that elements of poetics, hermeneutics and aesthetics all have a part to play in sensitively analysing games. However, for Kücklich it is not only the textual elements of digital games that make them literary-like. For him, the way both readers and gamers build resources for understanding conventions and develop expectations through which they order their engagement with the cultural object are similar. Only through playing digital games do we gain a tacit understanding of the 'rules' that govern them and their relationship to other texts.

Whereas literary studies can profitably be used to understand the lexical elements of the digital games text, Chapter 7 demonstrates the range of analytical approaches that exist within film studies through which to engage with their visual elements. The argument that King and Krzywinska develop is not that digital games are interactive films but that many games draw upon formal techniques, genres and conventions developed within film-making. As such, film studies provides a range of concepts which are available to aid their study. The chapter looks at how increasingly sophisticated in-game cut scenes are used to provide film-like establishing shots. It illustrates how filmic techniques are employed to develop narrative and how 3D rendering within the game, like film, uses an organization of point of view to manage different atmospheres and relationships between the viewer and the onscreen characters. Importantly, King and Krzywinska point out that some of the issues often raised in objection to application of film theory to digital games, such as the breaking of linear narrative or the emphasis on spectacle over story, are cinematic features which are also apparent in contemporary film.

Whereas the evolution of film has been profoundly intertwined with the development of film-making technologies, Chapter 8 examines digital games as a product of new media. Rather than emphasizing the continuity of digital games with other forms, Giddings and Kennedy argue that the computer-based medium of digital gaming offers new experiences which are not present in interactions with other cultural products. They highlight the ways in which digital games have offered new opportunities for consumers of texts to be simultaneously producers and consumers of new texts – most notably through the modding of games or design of new character skins. They also argue that by approaching digital games as new media it is possible to recognize the importance of the user's interaction with technology and the way in which it is vital to progressing and developing games and player experiences.

The final two chapters in this part of the book investigate how digital games fit within social and political contexts. Chapter 9 explores the playing of digital games as part of the organization, production, text and audience of culture. Crawford and Rutter explore the ways in which digital games can be seen as cultural products which are embedded within the political and social organization of our lives. To do this they detail how British and European cultural studies – from the politically informed work of Adorno and the Birmingham School to the theories of postmodernity put forward by Baudrillard and Baumann – can provide ways to understand the processes involved in the production and consumption of digital games culture. For them, the practice of 'doing' digital gaming involves a negotiation of the tension between the possibilities of digital games to control and commoditize gamers as consumers of a cultural product and the opportunity that they have as popular texts offering new forms of cultural resistance and expression.

The practices associated with playing digital games are an issue developed by Hand and Moore as they look at the role of community and identity in gaming environments. Examining digital gaming as a social activity, they explore how the sociological notions of communities of presence, imagined and virtual communities are useful in describing and understanding interactions including LAN parties and massively multiplayer online games. However, for Hand and Moore part of the importance of these gaming communities is to be found not only in the interactions themselves but in the possibilities they provide for identity development and identity play. They distinguish between the identity developed through engagement with gaming technologies – that is, being a gamer – and use of virtual environments to create characters, identities or 'multiple selves' online.

Key debates ●

The final part of this collection takes a more interdisciplinary orientated perspective by looking at several key themes which routinely reoccur in digital games research.

In Chapter 11, Bryce, Rutter and Sullivan explore the relationship between gender and digital gaming in a number of ways. After outlining an understanding of gender as a social rather than biological phenomenon, they examine measures of female participation in digital gaming and demonstrate how this differs from that of males and varies across different countries. They argue that this is due, in part, to gender differences in access to technology, space and leisure time in both domestic and public gaming environments. They also detail differences in the gendering of game content and consolidate literature that demonstrates the manner in which digital games are often designed to appeal to male leisure preferences and interests, or objectify female characters in a sexual manner.

Engaging with another recurrent debate, Bryce and Rutter turn their attention to violence and digital games in Chapter 12. They explore the literature which examines the proposed links between playing digital games and aggressive behaviour, placing it within the context of broader debates concerning media engagement. They critically review the often conflicting experimental research and associated literature. The authors explore this divergence by questioning the issue of causality which underpins claims for the negative consequences of exposure to game violence and the profound problem of claiming to define and measure aggression within a limited timescale and controlled environment. Bryce and Rutter conclude that despite the rigour of much of the experimental research exploring aggression and digital games, it has tended to reduce the social and contextual elements of digital gaming which inform so much of its real world context and enjoyment.

The final chapter of this book examines what is perhaps the opposite end of the games and media effects debate as it covers current developments in the use of digital games within an educational context. Dumbleton and Kirriemuir place digital games as a technology that most schoolchildren have grown up using and have a high level of competence and literacy in using. They explore the different types of digital games from educational simulations to the use of commercial games which can be used to develop skills for extracting and interpreting data, hypothesis building and testing. Through a series of case studies the authors examine the benefits of using digital games in the classroom and also the potential difficulties associated with establishing clear learning outcomes, providing training for teachers, and the cost of developing and implementing quality digital games within an educational context.

With this collection we have attempted to provide a valuable resource for those approaching the study of digital games for the first time or those wanting to develop an understanding of approaches outside their own discipline. However, like a guidebook to an unfamiliar destination, the full value of this book can only be realized as its readers take the information contained within and combine it with their own experiences and perspectives on digital gaming. It is only then that the potential of the multidisciplinarity of the work presented here becomes apparent and possible syntheses and contradictions present themselves. The perspectives which this book outlines will provide opportunities to develop the reflexive knowledge and skills necessary to understand digital gaming.

As one would expect from a research area so intimately linked with the development of new technologies and the communication potential of the Internet, both individual academics and research teams have developed a web presence for the study of digital games. A wide and expanding range of web sites are now online, each of which provides a different set of resources, perspectives and information on the current state of the art for digital games research. At the end of each chapter in this book there is a list of web sites that are of relevance to those wishing to further explore the ideas developed in the chapter. While every effort has been made to choose examples of well-established sites which have demonstrated a good level of stability, it is in the nature of the Internet that pages will move and sites become defunct. Where pages are no longer available, it is worth trying the 'Wayback Machine' offered at the Internet Archive – www.archive.org – which offers the ability to search archive versions of web pages by date.

Acknowledgements

Jo Bryce would like to express her gratitude to all those closest to her – family, friends and colleagues – who have supported her throughout her career, and in the work of editing this book. Too numerous to name, each of them knows who they are, as well as the importance of their support, guidance and good humour. She would also like to thank Jason Rutter for all his hard work on this and many other projects and for generally accepting her attempts at sentence trimming and punctuation.

Jason Rutter would like to thank his colleagues at the ESRC Centre for Research on Innovation and Competition at the University of Manchester, especially Stan Metcalfe, Rod Coombs, Ronnie Ramlogan, Dale Southerton and Bruce Tether for their interest and support of his curiosity for research into digital games. He would also like to thank Liz Fay. Thanks, of course, go to his organized co-editor, Jo Bryce, for curbing his worst excesses of verbosity and overly long sentences. Jason would like to dedicate his work on this book to his father, Derek Rutter, who, by buying him his first computer for educational purposes, is probably responsible for both his career as an academic and interest in digital games. He continues to be a powerful role model.

Together, the editors would like to express our indebtedness and thanks to Julia Hall, our commissioning editor at Sage, for allowing us to produce this book, her enthusiasm for the project and her continued patience when things did not entirely go to schedule. It has been a pleasure to work with her. Finally, we are also very grateful to the contributing authors who made this book possible. Their understanding of both digital games and their chosen discipline have enabled this collection to be both rich and varied and their ability to express their knowledge in a clear and coherent manner has undoubtedly enriched our understanding of digital games.

The editors and publisher wish to thank the following for permission to use their material:

Monolith Productions for Figure 6.3 from *No One Lives Forever, No One Lives Forever* is a trademark of Sierra Entertainment, Inc. in the US and other countries. *A Spy in H.A.R.M.'s Way* is a trademark of Monolith Productions, Inc.

Sony Computer Entertainment Europe for Figure 7.2 from *Primal Primal*™© Sony Computer Entertainment Europe. Developed by SCEE Cambridge Studio. All rights reserved.

EA Games for Figure 7.4 from *Black and White 2.*

The Entertainment and Leisure Software Publishers Association (ELSPA) for Figure 11.1.

Every effort has been made to trace all the copyright holders for permission to print material in this book but if any have been inadvertently overlooked the publishers will be grateful to hear from the copyright holder and will undertake to make the necessary arrangements in future editions of this book.

1 An introduction to understanding digital games

Jo Bryce and Jason Rutter

Academic interest in digital games has a history dating back to the early 1980s. Papers such as Hemnes' (1982) consideration of the application of copyright to support creativity in the digital games industry; the work of Sedlak et al. (1982) exploring the development of social integration through recreational programming for people with learning disabilities; the case report by McCowan (1981) of 'Space Invader wrist' (a minor ligament strain which we would probably now refer to as repetitive strain injury [RSI]); and Sudnow's (1983) much neglected book on the process of acquiring 'digital skill', indicate how rapidly researchers were responding to the new leisure technologies. There is also a pre-history that dates back as far as Alexander Douglas' PhD – part of which involved what appears to be the development of the first computer game in the early 1950s (see Kirriemuir, Chapter 2) – concerned less with social and cultural factors than elements of technology innovation and system design.

Unfortunately, this resource of digital games analysis is often not fully credited by contemporary authors. For example, Wolf and Perron (2003) suggest that their collection would not have previously been possible because of a lack of academics working on digital games and Newman (2004) suggests that academics have ignored digital games. The trope that digital games have been neglected by researchers and marginalized by the academy is problematic given the lack of substantive evidence provided. There is, of course, a difference between a topic being overlooked and being ignored – there is no malice or intentionality in the former. Suggesting that digital games have not received the academic attention they deserve because they have been framed as 'a children's medium' or 'mere trifles' (Newman 2004: 5) is difficult to accept without sources for these accusations. Neither does such a position help us explain how digital games are notably different from other ephemera and mundane practices that researchers have engaged with, such as music (Hatch and Watson, 1974; Sudnow, 1978) or humour (Jefferson, 1979; Sacks, 1978 – even Rutter, 2000).

Despite claims concerning a lack of research on digital games, examining the digital games bibliographies available on the Internet[1] makes it clear that research on digital games has for some time been thematically and disciplinarily diverse. Perhaps rather than a shift in the structure of academia, the recent surge in publications about digital games reflects the entry of researchers who grew up in the *Pong*, Atari, NES and BBC Micro years into academia.

A failure to address these existing bodies of digital games literature in contemporary research carries with it a number of consequences. First, it removes our ability to build upon this work or, to draw on the sociologist Robert Merton's phraseology, removes from us the possibility to 'stand on the shoulders of giants' (1965: 9).[2] Second, by not situating research in what has preceded, work runs the risk of unquestioningly assuming that this research has no precedents. This is a tenuous assumption and one which, unless critically evaluated, runs the risk of undermining contemporary academic research on digital gaming. Exploring a similar theme in the introduction to her collection, *Virtual Methods*, Hine writes about Internet research:

> Perspectives for the sociology of scientific knowledge are an important reminder not to take for granted the discontinuities between what we are doing now and what has gone before. These distinctions are achieved in the ways we research and write about the new technologies and the ways in which we organize our disciplinary boundaries. (Hine, 2005: 6–7)

Through recognizing previous work as well as discontinuities and understanding these as a process of academic development and evolution it is, however, possible to show that the amount of research on digital games is growing. A simple search of articles in the ISI Web of Knowledge's database of journal publication shows an almost twofold increase in peer reviewed papers on digital games when comparing the periods 1995–1999 and 2000–2004. In the earlier years there were 275 articles containing the phrases computer games(s) or video games(s) and this rose to a total of 535 during the following five years. While such a comparison may not be scientifically rigorous, it does offer an indication of a significant rise in research and publication activity in the area

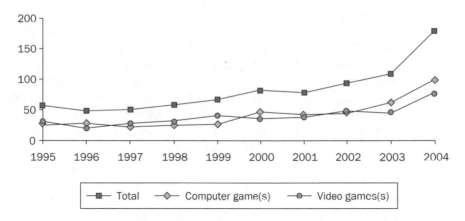

Figure 1.1   *Number of digital games articles published, 1995–2004*

of digital games. This is growth we can expect to be maintained for sometime, especially as research begins to include developments in new areas of technological innovation that have game relevance such as digital television and mobile telecommunications.

This publishing has taken place across disciplines. The growth in papers about digital games across the sciences, social sciences, and the arts and humanities serves to highlight the rich diversity of interest in digital games, as well as the great potential for work that involves cooperation between different disciplines and methodological perspectives. As Wolf and Perron convincingly point out:

> [T]he emerging field of video game theory is itself a convergence of a wide variety of approaches including film and television theory, semiotics, performance theory game studies, literary theory, computer science, theories of hypertext, cybertext, interactivity, identity, postmodernism, ludology, media theory, narratology, aesthetics and art theory, psychology, theories of simulacra, and others. (2003: 2)

We could spend time adding systematically to this list but it is perhaps more practical to adopt Aarseth's approach which suggests that interest in digital games is so broad that a 'more or less complete list reads like the A–Z list of subjects from a major university' (Aarseth, 2003: 1). Such a perspective highlights how digital games have become of empirical and theoretical interest for an impressively wide range of researchers, each of whom bring to the debate a different set of methodologies, theoretical perspectives and questions they seek to answer about/with digital games.

This book is an attempt to pull together the diversity and richness of research on digital games, and the disciplinary tools and approaches that can be used to investigate them. This collection celebrates the fact that research on digital games provides great opportunities for exploring the potential links and divisions between the different academic areas, which characterize this emerging disciplinarily diverse field. It attempts to avoid being over prescriptive about developing a single approach or set of methods or theoretical assumptions and is structured to encourage reading across chapters in order to explore the ways in which different disciplines investigate digital games. This approach, we hope, will encourage readers to explore both familiar and innovative paths of research and develop a broad background knowledge with which to investigate digital games, the practices of gaming, and the socio-economic and political factors that facilitate and control it. Our aim is that the chapters will provide the intellectual resources for multidisciplinary digital games research. We hope that the variety of theoretical and methodological approaches outlined by the included authors will provide knowledge of the various disciplinary perspectives available to those exploring the field, and encourage the reader to formulate their own research interests in digital games.

● A market context to digital games research

The growth in digital games research may be a reflection of changes outside academic research. Indeed, the placing of digital games research against the backdrop of the global digital games market is not unusual in writing in the area. The combination of impressive market value and increasingly powerful technology is a frequent starting point in a substantial amount of writing on digital games (Bryce and Rutter, 2003; Kline et al. 2003; Provenzo, 1991).

According to data published by the American-based Entertainment Software Association (ESA, 2005), the US digital games market was worth US $7.3 billion dollars[3] in 2004. Similar figures suggest that the value of digital games for Europe was €5.6 billion.[4] (ELSPA, 2005b) and highlight the UK as the world's third largest market for digital games (after the USA and Japan). In the UK software and hardware combined are worth more than £2.2 billion[5] (ELSPA, 2005a), with software accounting for £1.2 billion[6] of that figure (ELSPA, 2005b). In the UK, digital games account for approximately half of the market for toys and games (Euromonitor, 2004) and, for 2003, the market was estimated at being worth between £1.26 billion (ELSPA, 2004) and £2.1 billion (Euromonitor, 2004).

Such figures are almost ritually introduced at the beginning of many publications on digital games research and these figures are indeed impressively large. However, these figures are less frequently placed within a comparative context through which one can understand their implications. As research into digital games continues to grow it is useful to revisit these market overviews and question whether they actually demonstrate as much as we might hope or assume.

To support the idea of digital games as a cultural revolution represented by market worth, headlines in the press and some academic discourses claim that digital gaming is now 'worth more than the television or film industry' (Dimitrov, 2005). However, like many eye catching headlines, such claims only show part of the picture and report data in a slightly more spectacular manner than the generators of the data might be entirely comfortable with. The digital games market is indeed comparable to box office receipts – but this is just one element of revenue generated by the film industry. Recognizing that the market for pre-recorded DVDs in the USA was approximately equal to the global market for box office takings during 2002 places such claims into context. When other film industry revenues are added including hardware sales, video sales and rentals, licences, merchandizing, and so forth, on a global scale, the total market values become much less symmetrical.

Although a rationale for studying digital games is often based upon the reported size of the market, it is seldom made clear that the figures quoted compare to more mundane markets such as insurance, credit card services, large kitchen appliances or fast food. Comparing figures from Euromonitor and other industry sources gives a backdrop to the relative UK and global markets for consumer and business products and services. In the UK, digital games are worth approximately half as much again as 'paints and coatings', while the fast food market is worth about three and a half times more.

Such rankings of market values do not necessarily convert neatly into a similar ordering for unit sales, so we must be careful not to take market value as a proxy for number of people involved in an activity.

TABLE 1.1 Value of digital games and other UK markets

Market	Annual value	Year[1]
Credit and charge cards (UK)	£131.7 billion	2002
Insurance premiums (UK)	£125.5 billion	n.d.[2]
Advertising (UK)	£16.2 billion	2002
Kitchen appliances (UK)	£13.6 billion	2003
Mail order and home shopping (UK)	£12.1 billion	2003
DVD sale and rentals (USA)	£11.2 billion	2002[3]
Box Office (Global)	£11.1 billion	2002[4]
Digital games (Global)	**£10.2 billion**	**2002[5]**
Newspapers (UK)	£7.7 billion	2003[6]
Gambling (UK)	£7.7 billion	2003
Fast food and home delivery/takeaway (UK)	£7.4 billion	2003
Footwear (UK)	£5.1 billion	2003
Courier services (UK)	£4.8 billion	2002
Networking hardware (UK)	£3.0 billion	2002
DVD and video software (UK)	£2.9 billion	2004[7]
Digital games (UK)	**£2.1 billion**	**2003**
PC business software (UK)	£1.6 billion	2002
Paints and coatings (UK)	£1.4 billion	2003
Batteries (UK)	£0.4 billion	2002

[1] Year for which the estimate is given rather than year of publication of estimate

[2] Association of British Insurers, see www.abi.org.uk

[3] Converted from Digital Entertainment Group's estimate of US $20.3 billion, see http://www.dvd information.com

[4] Converted from Screen Digest estimate of US $20 billion, see http://www.screendigest. com/ezine/0311

[5] Converted from Screen Digest (2003) estimate of US $18.5 billion

[6] KPMG, see http://www.kpmg.co.uk/news/detail.cfm?pr=1954

[7] IVF (2004)

For example, whereas the average price for a DVD in Europe is €10.99 (IVF, 2004), digital games have tended to maintain a relatively high unit price for consumers. A top level console game may have an initial shelf price of almost US $50/€50/£40, while only older titles released as part of, for example, The Platinum Collection for the PlayStation 2, Xbox Classics, or Players' Choice for the GameCube, have prices comparable to those for general film DVDs.

There has developed a body of work examining digital games as an economic market (see for example Aoyama and Izushi, 2003; Castronova, 2006; Hayes and Dinsey, 1995; Kline et al., 2003; Readman and Grantham, 2004), but the success of this work lies in the way it has developed, refined and applied analyses to difference aspects of digital gaming and games. Each of these authors has taken a different approach to exploring the economics of the digital games industry, rather than justifying their research through headline figures. This differs from work that claims, sometimes implicitly, that digital games markets are notably large, and that this in itself justifies the investigation of their products as cultural artefacts.

Digital games are undoubtedly a successful market showing an impressive year-on-year growth, but this does not make them unique as an object of study – a solely economic rationale for studying games would, objectively, make them less interesting than washing machines and other white goods. However, one of the things that differentiate digital games from many of the other markets in Table 1.1 is that they are a leisure good purchased with disposable income. For both the economist and the socio-cultural researcher this opens up a variety of interesting questions concerning value, consumer choice, networks and so forth that tend to be hidden when relying on reporting market size alone. It is these implications, rather than the absolute value of the market itself, which are perhaps the most interesting of observations to develop.

Digital games as a new research challenge ●

A number of authors have argued that digital games present a departure from previous cultural or technological artefacts, and that in order to understand them we must develop a whole new research and practical approach (see, for example, Aarseth, 2003; Eskelinen, 2001; Lowood, 2002). The general rationale of such authors is that digital games present a new use of technology, which is profoundly linked to leisure, creativity and play and, as such, are a unique category without comparison. This has led to claims that, as Wolf (2001: 2) puts it, 'video games are already widespread and unique enough [sic] to deserve their own branch of theory'.

Wolf stresses the aesthetic content of digital games to suggest that research into digital games 'adds new concepts to existing ideas in moving imagery theory, such as those concerning the game's interface, player action, interactivity, navigation, and algorithmic structures' (2001: 3). However, this emphasis on discontinuity prevents any significant comparison with other new technologies. Digital games (or rather their design and play) may well draw on the issues Wolf highlights, but are they really unique in doing so? Do many of these issues have equal relevance to other forms of multimedia design, head-up displays in fighter planes (or racing driver's helmets) and programming structures in general?

Similarly, Aarseth argues that digital games are intrinsically different to other types of games. In his manifesto for the study of games he suggests that the aesthetics of games was not studied prior to digital games and, as such, it is digital games that have brought this change as they become 'much closer to the ideal object of the humanities, the work of art ... become visible and textualizable for the aesthetic observer' (2003: 1). While a stark contrast between digital games and their non-digital or earlier equivalents may seem plausible, closer inspection makes this contrast less straightforward. Indeed, when looking at the development of games it is not clear that a simple digital/non-digital divide is tenable or where the paradigmatic shift, so clear to Aarseth, from 'traditional' to digital contrast takes place.[7]

That digital games are unlike other games or sport in the manner in which they are built upon technology may be true but, made simply, this assertion can hide the fact that leisure and technology have long been linked in their development and practice. This relationship between technology and leisure, whether it be developments in tennis racket manufacture (the use of graphite-reinforced materials) the development (and legislation against) pinball machines in the USA or the use of technology to restrict access to leisure sites, has been discussed elsewhere (see Bryce, 2000).

As a games-related example, think of a simple shooting gallery game, such as one of the numerous Flash and shareware games that can be found on the Internet. As a game, this could be compared and contrasted with a game in which rocks are thrown at cans staked along the top of the fence. It may be clear that the digital game is a technological simulation of the low technology version of the game. In the digital game, technology replaces the physical action of throwing. However, by replacing the rocks with the shooting of an air rifle, we can mediate the throwing action with technology without going digital. A move towards mechanical arcade games, such as Midway's *Submarine* (in which the player looks through a periscope and 'fires' light at ships which have photosensitive cells on them), further pushes the mediated and simulated aspects of the game. It is also an example of a game that cannot be played outside the technological framework.

Of course, Aarseth is wise enough to refine his rhetoric into a more sustainable understanding of what digital games might be through his idea of 'games in virtual environments', which would include 'games from *Tetris* via *Drug Wars* to *EverQuest*, while computerized toys like

Furby and dice and card games like Blackjack are excluded. Non-computerized simulation games like Monopoly or Dungeons and Dragons would not be excluded' (Aarseth, 2003: 2). However, by shifting his definition Aarseth, intentionally or not, elides the definition of a phenomenon with his own interest in it. An understanding of game aesthetics that excludes games that have a massive user base – such as the version of Solitaire, which has been packaged with successive versions of Microsoft Windows, or online poker, which with US $15 billion of revenue in 2003 (McClellan, 2004) is worth a similar amount as the entire digital games industry – runs the risk of using a definition of games which does not actually include the majority of digital game playing.

This again highlights how drawing boundaries around academic fields is not necessarily a productive activity. Separating the aesthetic study of digital games for research into the aesthetics of other games – such as 'the beautiful game' of football/soccer (Inglis and Hughson, 2000) – does not necessarily help engage with that research, nor does it support mutual understanding with research carried out in other fields, which may provide insights for the study of digital games.

'Digital games studies' or multidisciplinary research? ●

The social sciences have long recognized that research methods, whether scientific or social scientific, are not neutral. Based upon empirical, theoretical and philosophical investigation researchers have argued that there is no simple way of separating science from the doing of science (Hine, 2002; Latour and Woolgar, 1986; Lynch, 1993; Merton, 1973). Kuhn (1962) has shown that when doing 'normal science' practitioners operate with a general set of shared assumptions governing how science is done, what understandings it is based upon and the world view it represents. However, at times anomalies may occur that call into question this previous paradigm, and present possible new and competing ones. An example of this was the shift from the understanding of space as one in which the Earth was the centre of God's creation, around which other heavenly bodies moved in perfect circles, to a heliocentric model of the solar system with planets having elliptical paths. The idea of paradigmatic shifts has been associated with the manner in which science, disciplines and accepted discourses develop not in a neutral fashion but through political and academic struggle.

Some researchers have argued that research on digital games has the power to cause paradigmatic shifts within a range of academic disciplines and that existing disciplines lack the tools, theory or application to fully address the research needs of understanding digital games. These writers have argued for the establishment of something that might be called 'computer game studies' (Raessens and Goldstein, 2005), 'video game theory' (Wolf and Perron, 2003) or 'games studies' (Aarseth, 2001), but which exists outside the established disciplines of academic research.

Perhaps the most famous proponent of this perspective has been Espen Aarseth. In his inaugural editorial for the online journal *Game Studies*, Aarseth (2001) drew a proverbial line in the sand, which he warned researchers not committed to establishing a new research discipline about crossing. He accused researchers from outside his own field of 'colonising' game studies:

> The greatest challenge to computer game studies will no doubt come from within the academic world. Making room for a new field usually means reducing the resources of the existing ones, and the existing fields will also often respond by trying to contain the new area as a subfield. Games are not a kind of cinema, or literature, but colonising attempts from both these fields have already happened, and no doubt will happen again. And again, until computer game studies emerges as a clearly self-sustained academic field. To make things more confusing, the current pseudo-field of 'new media' (primarily a strategy to claim computer-based communication for visual media studies), wants to subsume computer games as one of its objects. (Aarseth, 2001)

Aarseth is clear that the attempt to build game studies as a new and separate field is a political as well as an academic project. Indeed, an interesting aspect of Kuhn's paradigmatic shifts – as with the evolution of new fields, disciplines and university departments – is not merely the scientific change that underpins it but the recognition that such changes will profoundly benefit a few and disadvantage others. With new fields come funding investment, new professorial posts and other resources, as well as decisions about what forms the central core of the field.

Whether or not research into digital games will consolidate into a distinct field remains to be seen, but we can be certain that it will not happen without: (1) active work toward creating a hierarchy of digital games research and digital games researchers; (2) the institutionalization of what lies within and without the new field; and (3) the formation of academic practice that accepts certain methodologies and rejects others; focusing on certain aspects of digital games while marginalizing competing viewpoints.

However, given the academic, industrial, consumer and administrative diversity of digital games, would the reification of this dynamic research field be a productive endeavour, or does such movement seek to kill the enthusiasm, innovation and interdisciplinarity that currently characterize a great deal of digital games research?

Would it serve to prevent engagement with the broader development in academic interest in ephemeral issues of modern life from the visual (Ball and Smith, 1992; Emmison and Smith, 2000), the auditory (Bull, 2000; Bull and Back, 2003) and issues of taste (Bourdieu, 1984: Warde, 1997)? While it has been argued that the study of digital games has changed certain academic institutions, it is possible to view the growth in digital games research as simply part of a broader evolution of academic investigation into the routine and often taken-for-granted aspects of cultural life.

Discussing the development of cultural studies, David Morley, who with his colleagues at Birmingham University was highly influential from the 1970s onwards in laying the foundations for what we now regard as (British) Cultural Studies, warned of the dangers 'of the installation of a particular orthodoxy' (Morley, 1992: 2). Warning of the difficulties in prematurely drawing boundaries around research areas and translating findings from one area to another (academically, culturally and geographically) he argued:

> It would seem today, especially in the context of the North American Academy, cultural studies not only has become almost synonymous with a certain kind of postmodern theorizing but is now also referred to … simply as 'theory'. This fetishization of a rather abstract idea of theory is quite at odds with what Stuart Hall has described as the 'necessary modesty' which academic work in this field should properly display. (1992: 3)

Is the overenthusiasism of academic digital game researchers to create new disciplines around their own research concerns stopping the growth of research ideas? Is the keenness of some to erect boundaries around research into digital games only going to serve in making multidisciplinary work harder to develop? Will this isolationism retard the development of new ideas and maintenance of relevance to industry and policy users? Taken as a whole, the academic diversity of this collection would argue so.

The chapters in this book come from a diverse set of academic disciplines. One of their notable aspects is not that the authors compete for ownership of digital games research or present their own fields as providing definitive insight into digital games, but that they use the work from their own areas to enable them to answer different questions about the same phenomenon. The reader of this book is not asked to pick which of the viewpoints presented is correct to the exclusion of others, but to understand the multifaceted nature of digital games and that research methods and analysis must be chosen in line with the specific questions that one seeks to explore. For example, no amount of ethnographic-style participation observation with gaming communities and playing of digital games will help understand the economic models upon which the contemporary digital games industry is based. Of course, the converse is also true. Objectively, neither perspective is more useful until we decide which part of digital gaming we want to explore and the most appropriate methods for doing so. The chapters in this collection highlight the manner in which digital games do not exist in a space hermetically sealed from other aspects of culture, society and economics, but are a product of them and contribute to their reproduction and development.

While for convenience we can simplify our model of the world of digital games, draw largely arbitrary boundaries around the aspects we are most interested in and build our analysis on defined assumptions, factoids and simplifications, it is important to be clear that these are products of our analysis and are not the object of analysis itself. While it is often necessary for practical reasons to limit the focus of our investigation or simplify complex phenomena, it is good practice to remember that these boundaries are part of the research process and the questions and methods that we choose to ask. By focusing on a specific element of digital games, whether that be the technology; the onscreen text; the programmed text; the communities that are part of digital games; or their use in education, we deepen our understanding of the area. However, without sharing ideas with others outside specific research niches, we risk losing sight of the bigger picture upon which each niche depends for its structure.

One of the reasons why digital games have proved such a dynamic source of research and analysis in recent years is the manner in which they sit at a junction between a wide range of established academic interests. As Alloway and Gilbert point out:

> Video game narratives and the practices associated with video game culture form part of a complex interplay of discursive practices. They do not stand alone. They are part of a network of discourses and social practices that similarly construct violence, aggression, gender relations, ethnicity and power. It is because they dovetail so easily that they become so easily 'naturalized' in cultural practice. (1998: 96–7)

By unreflexively giving priority to one aspect of digital games we run the risk of convincing ourselves that our own perspective is, in actual fact, the defining one. While trying to understand digital games we must be aware of avoiding the situation of the six wise (but blind) men in John Godfrey Saxe's poem.[8]

Confronted with an elephant these men touch upon a different part of the animal and make the mistake of assuming that what they have found represents the whole of the creature. As such, the first man feels the elephant's side and assumes elephants are like walls; the second touches the tusk and so thinks the elephant is like a spear; the third concludes the elephant is like a snake having grabbed the moving trunk; the fourth, feeling the elephant's knee asserts the animal is like a tree; the fifth finds the elephant's ear and so believes the animal to be like a fan; and the final wise man finds the rope-like tail. Saxe warns that with the knowledge gathered:

> And so these men of Indostan
>   Disputed loud and long,
> Each in his own opinion
>   Exceeding stiff and strong,
> Though each was partly in the right
>   And all were in the wrong!

The lesson here, is not that any of the wise men were wrong in what they discovered or how they understood it, but rather that they did not see further than their own area. They assumed that their area could define the whole object and were prepared to take this partial knowledge as evidence of the ultimate perspective. In our attempt to gain a cohesive picture of digital games it is important that we show a keenness to talk to our fellow researchers and work together to develop a deeper understanding of our behemoth. This collection is an attempt to support and encourage such dialogue in order to strengthen our understanding of digital games.

Relevant web sites ● ● ●

Association for Business Simulation and Experiential Learning www.absel.org

Bristol Dyslexia Centre, Net Educational Systems www.dyslexiacentre.co.uk

Buzzcut www.buzzcut.com

Digiplay Initiative www.digiplay.org.uk

DiGRA (Digital Games Research Association) www.digra.org

DiGRA's digital games conferences www.gamesconference.org

ELSPA (Entertainment and Leisure Software Publishers Association) www.elspa.com

Euromonitor www.euromonitor.com

ESA (Entertainment Software Association) www.theesa.com

Games and Culture – A Journal of Interactive Media www.sagepub.com/journal.aspx?pid=11113

International Association for Game Education and Research (IAGER) www.iager.org

IGDA (International Game Developers Association) www.igda.org

Hard Core www.digra.org/hardcore

International Game Journalists Association (IGJA) www.igja.org

International Journal of Intelligent Games & Simulation www.scit.wlv.ac.uk/%7Ecm1822/ijigs.htm

ISAGA (International Simulation & Gaming Association) www.isaga.info

ISI Web of Knowledge isi22.isiknowledge.com

Interactive Software Federation of Europe www.isfe-eu.org

Journal of Game Development www.jogd.com

MEF (Mobile Entertainment Forum) www.m-e-f.org

Slashdot Games games.slashdot.org

TIGA (The Independent Games Developers Association) www.tiga.org

● Notes

1 See, for example, http://www.digiplay.org.uk/books.php, http://www.renreynolds.com/bibliography.htm or http://www.game-research.com/reference.asp.

2 This idea was revisited by Merton's son, Robert C. Merton, during his banquet speech on the occasion of his award for the Nobel prize for economics in 1997. See http:// nobelprize.org/economics/laurcates/1997/merton-speech.html

3 Approximately €5.8 billion or £4 billion.

4 Approximately US $7 billion or £3.9 billion.

5 Approximately US $4 billion or €3.2 billion.

6 Approximately US $2.2 billion or €1.7 billion.

7 What Aarseth's means by 'traditional' here is unclear but, like using 'natural' to mean 'usual' or refer to that which appears normal, care should be shown in not using 'traditional' when referring not actually to traditions but something which is chronologically earlier than now. For example, the traditions associated with playing the dreidel game at Hanukkah are not the same as those associated with an Easter egg hunt. Similarly, a historical view provides a different insight into understanding the traditions linked to lacrosse as a game played by Native Americans, as well as the differences in the UK between rugby league (traditionally a working class sport) and rugby union (the traditional choice of public, that is fee paying, schools).

8 Saxe's poem, 'The Blind Men and the Elephant' is based upon a tale originally Chinese or Indian in origin although its exact heritage is unclear. A Buddhist version can be found in the Udana but Hindu versions are recorded and the story illustrates well the Jain notion of Anekanta – the multi-faceted nature of reality.

References ●

Aarseth, Espen (2001) 'Computer game studies, year one', *Game Studies*, retrieved 15 March 2005 from: http://www.gamestudies.org/0101/editorial.html

Aarseth, Espen (2003) 'Playing research: methodological approaches to game analysis', paper presented at MelbourneDAC, the 5th International Digital Arts and Culture Conference, 19–23 May 2003, Melbourne.

Alloway, N. and Gilbert, P. (1998) 'Video game culture: playing with masculinity, violence and pleasure', in S. Howard (ed.), *Wired-up: Young People and the Electronic Media*. London: UCL Press. pp. 95–114.

Aoyama, Y. and Izushi, H. (2003) 'Hardware gimmick or cultural innovation? Technological, cultural, and social foundations of the Japanese video game industry', *Research Policy*, 32 (3): 423–44.

Ball, M. and Smith, G.W.H. (1992) *Analyzing Visual Data*. London: Sage.

Bourdieu, P. (1984) *Distinction: A Critique of the Judgement of Taste*. London: Routledge.

Bryce, J. (2000) 'The technological transformation of leisure', *Social Science Computer Review*, 79: 1–16.

Bryce, J. and Rutter, J. (2003) 'Gender dynamics and the social and spatial organisation of computer gaming', *Leisure Studies*, 22: 1–15.

Bull, M. (2000) *Sounding Out the City: Personal Stereos and the Management of Everyday Life*. Oxford: Berg.

Bull, M. and Back, L. (eds) (2003) *The Auditory Culture Reader*. Oxford: Berg.

Castronova, E. (in press) *Synthetic Worlds: The Business and Culture of Online Games*. Chicago, IL: University of Chicago Press.

Dimitrov, A. (2005) 'Influence of video games on children's health', *American Family Physician*, 71 (8). Retrieved 21 November 2005 from www.aatp.org/atp/20050415/lettersonline.html

ELSPA (2004) 'Video games continue to grow', press release, 6th January 2004, retrieved 15 March 2005 from: www.elspa.com/about/pr/pr.asp?mode=view&t=1&id=405

ELSPA (2005a) 'The UK games industry is in session', retrieved 15 April 2005 from: www.elspa.com/about/pr/pr.asp?mode=view&t=1&id=528

ELSPA (2005b) 'The games industry: a UK success story', retrieved 15 April 2005 from: www.elspa.com/about/pr/pr.asp?mode=view&t=1&id=524

Emmison, M. and Smith, P. (2000) *Researching the Visual: Images, Objects, Contexts and Interactions in Social and Cultural Inquiry*. London: Sage.

Eskelinen, M. (2001) 'Towards computer game studies', *Digital Creativity*, 12 (3): 175–83.

ESA (2005) 'Essential facts about the computer and video game industry', retrieved 26 May 2005 from: www.theesa.com/files/2005EssentialFacts.pdf

Euromonitor (2004) *Toys and Games in UK*. London: Euromonitor International.

Hatch, D.J. and Watson, D.R. (1974) 'Hearing the blues: an essay in the sociology of music', *Acta Sociologica*, 17: 162–78.

Hayes, M. and Dinsey, S. (1995) *Games War: Video Games – A Business Review*. London: Bowerdean Publishing Company Ltd.

Hemnes, T.M.S. (1982) 'The adaptation of copyright law to video games', *University of Pennsylvania Law Review*, 131: 171–233.

Hine, C. 2002 'Cyberscience and social boundaries: the implications of laboratory talk on the Internet', *Sociological Research Online*, 7 (2), retrieved 15 April 2005 from: www.socresonline.org.uk/7/2/hine.html.

Hine, C. (ed.) (2005) *Virtual Methods: Issues in Social Research on the Internet*. Oxford: Berg.

Inglis, D. and Hughson, J. (2000) 'The beautiful game and the proto-aesthetics of the everyday', *Cultural Values*, 4 (3): 279–97.

IVF (2004) 'European video market: the industry overview', retrieved 15 April 2005 from: www.ivf-video.org/EuropeanOverview2004.pdf

Jefferson, G. (1979) 'A technique for inviting laughter and its subsequent acceptance/declination', in G. Psathas (ed.), *Everyday Language: Studies in Ethnomethodology*. New York: Irvington. pp. 79–96.

Kline, S., Dyer-Witheford, N. and de Peuter, G. (2003) *Digital Play: The Interaction of Technology, Culture, and Marketing*. Montreal: McGill-Queen's University Press.

Kuhn, T.S. (1962) *The Structure of Scientific Revolutions*. Chicago, IL: University of Chicago Press.

Latour, B. and Woolgar, S. (1986) *Laboratory Life: The Construction of Scientific Facts*. Princeton, NJ: Princeton University Press.

Lowood, H. (2002) 'Shall we play a game: thoughts on the computer game archive of the future', retrieved 15 April 2005 from: www.stanford.edu/%7Elowood/Texts/shall_game.pdf

Lynch, M. (1993) *Scientific Practice and Ordinary Action: Ethnomethodology and Social Studies of Science*. Cambridge: Cambridge University Press.

McClellan, J. (2004) 'The hot favourite', *Guardian Unlimited*, retrieved 15 April 2005 from: http://sport.guardian.co.uk/horseracing/story/0,10149, 1182988, 00.html

McCowan, T.C. (1981) 'Space Invaders wrist', *New England Journal of Medicine*, 304: 1368.

Merton, R.K. (1965) *On the Shoulders of Giants*. New York: Free Press.

Merton, R.K. (1973) *The Sociology of Science: Theoretical and Empirical Investigations*, ed. N.W. Storer. Chicago, IL: The University of Chicago Press.

Morley, D. (1992) *Television Audience and Cultural Studies*. London: Routledge.

Newman, J. (2004) *Videogames*. London: Routledge.

Provenzo, E.F. (1991) *Video Kids: Making Sense of Nintendo*. Cambridge, MA: Harvard University Press.

Raessens, J. and Goldstein, J. (eds) (2005) *Handbook of Computer Game Studies*. Cambridge, MA: MIT Press.

Readman, J. and Grantham, A. (2004) 'Strategy frameworks and the positioning of UK electronic games super developers', Centre for Research in Innovation Management working paper, University of Brighton, retrieved 15 April 2005 from: http://centrim.mis.brighton.ac.uk/publications/abstracts/ 041abs.shtml

Rutter, J. (2000) 'The introductions of stand-up performers: comparing comedy compères', *Journal of Pragmatics*, 32 (4): 463–83.

Sacks, H. (1978) 'Some technical considerations of a dirty joke', in J.N. Schenkein (ed.), *Studies in the Organization of Conversational Interaction*. New York: Academic Press. pp. 249–70.

Sedlak, R.A., Doyle, M. and Schloss, P. (1982) 'Video games – a training and generalization demonstration with severely retarded adolescents', *Education and Training in Mental Retardation and Developmental Disabilities*, 17: 332–6.

Sudnow, D. (1978) *Ways of the Hand: The Organization of Improvised Conduct*. Cambridge, MA: Harvard University Press.

Sudnow, D. (1983) *Pilgrim in the Microworld*. New York: Warner Books.

Warde, A. (1997) *Consumption, Food and Taste: Culinary Antinomies and Commodity Culture*. London: Sage.

Wolf, M.J.P. (ed.) (2001) *The Medium of the Video Game*. Austin, TX: University of Texas.

Wolf, M.J.P. and Perron, B. (2003) *The Video Game Theory Reader*. London: Routledge.

Part one

History and production

2 A history of digital games ● ● ●

John Kirriemuir

Introduction ●

The history of digital games is filled with experimentation and innovation. As each new electronic device, such as the valve, silicon circuit, television, radio and so forth was invented, so the inclination of many researchers and users was to seek out whatever entertainment value could be had from the new technology. Thankfully, many older video games are playable today either through purchase on online auction houses or retro gaming companies, on updated versions on contemporary machines or through emulation software or websites. Video games have been available for (depending on where you take the starting point) between 35 and 50 years and so a rich and often subjective history has accumulated.

This chapter weaves a course through some of the developments, key products and companies in this field. It explains some of the frequently used jargon of the video gaming industry, both contemporary and historical. It cannot feature every video game console (of which there have been hundreds) or video game (of which there have been hundreds of thousands) but it gives a flavour of how we moved from a dot on the screen, to games which share the style and technology of many Hollywood blockbusters.

● In the beginning there was a dot...

Commercial, and widely used, versions of digital games did not, as we shall see, emerge until the late 1960s. However, while digital games precipitated the creation of many digital game-related development and production companies, several of the major companies of today incorporated these new entertainment technologies into their existing main business. For example, Nintendo, a Japanese company with origins in the 19th century, produced playing cards for nearly 80 years before diversifying into electronic technologies. Similarly, in 1956, Tokyo Telecommunications Laboratory, a business increasingly occupied with transistor-based products, changed its name to Sony, though its involvement with games consoles would not begin until the last decade of the century.

The pinpointing of the 'first' computer game is a contested issue with claims drawing on definition as well as chronology. In 1952 Alexander (Sandy) Douglas, then a PhD student at Cambridge University, produced a version of noughts and crosses (Tic-Tac-Toe) which ran on the EDSAC, the world's first stored-program computer to operate a regular computing service (Bryce and Rutter, 2003).

Six years later in 1958, William Higinbotham, a physicist at the Brookhaven National Laboratory, invented a basic simulation of tennis that functioned on a laboratory oscilloscope. The game quickly became a main attraction to visitors to the laboratory and is often claimed in literature to be the first computer game (Brookhaven National Laboratory, n.d.). In 1962, the game *Spacewar* was written by a team of researchers at Massachusetts Institute of Technology led by Steve Russell. *Spacewar* ran on a PDP-1, a large research computer within the faculty. The aim of this two-player game was to shoot at your opponent's ship, while avoiding falling into the sun. The game was copied, or modified, throughout a number of US academic institutions over the next few years making it the first game to be available outside a single research institute.

However, a major shift for the evolution of digital games came in 1967 when a text-based adventure game called *ADVENT* (short for 'adventure') was developed to run on mainframe computers. The game was so called because the original DECsystem-10 operating system it ran under only supported filenames of six characters but became *Adventure* (and variously *Colossal Cave Adventure*, *Colossal Adventure* or *Classic Adventure*) with its release into the young personal computer market in the early 1980s.

It is increasingly hard to remember that home computing is still relatively new. In the 1950s and 1960s, computers were few and far between, tending to be the size of a small room or large car. Few businesses could afford to purchase one computer, and many were owned by affluent research or military institutions. Processing power and memory size was primitive compared to the capabilities of the mobile phone handsets of today. Data entry was laborious, being through punched cards or paper tapes. It often took several hours, and regular maintenance and repairs, for example when changing valve tubes, to run one program.

Throughout the 1960s, an increasing number of people created basic digital games but struggled to find commercial funding or outlets for these. For example, in 1967 Sanders Associates created a television-based hockey simulation game, but failed to obtain a commercial outlet or funding from either television manufacturers or channel/content providers. It would be five years before the game would become commercially available, eventually appearing on Ralph Baer's Magnavox Odyssey home games console.

In 1969, Rick Blomme wrote a version of *Spacewar* which ran over the PLATO (Programmed Logic for Automatic Teaching Operations) network, an early computer-based learning system which had been built at the University of Illinois. The game marked the advent of online gaming, an area of gaming history we will return to in more detail later.

The first rise of the consoles ●

The Magnavox Odyssey was the first commercial home video game system. Launched in 1972 it sold over 100,000 units within the year. The console came with controllers and translucent screen overlays. These overlays added context to whatever game was being played; for example, the overlay for the tennis game included the court and net markings. In 1972, Nolan Bushell formed the company known as Atari. Atari are perhaps the most well-known company in video gaming history, certainly from the USA. One of their first creations was an arcade machine version of *Pong*, an extremely simplified tennis simulation. Over the next few years, dozens of companies created clones of the game for use in either arcades or the home. *Pong* also marked the start of the long relationship between the gaming and legal industries, as companies such as Atari and Magnavox disputed the origins and ownership of *Pong* and other games.

In 1977, Atari launched its Video Computer System (VCS), otherwise known as the 2600.[1] The console, with its sleek faux wood finish, proved immensely popular and arguably became the first games console to be bought in significant numbers. The console was marketed under a business model whereby most of the revenue was gained through sales of the associated games – a model still frequently employed in the digital games industry (see Alvisi, Chapter 4). The low price of the VCS encouraged sales of the console and consequently the software that it used.

BREAKOUT BOX 2.1 ● ● ●

Cartridge

Many of the early home-based video game consoles incorporated a slot. The console would plug into the television and into the slot would be put a cartridge (effectively a circuit board with the game hard coded into a chip), which contained the game. Game loading time was non-existent. However, as each game cartridge was effectively a piece of hardware, production costs were high. Over time, consoles gradually moved towards CD-like disc-based methods for selling games software as production costs were lower (though this made games vulnerable to disc-copying piracy). The Nintendo 64 machine of the mid to late 1990s was the last mainstream console to use cartridges.

The three years of 1978 to 1980 became, for historians of entertainment, a golden period of gaming development. During this time enduring popular games such as *Space Invaders, Zork, Pacman, Asteroids and Battlezone* were released. Versions of these games would appear on gaming consoles and other devices for the remainder of the century. By 1981 in the USA alone, US $5 billion per year was being spent in games arcades and an additional billion dollars on home video gaming systems.

However, by the early 1980s, the games produced in-house by Atari were rapidly receding in terms of quality, customer appeal and, therefore, popularity. Many other companies struggled, merged or (increasingly) went bankrupt. Atari was not alone. However, several poorly selling games left Atari with large amounts of unsold games, much of which (according to Internet legend) it buried in a pit in the New Mexico desert. The company continued to produce games and released a number of other consoles and home computers, though none matched the popularity of the early VCS days. Throughout the 1980s and 1990s, Atari was sold to a succession of parent companies and as with other games from that era, copies of its earlier titles command respectable prices on retro gaming web sites and online auction houses.

BREAKOUT BOX 2.2 ● ● ●

RAM: random access memory

Temporary memory in which programs and relevant data are stored. When the computer was switched off, the memory was wiped. RAM is measured in K or Kilobytes: 1 K equals 1024 bytes (2^{10} bytes = 1024 bytes = 1 KB), where each byte was the equivalent of one character or number. In the early 1980s, 32 K to 64 K of RAM was available in popular machines such as the Sinclair Spectrum, BBC Micro and Commodore 64. The Xbox and PlayStation 2 have 64 Mb (1 Mb = 1024^2 bytes) of RAM as standard and, at time of writing, it was rumoured that the Xbox 360 and PlayStation 3 will each use 512 Mb.

Home computing, PCs and PC gaming ●

The early 1980s saw a boom in ready-made home computers. In the UK, Sir Clive Sinclair launched a range of low-cost computers including the ZX80 (1980; in kit form), ZX81 (1981) and Spectrum. These computers were among the first to incorporate a keyboard, thus allowing the entry of programmes which could then be saved onto cassette tape. Though many of these were bought on the premise of being used for educational or work purposes, most primarily became home video game machines.

The Sinclair Spectrum, in particular, became a popular platform for games developers. Many of the leaders of UK and European game development houses today began their careers by writing games for these machines, often from home and working on their own.

Meanwhile, 1981 saw the launch by IBM of its 8088 processor-based PC. Though these were priced at a level to make them affordable to medium and large businesses only, increasingly, personal computers (PC) began to appear in the home and almost immediately became a platform for keen games developers.

Throughout the 1980s, various PC-clones (machines that could handle software developed for IBM PCs) were produced by hardware manufacturers as the market for these devices rapidly expanded. It was a computer game that was used as a calibration of compatibility: as *Spacewar* had been used as a diagnostic tool for PDP-1 machines so one of the new personal computers was not considered a hundred percent compatible with IBM machines unless it could run Microsoft's *Flight Simulator*.

Throughout the 1980s, the line between home computers and video games consoles became blurred; to this day, the phrases 'computer games' and 'video games' are often used interchangeably.

BREAKOUT BOX 2.3 ● ● ●

MUD: multi-user dungeon

A type of game, typically played online via a PC in the 1980s and 1990s. MUDs were quest-based games, primarily textual in appearance, that usually involved interacting with other characters in a pseudo-medieval Tolkienesque setting. The draw of MUDs involved making your character rise through the ranking system of the game, from a humble labourer to a grand wizard or necromancer, accumulating extra skills and powers on the way.

● The second rise of consoles in the home

In 1983, Nintendo released the Famicom (short for 'Family Computer') in Japan. The Famicom marked an early outing for Mario, a Nintendo character who would become synonymous with the company. Soon afterwards, Nintendo released the US version of the Famicom, known as the Nintendo Entertainment System (NES).

The mid-1980s are regarded by most digital games historians as a period which was dominated by Nintendo. This was partially because the Famicom and NES were pitched with a retail tag of around US $100, the console selling solidly in all territories where it was released. However, Nintendo was also a dominant market force due to the rapid contraction in Europe and the USA of the video game market (and consequently the supporting industry) in the mid-1980s. This was due, to an extent, to customer disillusionment in the quality of many games but also because of the rapid increase in sales of now-affordable PCs, which could play games and be used for more serious applications.

Against this backdrop of a struggling industry, another Japanese company, SEGA, was making some headway in the games console market. In 1985 it released the SEGA Master System, followed by the Genesis in 1989. SEGA also took on Nintendo in the emerging hand-held console market, pitching its SEGA Game Gear (1990) against the Nintendo Game Boy (1988). Like Nintendo, SEGA introduced strong character branding through its games, the most well-known example being Sonic the Hedgehog. In 1991, Nintendo responded to the competition from SEGA with the Super NES (SNES) an enhanced version of the Famicom.

BREAKOUT BOX 2.4 ● ● ●

Bit

The 'bit' size of a console or gaming machine is often used as a rough benchmark by the public and the media for how powerful the machine is (replacing the 'RAM' benchmark of the 1980s). The more 'bits', the larger the numbers that the processor within the machine could handle and – at least in theory – the more complex games could be developed for the machine.

The year 1993 saw the launch of the first 64-bit console, the Jaguar, by Atari. The console proved too expensive for many gamers. With the limited range of software available compared to existing consoles, sales were disappointing, and Atari eventually withdrew from the hardware manufacturing side of the gaming industry.

Two years later, SEGA responded with the 32-bit Saturn. This console, like its successor the Dreamcast, contained facilities which enabled basic Internet access. Though the Saturn proved promising, and played host to a clutch of classic games such as *NiGHTS*, the emergence of Sony's PlayStation in 1994 would limit the lifespan of SEGA's penultimate hardware platform.

The entry of Sony into the video game market is an interesting one. In the early 1990s, Sony and Nintendo negotiated to form an alliance and went into partnership on hardware development for the digital gaming sector (a move which, in retrospect, would have arguably led to a dominating or single-platform, market). However, the partnership broke down – games historians differ on why – and Sony decided to go it alone in producing a console.

Initially expensive, and released to a mixed reception from the public and industry, the PlayStation would gain momentum largely through the sheer number of games developed for it and aggressive marketing and pricing by Sony. High profile games and characters, most notably *Crash Bandicoot* and Lara Croft of *Tomb Raider* fame, helped the console to sell in large numbers to previously non-gaming players. The console was effectively remarketed as the PS One in the early part of the next decade, continuing to sell well to date despite the emergence of considerably more powerful consoles.

The closing years of the 1990s saw the global launch of a number of consoles. The two which attracted the lion's share of publicity and sales were the Nintendo 64, and the SEGA Dreamcast.

BREAKOUT BOX 2.5 ● ● ●

Tomb Raider and Lara Croft

If one game character is synonymous with 1990s video gaming, it would be Lara Croft. The first Tomb Raider *game appeared on the Sony PlayStation in 1996, selling rapidly in large quantities. This featured Lara, a heavily-armed Indiana Jones type character with tight fitting clothes and large breasts. Despite suspicions, the developers deny that the character was designed for a core market of male teenage game players. Lara was the first game character to appear frequently across the general, non-gaming media, such as on magazine covers and in adverts. However, later updates of the* Tomb Raider *game have steadily diminished in popularity. While Lara Croft is often credited with making video games more 'mainstream', increasingly she is seen as a top-heavy throwback to a less intelligent and refined gaming concept.*

Nintendo 64 ●

Nintendo launched the Nintendo 64 (otherwise known as the Ultra) in 1996. Though often thought of as a failure when sales figures are compared with the PlayStation, the Nintendo 64 did become the fifth best selling video game console in history. As games for the Nintendo 64 were still being released on cartridges, the take-up of the console was hindered by the software format: games which incurred production delays and high costs that were reflected in shop prices. However, a clutch of classic titles, including *Super Mario 64* (a 3D platform game), *GoldenEye* (a first person shooter) and *Zelda: Ocarina of Time* (a multi-genre game, still regarded by many as the best video game ever developed) helped the console achieve a significant user base.

SEGA Dreamcast ●

The SEGA Dreamcast had a spectacular though relatively short lifespan, being marketed from 1998 to 2002. Unusual marketing and advertising strategies (often referring to play in an abstract sense, but not to digital games) confused many game players. Despite a number of games that were graphically superior to comparable titles on rival platforms, many developers avoided or dropped development work for the console, leaving SEGA with an uphill struggle to see a return on its considerable investment. One critical failure of the console, which was marketed on the premise of offering online gaming, was the lack of such games in any quantity until near the end of its life when key titles such as *Phantasy Star Online* appeared. Despite the acclaim achieved by this title, which enabled easy and seamless online gameplay with and against people from around the world, the console was dropped in 2002 and SEGA moved solely into producing games software for other platforms.

The early years of the new millennium saw three key manufacturers each releasing one television-based video gaming console. The PlayStation 2 (PS2) is Sony's successor to its previous console. Sales of the console have grown to the extent that it has a probably unsurpassable lead over its contemporary competitors. A key feature of the console is the ability to play games developed for the original PlayStation. Added to this was the support of more developers than the other consoles and the continuation of several key game franchises, such as *Grand Theft Auto*, *FIFA* (football/soccer) and *Gran Turismo*.

The Xbox is the console developed and marketed by Microsoft. The Xbox is unusual for a games console in that it contains a hard drive. This allows soundtracks and game components to be saved and used in-game. Microsoft promoted the Xbox with the largest marketing and advertising campaign of any console launch. The launch proved successful in the USA, though sales in Europe have taken time to build momentum and the Japanese market is still insignificant. In this territory the unusually large size of the console was one of the reasons often given for its slow sales, as Japanese homes and culture are traditionally more accommodating to smaller, more compact devices.

A key factor which attracted early adopters of the Xbox at the launch was the game *Halo*, which received critical acclaim from nearly all quarters of the gaming industries and media. Microsoft has either brokered deals with, or acquired, a number of development and production companies, such as Rare, thus ensuring a steady stream of games for the console.

The GameCube was Nintendo's successor to the N64. Unlike the Xbox and the PS2, the GameCube did not have the facility to play CDs or DVDs, using a proprietary disc format instead. In the early period of its life, this limitation was used by business analysts to often negatively forecast its future against its rivals. However, the GameCube has made strong use of Nintendo game character brands and franchises, such as Mario and Zelda, and has subsequently enjoyed reasonable success in the console marketplace. The development of more games aimed at an adult market, such as titles in the *Resident Evil* series, has shown that the console is not exclusively aimed at a schoolchild audience.

However, by the end of 2004, speculation was rife about the next generation of consoles, and possible successors to each of these three predominant machines of the age.

The ubiquitous game

Games as accessories

Digital games appear periodically in a number of forms. In the 1970s and 1980s, digital games were produced in watch format, as LCD panels and as self-contained toys and games. Examination of the catalogue of any major toy store or in-flight trolley sales brochure, often reveals a variety of such games. Some games, and gaming brands, have become phenomenally popular for short periods of time. In 1996, Bandai released Tamagotchi. This game, available on a key ring-sized device, involved 'growing' a digital animal and ensuring it was fed and generally looked after various times of the day and night. Despite the game appearing to be more work than play it sold at a rapid rate shipping around 20 million units in its first year.

The following year, Nintendo released Pokémon, a similar 'creature nurturing' game on its Game Boy and Nintendo 64 consoles. Nintendo used the Pokémon brand in a wide range of products, including movies, books, cartoons, food and toys. As of the end of 2001, Nintendo had released over a thousand Pokémon tie-in licences with total sales of some US $20 billion. The potent combination of collecting items, and defeating opponents with your collection, ensured sales that have only recently begun to abate.

Handheld consoles: gaming goes mobile ●

In the early 1990s, Nintendo launched the Game Boy. This offered a two-colour display and a small but rapidly growing selection of cartridge-based games, the most well-known being *Tetris*, which helped to cement the popularity of the console. Later on in the decade, the Pokémon series of games (based around the concepts of digital trading cards and monster fighting) greatly increased sales. The original console was followed by a version offering games in colour, then a version (Game Boy Advance) enabling considerably more complex and detailed games to be developed and sold.

Throughout the life of the Game Boy other handheld consoles were launched by rival companies. Consoles such as the Neo Geo were arguably superior in terms of processor power, game depth, detail and colour. However, the extensive collection of titles available for the Game Boy has ensured that no competing handheld console has so far provided a serious challenge. The Game Boy Advance, while having a battery life of over 20 hours, drew complaints over it not containing back lighting to make the screen easier to see, which often made games difficult to play. In 2003 Nintendo launched the Game Boy SP, a version containing a backlight and sales proved impressive with a number of countries experiencing initial stock shortages.

The end of 2004 and the start of 2005 saw a new rivalry in the handheld console market, with products by both Nintendo and Sony. Nintendo launched the DS, which featured two screens (one of which was touch sensitive). The console made use of both wireless technologies – allowing a classroom of children to play the same game – and online technology for more remote and larger user base games. Sony launched the PSP, a console relying on the strong branding of many PlayStation game franchises.

Converging the game

Early mobile phones often included simple monochrome games such as *Snake*, which were similar in nature, complexity and visual style to games on early home computers such as the ZX80 and ZX81. As mobile phones have rapidly increased in functionality and technical power so the games they support have become more complex. However, three restrictions have impeded the emergence of games which can rival those found on handheld and television-based consoles:

- the processing power within the mobile phone;
- the speed of download of games and upgrades, though faster 3G networks promise to eradicate this problem; and
- the small screen size

In 2003 Nokia released the N-Gage, a handheld gaming device with mobile phone facilities. Reviews of test and early games were mixed (see, for example ZDNet Australia, 2003), though the appearance of key gaming franchises such as *Tomb Raider* and *Sonic* show that some of the larger gaming industry developers are investing in developing for such a platform. An upgrade of the N-Gage has helped sales, but at the same time several other similar devices have entered the market, thus making it unclear as to any long-term dominating device. The advent of mobile games offers great possibilities, especially as the mobile phone is becoming a significant platform for gaming and the majority of children possess such a device. Here, there is already intense social collaboration around this device, through the use of SMS (short message service), between school children. Bluetooth enables synchronous mobile phone play between some handsets over short distances and emerging mobile technologies will make more wide-spread and develop the range of digital gaming.

> ## BREAKOUT BOX 2.6 ● ● ●
>
> ### MMORPG: massive multiplayer online role-playing game
>
> *This clumsy acronym adequately describes this particular type of game. Primarily through personal computers (though some console-based MMORPGs are starting to become available), thousands of people 'log on' to a virtual world. Here, they control an avatar (a configurable person) within a graphical landscape. The avatar can trade, communicate, fight and interact in other ways with avatars controlled by other players. A MMORPG can be thought of as the modern version of the MUD.*

Online games ●

As we have seen, through games such as MUD-type games, online gaming is not a new concept. Typically, online gaming has been regarded until recently as a niche form of gameplay on personal computers, as consoles did not offer online capabilities.

However, starting with the SEGA Dreamcast, all popular video game consoles now offer such an option, though the proportion of games that use it is still not high. Online gaming is fiscally attractive to game and console developers: the financial return for committed players is far higher than for single discrete offline games as monthly subscriptions generate ongoing income. Partly because of this, for the last few years, online games have been widely predicted as the future of mainstream, or mass public, digital game playing.

Perhaps the best-known online game is *EverQuest*, a massive multiplayer online role-playing game often played simultaneously (and for long periods of time) by several hundred thousand people. The game has become a contemporary cultural reference point. It has also generated a (real world) economy comparable to that of a medium-sized country (Lichtarowicz, 2002). Such games are often characterized by the dedication and commitment exhibited by the players. For example, about one third of the adult players of *EverQuest* spent more time in a typical week in the virtual world than in paid employment (Castronova, 2001).

While MMORPGs (massive multiplayer online role-playing game) dominate online gaming, other types of games that use this remote media are emerging. Anecdotal information points to online card games, typically played by middle aged and elderly American citizens, as being a large market (though precise figures are more difficult to come by). Increasingly, games are being developed for both PCs and for video consoles where the multiplayer aspect is the primary driver of the game (whereas the traditional approach was for the single player to be the key feature, with a few static online features as an added bonus).

However, the largest factor in the rapid emergence of online gaming for the general public is the take-up of domestic broadband access in recent years, making it possible to play complex games against large numbers of opponents with little or no delay or 'lag'. It is with this emerging method of game-playing that the next chapter of the history of this form of entertainment will be written.

Relevant web sites ● ● ●

Atari History Museum http://www.atari-history.com
Brief History of Video Games http://www.geekcomix.com/vgh
Digiplay Initiative, Computer Gaming Timeline http://www.digiplay.org.uk/timeline.php
Dot Eaters, Classic Video Game History http://www.emuunlim.com/doteaters
Edsac Simulator http://www.dcs.warwick.ac.uk/~edsac
Emulators Unlimited http://www.emuunlim.com
Game Archive http://www.gamearchive.com/vault
Gamespot, History of Video Games http://www.gamespot.com/gamespot/features/video/hov
Nintendo Land http://www.nintendoland.com
PONG-Story http://www.pong-story.com
Ralph H. Baer http://www.ralphbaer.com
Spacewar! http://lcs.www.media.mit.edu/groups/el/projects/spacewar
Video Game Museum http://www.vgmuseum.com
Videogames.org http://www.videogames.org

● Note

1 It is important to note that a significant number of video game consoles were released with different names in the three main 'territories' of the USA, Japan and Europe.

References ●

Brookhaven National Laboratory (n.d.) 'Video games – did they begin at Brookhaven?', retrieved 15 March 2005 from: http://www.osti.gov/accom plishments/videogame.html

Bryce, J. and Rutter, J. (2003) 'Editorial comment', *Information Communication & Society*, 6 (4): v–x.

Castronova, E. (2001) 'Virtual worlds: a first-hand account of market and society on the cyberian frontier', CESifo working paper No. 618, December.

Lichtarowicz, A. (2002) 'Virtual kingdom richer than Bulgaria', retrieved 15 March 2005 from: http://news.bbc.co.uk/1/hi/sci/tech/1899420.stm

ZDNet Australia (2003) 'First look: Nokia N-Gage', retrieved 15 March 2005 from: http://www.zdnet.com.au/reviews/coolgear/mobiles/story/0,2000023537, 20271872,00.htm

3   The business of making digital games

Aphra Kerr

Introduction

Journalists have written many books on the digital games industry. Some of these books focus on one company (Asakura, 2000; Sheff, 1993; Takahashi, 2002), while others give a broad history of the technologies, key players and significant games (Herz, 1997; Poole, 2000). Although useful, these texts do not provide an understanding of the overall structure of the industry, the relationships between the main players and the process by which a game gets produced. In addition, very little attention is given to new markets like games for mobile, web and interactive television (i-TV). One is more likely to find information on these sub-sectors in trade magazines or on specialist websites (such as http://www.gamasutra.com and http://www. games-industry.biz).

The aim of this chapter is to give the reader an insight into the growing economic significance of the global games industry, to explore the process by which games get produced and to examine the dynamics operating in each sub-sector of the industry. Thus the 'business' of making games is defined rather broadly. The sections below explore growth in the games industry and claims that it is now larger than the film industry before analysing its structure and the key industrial dynamics operating across the main sub-sectors. Finally, the chapter examines the latest trends in the industry focussing on consolidation and licensing.

This chapter takes a political economy approach to the business of making games. Political economy is a branch of economics, which has been used extensively to study the media. According to Mosco, political economy is the study 'of the social relations, particularly the power relations, that mutually constitute the production, distribution and consumption of resources' (1996: 25). Political economists often identify the location, use (and in some cases abuse) of power by companies at various stages in the production cycle and they draw attention to the influence that corporate consolidation and certain business strategies can have on the range of content available on a media platform. This perspective underpins the analysis in the following sections.

Sales and growth in the digital games industry ●

Constructing an accurate picture of the size of the global games industry in terms of software and hardware sales is a difficult task. The information contained in government, consultancy and press reports usually fails to give a global perspective on the industry and, indeed, often offers contradictory information. This section explores data commissioned by the industry umbrella bodies; the Entertainment Software Association (ESA) in the USA and the Entertainment and Leisure Software Publishers Association (ELSPA) in the UK, and government reports from the UK and Japan.[1] Despite the caveats already mentioned it is clear that sales, both in monetary and unit terms, across all platforms have grown significantly over the past ten years and currently the digital games industry is seen as both a threat and an opportunity by traditional media companies.

A UK government report suggested that the global 'leisure software' industry in 2000 was worth approximately £13 billion of which almost £10 billion was accounted for by games software (Spectrum, 2002: 10). Within this total the US market accounted for 35 per cent of total sales, Europe 31.5 per cent and Japan 18.5 per cent. These figures are collaborated by figures published by Deutsche Bank in 2001, but this report estimated that the USA accounted for 40 per cent of total sales followed by Japan at 33 per cent and Europe at 26 per cent. A third source estimated that total games software sales in 2001 were worth US $17.7 billion and indicated that the largest market was the Asia Pacific market with sales of US $7.6 billion in 2001 (DataMonitor, 2002). A fourth source of estimated that the global interactive software market was worth US $18.2 billion in 2003 (Screen Digest, 2004). Table 3.1

TABLE 3.1 Summary of global sales (EUROS)

	Software sales (€ billion)	Hardware, software and peripherals (€ billion)	Source
2000	18.6		Screen Digest 2001; Spectrum 2002
2001	13.4	21.4	Deutsche Bank 2002
2001	16		DataMonitor 2002
2003	15.56		Screen Digest, 2004

converts these figures to euros for ease of comparison. From an industrial and policy-making perspective this variance in data and definitions as to what constitutes game software makes strategic planning and comparison with other industrial sectors difficult.

So how big is an industry which generates between €13 and €18 billion annually in software sales? These figures become more meaningful when we compare them to sales figures for traditional media products. Unfortunately there is no source for such data on a global scale and so we will focus on the USA and figures provided by a number of industry associations.

The National Purchase Diary (NPD) Group, a consultancy based in New York, estimates that total sales of hardware, software and accessories in the USA in 2002 generated US $10.3 billion, of which about US $6 billion was earned by game software (http://www.npdfunworld.com). By comparison, the US domestic box office in 2002 generated US $9.5 billion (MPAA, 2002). The figure for total hardware and software game sales is often used to suggest that the digital games industry is now worth more than the film industry. Indeed the claim is made so often in the popular press and game magazines that it demands closer investigation. It turns out that these comparisons usually fail to point out that 'total game sales' includes sales of game hardware, accessories and leisure software, such as photography libraries. In addition, they often fail to explain that cinema receipts only form a small percentage of the total revenues made by a film. Indeed box office receipts only account for approximately 25 per cent of total revenues and typically video and DVD sales/rentals, network and cable TV and pay-per-view are all important additional sources of revenue (Deutsche Bank, 2002: 29). Further, while growth in the digital games industry has been fairly steady since 2001 the US box office has fallen from 13.2 per cent between 2001 and 2002 to almost no growth in the

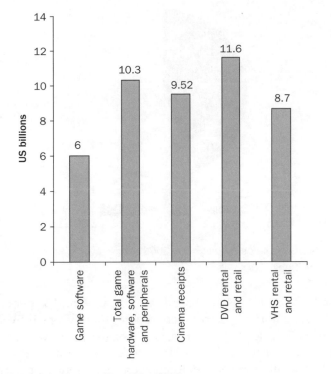

FIGURE 3.1   *Total sales by media, USA, 2002*

Source: Game software and total game hardware, software and peripherals: NPD Funworld and the Entertainment Software Association, http://www.npdfunworld.com; http://www.theesa.com/; cinema receipts: Motion Picture Association of America, http://www.mpaa.org/useconomicreview/index.htm; DVD and VHS rental and retail, http://www.dvdinformation.com/news/index.html

past four years (ESA, 2004; OECD, 2004). Figure 3.1 gives an overview of total sales by media sector in the US in 2002.

What the various reports do agree on is the significance of console games in comparison with games sold for other platforms. The various reports analysed estimate that between 57 and 78 per cent of total global software sales are console games. At present the main consoles are Sony's PlayStation 2 (PS2), Microsoft's Xbox 360 and Nintendo's GameCube (GC). Some reports group handhelds, such as the Game Boy Advance (GBA), with the other console platforms. Interestingly, not all markets demonstrate the same affinity with console games. While console games dominate in Japan with almost 94 per cent of

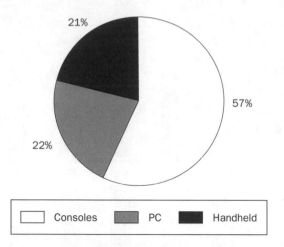

FIGURE 3.2 *Software sales by platform, 2001*
Source: Deutsche Bank, 2002

total sales; this falls to 80 per cent in the USA and 55 per cent in Europe (ESA, 2003). The Spectrum report notes that Europe is by far the largest market for sales of PC games, at 47 per cent, followed by the USA at 35 per cent (Spectrum, 2002: 11). Sales of games on other platforms form only a small proportion of total revenues currently. Spectrum (2002: 15) estimate that the mobile games market in Europe, the USA and Japan was worth £73 million in 2001, with Japan constituting over 50 per cent of this total. They predict that the mobile games market would double in value by 2005 and that the online games market would grow from £0.5 billion in 2001 to £0.89 billion in 2005.

● Understanding the structure of the digital games industry

In May each year game developers from around the world meet at the Electronic Entertainment Exposition (E3) in Los Angeles to pitch their ideas to publishers, sneak a preview of other games and do licensing deals with hardware companies and Hollywood studios. The show has much in common with the main international film festivals Melia, Cannes: it has all the glitz, the hype and the, albeit digital, stars. In Europe the London Games Week and the Lyon Game Connection offer less glitzy industry fora. In Asia, Japan hosts the biannual Toyko Game Show, which Steven Poole (2000) describes in detail in his book *Trigger Happy*.

The UK, the USA and Japan are the main centres of digital game production and all have substantial numbers employed both directly and indirectly in the digital games industry. In the UK the digital games industry employs more than 20,000 people across all sectors, with 6000 employed directly in game development (Spectrum, 2002). The same report claimed there are 270 independent and publisher owned studios and that the average UK development studio employs 22 people with the largest studios employing over 100 people. In the USA the industry employed 29,495 directly in computer and video game software development and publishing with a further 195,000 indirect jobs in the information, trade and transportation sectors in 2000 (IDSA, 2001). In Japan game hardware and software employs an estimated 30,000 people (Aoyama and Izushi, 2003). Other growing centres of game development include Australia, France and South Korea.[2]

In the next section we will describe the digital games production cycle, which is the cycle of activities involved in creating a game and delivering it to the customer. Following this, we will examine the structure of the digital games industry; dividing it into a number of different market segments and analysing the dynamics operating in each. In line with our political economy of the media approach we are concerned not just with production, but also with the interaction between production, finance, distribution and retail. In addition, we are concerned with the degree of concentration within and across each market segment.

The vertical structure of the digital games industry: ● the production cycle

The Spectrum report (2002: 9) compares the production cycle of the games industry to the film, music and book industries. In all these industries a publisher provides advance finance to a creative artist and takes on the role of marketing and distributing the final product. Once costs have been recouped the artist will receive a percentage of royalties. A similar process takes place in the digital games industry although the artist is usually a team of people. The core stages in the production of games software include pre-production, production, publishing, distribution and retail (Figure 3.3 lists the types of activities that occur at each of these stages in the development of a console game).[3]

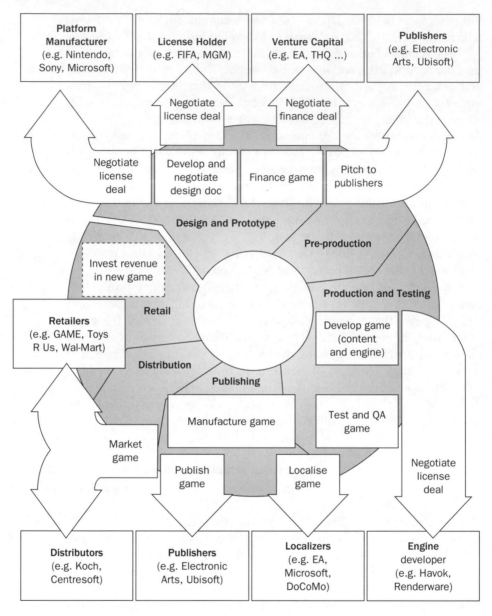

FIGURE 3.3   *The Digital Game Production Life Cycle*

Production of a console game can take approximately 18 months while PC and mini games take on average 15 and 3 months, respectively, to complete. The size of development teams again can vary widely but 12–20 people is average for a console game with at least half of these engaged in content development and design and the balance in programming and management (Tschang, 2003). Again there are variations from country to country.[4] In the UK, development teams are multi-functional and include all the skills needed to complete a project while in Japan companies tend to keep their core teams small and engage people with specialist skills only when they are needed (TerKeurst, 2002a).

The development of a game involves a number of pre-production decisions. Choosing the platform for which one wishes to develop is a crucial decision as it affects the design and technologies used to develop the game as well as the partners and channels one must negotiate with. For example, if a developer wishes to develop for one of the major console platforms they must negotiate with the manufacturer, pay a licence fee, acquire a specific development kit and follow their quality approval process. However, the costs of negotiating with the hardware manufacturer must be weighed against the potential profits to be gained from accessing the largest market segment.

The next major hurdle is to negotiate a publishing/distribution deal. There are three types of development company: first-party developers who are fully owned by a publishing company; second-party developers who are independent companies who are contracted to create games from concepts developed by a publisher; and third-party developers who are independent development houses who work on their own projects. For each, the source of the finance may vary, but all games begin as a concept or game proposal briefly described on a few pages of paper. Ten years ago this might have been sufficient to obtain some degree of funding, but today an advanced technical prototype must also be produced. Third party developers use this demo to secure a financial advance from a publisher although, as in more traditional media industries, it is easier for a developer with an established reputation to negotiate a larger advance and a higher percentage of royalties. Sometimes developers obtain finance from venture capitalists or private sources.[5] The extent of first-, second- or third-party development varies from market to market but one source suggests that almost two thirds of game development is done by first-party developers (Williams, 2002: 47). In other words, a majority of games are developed by teams working within or fully owned by a publisher.

If a publishing deal is agreed with a second- or third-party developer, the publisher becomes involved to varying degrees in the production process. Sometimes the publisher will try to get the developer to change the original game concept to fit with the portfolio of titles they already have in production. Usually they will appoint a producer to the project who will provide both technical and creative input and assist in the management of milestones. Publishers may also take charge of ensuring that a game meets the quality thresholds demanded by the console manufacturer and generally they organize user testing, market research, marketing, localization, manufacture of the game and negotiations with distributors and retailers.

The average development cost of a console game ranges between US $3–5 million but some games cost considerably more, particularly when the game is based on a film, book or sports licence. Increasingly developers or publishers licence intellectual property (IP) rights from another media for their game, for example, the right to use the voice and image of James Bond in a game (Kerr and Flynn, 2003). Developers may also try to reduce the amount of time it takes to programme a game by licensing a 3D graphics engine or middleware, that is software which provides a library of pre-programmed behaviours and plug-ins. These tools enable developers to reduce development time. For example *Harry Potter and the Philosopher's Stone*, published by Electronic Arts (EA) in 2001 for the PlayStation, PC, GBA and Game Boy Colour (GBC), was based on the Harry Potter licence and the developers of the PlayStation game licensed the UnReal Tournament 3D graphics engine.[6]

Many publishers, almost 80 per cent according to one estimate (Deutsche Bank, 2002: 26), own their own distribution channels and so this stage in the cycle may also be fully controlled by the publisher. The retail stage is more and more the preserve of large supermarket and specialist chains such as WalMart and Best Buy in the USA; GAME and Dixons in the UK. As the main access point to consumers retailers can significantly influence the success of a game through their allocation of shelfspace and in-store marketing. As supermarkets and specialist chains grow in size they have more power to negotiate discounts on wholesale products and returns. While variations on this production cycle exist the majority of games follow these production stages, as outlined in Figure 3.4.

The production cycle can also be viewed as a value chain. At each stage in the production cycle intermediaries add value to the core product and contribute to the final cost paid by the consumer. Figure 3.4 provides an estimate of the value added by each intermediary in the console value chain. According to this analysis, the developer/publisher and the retailer are the two key sources of value added in the digital game chain.

Console manufacturer	Developer	Publisher	Distributor	Retailer	Customer
↓	↓		↓	↓	↓
€10	€20		€6	€14	€50

FIGURE 3.4 *The digital games industry value chain – what each stage contributes to the final price of a game*

Source: Deutsche Bank, 2002: 18

The horizontal structure of the digital games industry: ● key market segments

While the previous section analysed the production of a product vertically from concept to market another way to analyse the games industry is horizontally and divide it into a number of different market segments. Williams (2002) divides the games industry into three market segments: consoles, handhelds and PCs, and describes each segment in terms of market share, competition and product. In what follows we will develop a slightly different segmentation taking games as our starting point and not the hardware or platforms (Kerr, 2006). In this segmentation we will group single and multiplayer console and handheld games together and extend the number of segments to include new markets around massive multiplayer online games and emergent games (MMOGs) and mini games played on PCs, i-TV and wireless/mobile platforms. There are two reasons why this segmentation makes sense. First, while sales of console and handheld games are the most significant in terms of sales at the moment (see Figure 3.2) it is clear that other markets are emerging which offer alternative business models, new types of games and are attracting new types of players. It is important that academics, policy-makers and game companies realize that opportunities exist outside segment one. Second, a hardware-based segmentation is unsatisfactory given the tendency for hybrid and new platforms to emerge at fairly regular intervals (see also Alvisi, Chapter 4). The development of MMOGs, for example, combines online and PC platforms to produce a new market segment with unique characteristics. In the future consoles may also allow one to play MMOGs.

TABLE 3.2 Key segments of the digital games industry

	Examples of platforms and games	Market concentration	Revenue model	Openness of hardware system	Software production process
Segment 1 – console games					
1A	Console/Video *Final Fantasy* on PS2 *Halo* on the Xbox *Donkey Kong* on the GameCube	Hardware numerous Sony, Microsoft, Nintendo	Hardware developed as a loss leader and money made on sales of software Games sold on CD through shops Many games now adding online and multiplayer functionality Premium retail price	Closed Proprietary and non-interoperable hardware systems	Games expensive to develop, little follow-up service costs Average length of development 18 months Average team size 12–40
1B	Handheld *Pokémon* on GBC, GBA, GBASP Also Gamepark, N-Gage and Zodiac Sony's PSP Nintendo's DS	Until recently a Nintendo hardware monopoly New entrants Nokia, Tapwave and Sony	Hardware developed as a loss leader and money made on sales of software Games sold on cartridges through shops Newer handhelds include multiplayer functionality Premium retail price	Closed Proprietary and non-interoperable hardware systems	Games expensive to develop, little follow-up service costs Average length of development 9 months Average team size 12–20
Segment 2 – standard PC games					
2	*Harry Potter and the Philosopher's Stone, Quake, Black and White, Diabhlo II and battle.net*	Numerous	Games sold on CD through shops Many games now adding online functionality and downloadable elements Cheaper retail price than segment 1	Common standards, non-proprietary technology	Games less expensive to develop than console and handheld Average length of development 15 months Average team size 12–15

TABLE 3.2 *(Continued)*

	Examples of platforms and games	Market concentration	Revenue model	Openness of hardware system	Software production process
Segment 3 – MMOGs					
	World of War craft Blizzard/ Vivendi *Lineage II* NCSoft	Numerous EA, Sony, Microsoft, NCSoft, Vivendi	Games sold on CD through shops but played online Consumers pay monthly subscription fee and online service charges to a telecoms operator	Common standards, non-proprietary technology Developed mainly for PC	Very expensive to develop and significant ongoing costs[1]
Segment 4 – mini casual games					
4A		Numerous players including the major players in other segments	Advertising used to support free games distributed via portals on the Internet Also pay-per-play and monthly subscriptions	Common standards, non-proprietary technology	Inexpensive to develop and small teams
4B	Mobile *Snake*, *Frogges*	Numerous players DoCoMo in Japan, Sprint in the US, also Sega and Sony	Games sold online and pay-per-download model Revenue divided between developer and operator	A number of competing proprietary technologies	Inexpensive to develop and small teams Average length of production 6 weeks to 3 months
4C	Digital television PlayJam in the UK and CableVision in the USA	Numerous players	Games channels offered as part of a digital subscription package Advertising an important revenue source as is SMS and telephone calls	A number of competing platforms and input devices	Inexpensive to develop and small teams

[1] Kline et al. (2003: 161) note that *Ultima Online* took two years to develop, was beta tested with 25,000 players and support staff costing one million dollars annually. Industry interviews have suggested initial development costs of approximately €15 million. Other sources estimate that *EverQuest* costs US $10 million annually to run, see http://www.gamespy.com/amdmmog/week3/

The four market segments identified in Table 3.2 are grouped according to the following four characteristics:

(1) Market concentration – monopoly, oligopoly or numerous companies.
(2) The revenue model – shop sales, online sales, subscription, pay-per-play, free, advertising.
(3) Degree of openness in hardware system – open, mixed, closed.
(4) Characteristics of the software production process – cost, length, team size.

Segment 1 includes games developed for both handheld and console platforms and is clearly the most significant in terms of market share at least according to current industry reports. These two platforms are combined into one segment given their similarities across the different criteria in all but their storage device. This segment is an oligopoly with three companies currently operating as hardware manufacturers, software publishers and game developers: Nintendo, Sony and Microsoft.[7]

The additional licence fee per unit sold that developers must pay to console manufacturers means that console games are sold at a premium price as boxed CDs or cartridges through specialist and non-specialist shops. The last section noted that the retailer is playing an increasingly important role in the production cycle and the value chain and an interesting development therefore is the growth of console games with online functionality. To date both Sony and Microsoft have launched online multiplayer services namely Xbox Live and PS2 Network Gaming, whereby people can play games online against other players and download additional game content. This development may ultimately change the revenue model in this segment and challenge the growing power of the retailer although a key barrier in many markets is access to broadband networks.

Segment 1 is also marked by the fact that there are a small number of competing and non-compatible technological systems which are upgraded every four to five years. Hardware lifecycles are a unique characteristic of this segment and pose considerable challenges to both developers and the market. While games can be 'ported', or translated, from one platform to another, hardware manufacturers usually try to make some games exclusive to their platform. Software exclusivity is a key selling point for hardware systems. Console manufacturers sell their systems as 'loss leaders' in order to build a large installed base of users.[8] The success of a hardware platform is both dependent on the number of units sold and the number of games sold for the platform (for further discussion of this, see Alvisi, Chapter 4). Indeed, sales of consoles are directly related to the number of high quality titles available for that console and hardware manufacturers work hard to ensure that there are a number of high quality titles available for their consoles on launch.

Segment 2 includes offline and multiplayer/networked PC games but not MMOGs. Current statistics suggest that this segment has a much smaller market share than segment 1, particularly in Japan and the USA. However, developers do not need specialist development kits to develop for a Windows or Apple personal computer given that they are based on common standards and open architecture. In addition, developers do not have to pay a licence fee to a hardware manufacturer. These facts are reflected in a cheaper retail price than console games. The downside of this openness is that there are a greater number of games competing for shelf space and sales. PC games are generally sold as boxed CDs through specialist and non-specialist retail outlets although many companies release upgrades and patches online. Companies also provide important development resources and roots to India and Far East developers.

Despite the fact that the console and PC market is developing online elements, MMOGs are marked by specificities that require classification as a separate segment; not least the fact that they are persistent. **Segment 3** is strongly vertically integrated and a small number of large companies control development, publishing and distribution. However the underlying technologies are open platform, as in segment 2, and currently based on PC and Internet common standards. Developing a persistent world requires significant investment not only in initial development but also in ongoing costs including maintenance, expansions and customer/community support. Finally, while most MMOGs are sold on CD through shops the consumer must also pay a monthly subscription fee and ongoing telephone charges to play in the persistent world.

The final segment, **segment 4**, covers the development of mini or casual games for platforms like i-TV, mobile phones, PDAs and the Internet. This sector is embryonic but in general is characterized by shorter development cycles and lower production costs than other segments. There are numerous players and a mixture of open and proprietary technologies. There are also many revenue models: pay-per-download, pay-per-play, advertising. For example, most telecom operators offer users access to mobile games on a pay-per-play or pay per-download basis. In most cases developers are not paid a cash advance and rely on a share of the revenues generated by the game; a share which varies from operator to operator and territory to territory. In Japan the i-mode model adopted by NTT's DoCoMo is generous and content developers may receive up to 90 per cent of revenues. In Europe the revenue share obtained by developers varies widely from a low of 20 per cent to 50 per cent. In the USA the rate is closer to 80 per cent (TerKeurst, 2002b). Some mobile developers have indicated in interviews that as mobile handsets improve technologically mobile games may be sold through specialist and non-specialist shops.

On the Internet and i-TV platforms mini games are often provided for free and the service paid for through advertising or costs associated with registering (ringing) in one's high score. Another development is advergaming – the development of free games which are paid for in advance by a client in order to advertise a particular brand such as the Nokia Game. So far I have analysed the structure of the digital games industry along vertical and horizontal axes. However, some companies operate in more than one stage of the production cycle and in more than one segment, as Breakout box 3.1 illustrates. Expansion and growth through company acquisitions is just one of the key trends in the games industry which we will examine in the next section.

BREAKOUT BOX 3.1 ● ● ●

Case study: Microsoft

Microsoft currently has a presence in all four of the segments outlined above and in all stages of the production cycle. Microsoft entered the games industry as a software developer and publisher of PC games (segment 2) and one of its biggest hits in this market was Flight Simulator *launched in 1983. The launch of the Xbox in 2001 and Xbox 360 in 2005 signalled a move upstream in the production cycle into hardware manufacturing and horizontally into segment 1. The company has extended the multiplayer capacity of its console with the launch of Xbox Live in 2002. A closed subscription-based service, Xbox Live allows users to play against players around the world over broadband networks.*

Microsoft also publishes the MMOG Asheron's Call, *developed by Turbine Entertainment Software Corporation from Boston. In addition, the company has ongoing interests in interactive television/WebTV and distributes free web games on 'The Zone' on MSN. This horizontal move into different industry sub-sectors and vertical moves upstream and downstream is illustrative of trends more generally in the industry as uncertainty over future delivery platforms grows and companies attempt to minimize risk.*

Further sources of information: Takahashi (2002);
http://www.xbox.com;www.xboxlivecommunity.com;www.microsoft.com/games/ac;
zone. msn.com/en/root/default.html

Key trends in the digital games Industry ●

Different industrial reports highlight different trends in the digital games industry. The Spectrum (2002) report notes that the digital games industry is increasingly hits driven, that production costs are rapidly increasing, that demand is broadening and that there are an increasing number of platforms. The Deutsche Bank (2002) report notes that publishers are getting bigger, R&D and marketing costs are rising, games are increasingly being sold by non-specialist retailers and that next generation consoles will be complex boxes capable of providing multiple entertainment options. In the space that remains, this chapter will briefly analyse two key trends: industrial consolidation and licensing.

Consolidation: vertical and horizontal integration ●

In the last section we saw that both monopolies and oligopolies have emerged in the digital games industry, particularly in segment 1. However, across all segments it is clear that the dominant corporate strategy is vertical integration up and down the production cycle and to a somewhat lesser degree horizontal integration across market segments. An analysis of the digital games industry across all the segments over the past five years reveals that in order to compete with Sony, Nintendo and Microsoft, and offset the growth in retailer size, independent publishers are scaling up through acquisitions and globally there are now a core of between 10 and 20 independent publishers (Cornford et al., 2000; Kerr and Flynn, 2003; Pham, 2001). Publishers have also been taking on other functions in the production cycle. For example, publishers have been acquiring distribution channels in order to ensure that their products reach retailers and they have been buying into, or taking over, development studios. Ownership of development brings two benefits: a means of maintaining control over production and deadlines (Cornford et al., 2000) and a means of retaining more of the revenue gained from the sale of a game. Publishers may also acquire development studios in order to gain access to intellectual property; as in the purchase by Infogrames of Shiny Entertainment for US $47 million in 2002 to obtain exclusive publishing rights to the Matrix games. This increasing vertical integration along the production cycle suggests that over time a situation may emerge where a small number of publishers dominate the industry; as the majors do in the film industry.

Vertical consolidation is driven by a desire to control more aspects of the value chain and to create economies of scale whereby increased distribution of a game leads to increased sales, lower per-unit production costs and greater profits. This drive for economies of scale is nothing new. Garnham (1990) argues that capitalism tends to encourage concentration whereby a small number of firms effectively control enough of the market to manipulate it in their favour. Murdoch and Golding (1997) point out that all media industries have gone through a process of growth from small-scale production to large concentrated corporations. The move to create economies of scale in the games industry is being driven by the increasing costs of producing and marketing games, especially console games, the increasing power of retailers and other distribution gatekeepers and the related downward pressure on prices in the marketplace.

A related strategy is the creation of economies of scope. Economies of scope are a fundamental means by which the media industries more generally, and publishers in particular, reduce uncertainty of demand. The development and publishing of a console and PC game is costly while reproduction is relatively cheap, especially of games sold on CD (Cornford et al., 2000). Publishers, as the main source of finance for game development, shoulder most of the investment risk. However, there is no guarantee that a game will make a profit: indeed a very high percentage of games fail to make a profit. As a result publishers must develop a broad catalogue of titles in different genres and across different sub-sectors in order to ensure they have at least one successful title. This provides an incentive for games companies to grow through acquisitions in different media markets. Table 3.3 illustrates how horizontal consolidation in the ten largest media corporations in the world operate across multiple media markets. Both Sony and Vivendi Universal, for example, operate at many levels of the digital games business but they are able to achieve economies by exploiting synergies with their business interests in film, broadcasting and music. Indeed, the trend towards horizontal consolidation, especially prevalent in the 1990s and early part of this decade, and the growing economic significance of the digital games industry have helped to stimulate the next trend that we shall look at, licensing.

● Licensing

A further strategy which publishers and developers use to overcome the uncertainty of demand for games is to associate the game with a high

TABLE 3.3 Percentage of turnover by media

	AOL Time Warner	Walt Disney	Viacom	Sony[1]	Bertelsmann	Vivendi Universal[2]	News Corp.
Filmed entertainment	24.5	26.4	14.8	28.8		34.5	26.6
Cable channels		18.6	19.2			12.3	18.0
Broadcasting		20.0	30.4		23.8	26.6	28.1
Cable	17.2						
Interactive (games, online, new media)	22.2			44.6		4.4	
Theme parks		25.5					
Music	10.3			26.6	14.8	34.5	
Radio			15.3				
Publishing	13.2				30.2		28.7
Retail		9.6	22.6		14.8		
Other					20.3		4.3
Intersegmental elimination	−6.1		−2.4		−3.9		

Source: Screen Digest, 2003

[1] Game, music and pictures only.

[2] Excluding telecoms

profile intellectual property purchased from another cultural sphere, what film historian Thomas Schatz has called 'pre-sold' properties (1993). Kline et al. (2003) note that drawing on pre-existing cultural goods reduces marketing costs because the most expensive element, building awareness, has already been done. From real world properties, such as David Beckham, to television properties, such as *Starsky and Hutch*, to film properties, such as *The Matrix*, it would appear that licensing is becoming increasingly widespread. Screen Digest notes that in 2000 'licence-based titles accounted for 45 per cent of all-formats UK top 100, up from 28 per cent in 1997 and 42.5 per cent in 1999' (Screen Digest, 2001). Table 3.4 lists the top selling digital games in the UK in November 2005. The two top selling games are both based on licences from other media and the list includes games based on licences from films, books and sport. The trend towards licences is particularly evident in the top-selling console games and games for mobile phones and less so in the top ten PC games. Increasingly, the top-selling titles are sequels released annually or bi-annually. Similar trends can be observed from US game charts although top-selling sports licences are different.

One viewpoint is that increased cross-media licensing or 'intertextuality' – where a media text draws upon the user's knowledge of other

TABLE 3.4 UK Games Charts, top selling games on all platforms, November 2005

1. Harry Potter and the Goblet of Fire
2. Star Wars: Battlefront 2
3. WWE SmackDown! Vs Raw 2006
4. Pro Evolution Soccer 5
5. FIFA 06
6. The Matrix: Path of Neo
7. World Tour Soccer
8. The SIMS 2
9. Gun
10. Grand Theft Auto: Liberty City Stories

Source: www.elspa.com

media texts – is a good thing as it helps to broaden the market by providing themes, narratives and characters of which non-gamers are already aware. Clearly publishers and developers feel that the addition of a licence increases their chances of having a hit. A political economic perspective however would ask if the increasing interdependence between media products in different media industries is leading to a reduction in the overall diversity of texts and the scope for radical innovation (Wasko, 1994). Recent research would appear to suggest that the growth of licences combined with consolidation in the digital games industry is making it increasingly difficult for new ideas and third-party developers to enter the market, particularly in segments 1, 2 and 3 (Kerr and Flynn, 2003). This works on a number of levels. It can make it increasingly difficult for new ideas to get a publishing deal, regardless of the developer's reputation. Indeed the idea for *The Sims* was initially rejected as unworkable and unmarketable. It can also mean that larger and larger companies are content to build brands, produce sequels and license properties between their different media operations while smaller independents struggle to compete. When one examines recent media projects by global companies, for example, Vivendi Universal's film and game *The Hulk*, one can see how companies actively exploit synergies between their different media divisions. For large corporations it would appear that the business of making digital games fits quite nicely alongside the business of making other media products. For everyone else content innovation and securing access to markets are key challenges.

Relevant web sites ● ● ○

Academic Gamers www.academic-gamers.org
Computer Entertainment Suppliers Association www.cesa.jp/english/
Entertainment & Leisure Software Publishers Association www.elspa.com
Entertainment Software Association www.theesa.com
Gamasutra www.gamasutra.com
Gamebiz www.gamesbiz.net
Games Investor www.gamesinvestor.com
Korean Game Development Institute www.gameinfinity.or.kr/en/index.php
NPD Funworld www.npdfunworld.com
Screen Digest www.screendigest.com
Terra Nova terranova.blogs.com/terra_nova

Notes ●

1 The ESA was formerly known as the Interactive Digital Software Association (IDSA).
2 See http://www.gameinfinity.or.kr/en/sub2_1.php
3 Kline et al (2003) provide an alternative to Figure 3.3 in their book.
4 See http:// www.gameinfinity.or.kr/en/pdf/Chapter%202(18%7E32).pdf
5 Some third party developers, such as Vis Entertainment plc in Scotland, are developing alternative funding models in an effort to avoid relying solely on publishers for funding. For the sequel to *State of Emergency* (2002), Vis has created a special function company funded by shareholders. See http://www.gamasutra.com/php-bin/news_index.php?story=2205
6 For more information on this title, see http://www.mobygames.com/game/versions/gameId,5416/
7 An oligopoly exists where control or power rests with a small group of companies.
8 A loss leader is a product sold below cost to attract customers.

References ●

Aoyama, Y. and H. Izushi (2003) 'Hardware gimmick or cultural innovation? Technological, cultural and social foundations of the Japanese video game industry', *Research Policy*, 32: 423–44.
Asakura, R. (2000) *Revolutionaries at Sony: The Making of the Sony Playstation and the Visionaries Who Conquered the World of Video Games*. Hampshire: McGraw-Hill.

Cornford, J., Naylor, R. and Driver, S. (2000) 'New media and regional development: the case of the UK computer and video games industry', in A. Giunta, A. Lagendijk and A. Pike (eds), *Restructuring Industry and Territory. The Experience of Europe's Regions*. London: The Stationery Office. pp. 83–108.

DataMonitor (2002) *Global Electronic Games, 2001–2007. Riding the Next Generation Wave*. London: Datamonitor Corporation.

Deutsche Bank (2002) *The Video Games Industry. Game Over or Extended Play?* Frankfurt: Deutsche Bank.

ESA (2003) 'Industry sales and economic data, 2003 consumer spending poll', retrieved August 2003 from: http://www.thesa.com/pressroom.html

ESA (2004) *Essential Facts About the Computers and Video Game Industry*. Retrieved 20 July, 2004, from: www.theesa.com

Garnham, N. (1990) *Capitalism and Communication. Global Culture and the Economics of Information*. London: Sage.

Murdock, G. and Golding, P. (1997) 'For a political economy of mass communications', in P. Golding and G. Murdock (eds), *The Political Economy of the Media*. Cheltenham: Edward Elgar. Vol 1: 3–50.

Herz, J.C. (1997) *Joystick Nation*. London: Abacus.

IDSA (2001) 'Economic impacts of the demand for playing interactive entertainment software', Accessed 16 May 2001, www.idsa.com/pressroom.html

Kerr, A. (2006) *The Business and Culture of Digital Games: Gamework/ Gameplay*. London: Sage.

Kerr, A. and Flynn, R. (2003) 'Revisiting globalisation through the movie and digital games industries', *Convergence: The Journal of Research into New Media Technologies,* (2): 91–113.

Kline, S., Dyer-Witheford, N. and de Peuter, G. (2003) *Digital Play: The Interaction of Technology; Culture and Marketing*. Montreal: McGill Queen; University Press.

Mosco, V. (1996) *The Political Economy of Communication. Rethinking and Renewal*. London: Sage.

Motion Picture Association of America (MPAA) (2002) '2001 US economic review. Box office', retrieved 6 March 2002 from: www.mpaa.org/useconomicreview/ 2001Economic/sld002.htm

OECD (2004) Digital Broadband Content: Music. Unpublished internal report. Paris: OECD.

Pham, A. (2001) 'Video game firms power up; amid sector's consolidations craze, a contest of survival intensifies', retrieved 22 May 2002 from: http:// web.lexis-nexis.com/professional/

Poole, S. (2000) *Trigger Happy, the Inner Life of Videogames*. London: Fourth Estate.

Schatz, T. (1993) 'The new Hollywood', in A. Colins (ed.), *Film Theory Goes to the Movies*. New York: Routledge. pp. 8–36.

Screen Digest (2001) *Interactive Leisure Software: Market Assessment and Forecasts to 2005*. London: Screen Digest.

Screen Digest (2003) 'AOL/TW stretches lead as top media company', in *Screen Digest*, 197, July.

Screen Digest (2004) 'Interactive leisure software report, 4th edition', retrieved 8 May 2005, from: www.elspa.com.serv.screendigestinevo.asp

Sheff, D. (1993) *Nintendo's Battle to Dominate an Industry*. London: Hodder and Stoughton.

Spectrum Strategy Consultants (2002) *From Exuberant Youth to Sustainable Maturity. Competitiveness Analysis of the UK Games Software Sector*. London: Department of Trade and Industry (DTI).

Takahashi, D. (2002) *Opening the XBox: Inside Microsoft's Plan to Unleash an Entertainment Revolution*. Roseville, CA: Prima Publishing.

TerKeurst, J. (2002a) *Games Are Like Fruit. Japanese Best Practice in Digital Game Development*. Dundee: DT, International Technology Service Mission, IC CAVE.

TerKeurst, J. (2002b) *Mobilising Entertainment Content. North American Best Practice in Mobile Entertainment*. London: DTI, TIGA, IC CAVE.

Tschang, T. (2003) 'Beyond normal products and development processes: computer games as interactive experiential good and their manner of development', paper presented at What Do We Know about Innovation? A conference in honour of Keith Pavitt, Freeman Centre, University of Sussex, UK, retrieved from: www.sussex.ac.uk/units/spru/events/kp_cont_03/documents/Tschang.pdf

Wasko, J. (1994) *Hollywood in the Information Age: Beyond the Silver Screen*. Oxford: Polity Press.

Williams, D. (2002) 'Structure and competition in the US home video game industry', *The International Journal on Media Management*, 4 (1): 41–54.

4   The economics of digital games

Alberto Alvisi

Some may wonder why there is a need to dedicate a chapter to the economic aspects of digital games: after all, digital games are about creativity, eye-to-hand coordination, skill and fun, and, to some extent, can be considered a new form of art. Nevertheless, one must not forget that the digital games business is worth several billion dollars per year, that the players are giants such as Microsoft, Sony and Nintendo, and that games are essentially an industrial product created by companies who, in the long run, must cover all the costs they bear.

The aim of this chapter is to introduce the reader to the critical factors that drive competition and determine the success or failure of companies, and to shed light on the quite peculiar business model of the digital games industry. This will be achieved by the use of basic tools to examine analytically the various aspects of the economic environment linked to digital games. For a detailed description of the industry, it is necessary to analyse the supply side separate from the demand side, paying particular attention to the distinction between hardware and software, since digital games are typical systemic products, that is, a combination of two, equally important, elements for the end product. The chapter will look at digital games as a system, integrating these concepts and explaining their interaction to formalize the business model of the industry.

The supply side

Cost structure: consoles

Consoles are the 'hardware' side of digital games, which means that a significant number of physical components are needed such as graphic chip, memory, case, cables, and so on. Consoles can be classified as typical production goods in that huge investments are needed to design, engineer and test the product, and production facilities have to be set up to meet demand. Effectively forecasting the demand level is a crucial factor, since a production plant has a *minimum efficient plant size*. Of course, lower than expected sales mean higher 'per unit' costs due to the under optimization of production capacity. Plants, marketing expenditures, engineering and design investments are examples of fixed cost and their effect on unitary costs is inversely proportional to the output volume. That is to say, unitary costs decrease as production increases.

On the other hand, if demand exceeds the predicted level, *diseconomies of scale* may arise, as capacity cannot be quickly adapted due to the large investments needed, and costs may be higher than expected. Furthermore, supply may be eventually unable to cope with demand resulting in a scarcity of goods on the market. To some extent, this could be to the producer's advantage, since scarcity could add to the product's appeal as with PlayStation 2's European launch. On the other hand, the lack of products on the shelves may encourage consumers to buy a competitor's product.

We can also note that consoles very seldom sport custom chips and instead rely on established firms for integrated circuits.[1] Sony's decision to internally produce the hardware of PlayStation 2 can be interpreted as a decision to convert the variable costs for the supply of chips into a fixed cost so as to better exploit cost reductions triggered by *economies of volume* (the possibility of spreading fixed costs over a large number of units).

BREAKOUT BOX 4.1 ● ● ●

Glossary

Barriers to entry   Obstacles to the entry of new firms into a market. Barriers can be technical, legal, financial or strong branding of the existing product.
Diseconomies of scale   An increase of costs per unit caused by operating beyond the optimal level.

(Continued)

(Continued)

Economies of scale   *A decrease of unitary costs caused by economies generated by a larger scale of operations.*

Economies of volume   *A decrease of unitary costs caused by spreading the fixed costs over a higher output volume.*

Fixed cost   *Cost that does not vary with the volume produced.*

Killer application   *A game title whose appeal is strong enough to justify the purchase of the console just to play it. A killer application must be platform exclusive.*

Minimum efficient plant size   *The output level at which most scale economies are exploited.*

Sunk cost   *A cost that is not recoverable once sustained.*

Tie-ratio   *The average number of games purchased by each user.*

Variable cost   *Cost that does vary with the volume produced.*

Cost structure: games

Games represent the 'software' side of a digital games system. The cost structure of software production is strikingly different to that of hardware. First, the physical support has little effect on total costs. Furthermore, the vast majority of costs are incurred while creating the very first copy (the same cost pattern applies to books, records and movies). High budget games (as well as high budget movies or records) can be duplicated for a fraction of the cost of the first copy, which is both a *fixed cost* and a *sunk cost*. The unbalanced ratio between fixed and variable costs implies the extreme importance of economies of volume and the minimal effect of marginal costs.

Royalties requested by hardware manufacturers represent an extremely important part of the cost structure. While PCs are an open system, in that everyone is allowed to develop and market any kind of software for them, no firm is allowed to publish a game for a console, unless the firm is legally authorized to do so by the owner of the hardware's copyright – typically the producer of the console itself. For each copy sold, the publisher must pay a fixed amount, ranging from approximately €5 to €10. This is, by far, the largest variable cost of producing console games and central to the business model.

Over the years, console software has abandoned Mask ROM cartridges[2] in favour of optical solutions (with the notable exception of handhelds, however, the situation may change in the near future, if Sony PSP should prove itself successful). As a result, CD- and DVD-based games are not only much cheaper to produce, but diseconomies of scale have no effect on production as increasing press runs is a routine task. This consideration was a crucial factor in many companies' decisions to discontinue their support of Nintendo in the Nintendo 64 era, due to the high risks connected to the advance production of a large number of relatively expensive copies of the game. Rumours indicate an area in the New Mexican desert, Alamogordo, where Atari buried millions of unsold *ET* cartridges.

Pricing policies: consoles

The main difference between PCs and games consoles lies in their architecture. From a technological standpoint, there is next to no difference between an Xbox and a PC. However, consoles are 'closed systems' which means that the hardware architecture must remain basically the same for the entire life-span of the machine to ensure software compatibility to all users from early adopters to laggards. The hardware may go through several modifications in order to solve problems, save costs or reposition the product (as with the PS One and Megadrive II) but the architecture must remain the same.

Some consoles aged better than others, but all shared a common trait: they were quite ahead of their time in terms of graphical capabilities/ sale price. The Atari 2600 had little competition, but the SEGA Megadrive (1988) rivalled (and in many cases surpassed) the Commodore Amiga (1987) at less than half the launch price (US $199 versus US $799). Similarly, the Sony PlayStation (1994) showed performances comparable to a Pentium 133, 8 MB graphic card PC, a cutting edge configuration until early 1996. This is possible due to the fact that consoles are launched at a price which does not cover all costs, but rather, is determined by a psychological threshold in the consumer's mind. We can easily compare the success of consoles priced *within* the limit to those that were priced *beyond*. The arcade-based Neo-Geo and its huge and pricey cartridges, the Atari Jaguar, 3DO, and SEGA Saturn all suffered the consequences of an excessive retail price. SEGA Master System, Super Nintendo, and PlayStation were all priced on a par (or lower) than the competition. This does not mean that a reasonable launch price is a guarantee for success but rather that an excessive price could severely hamper the chances of success for new hardware. For example, in the case of Nintendo's GameCube the competitive price was not sufficient to compensate for the near 20 million PlayStation 2s already sold.

To summarize, consoles are basically launched at a price determined by psychological factors, more than by economic considerations. Game enthusiasts and novelty fanatics are typical early adopters of the newly released consoles. In marketing terms, these kinds of customers are referred to as 'pioneers'[3]: their relative low price-sensitivity can be used by manufacturers to ask for a relative high price, so as to minimize losses on hardware sales. Nevertheless, it is impossible to fully exploit their revenue-generating potential because of the necessity to quickly increase the installed base in order to attract independent developers.

Further on in the console's life cycle the price is lowered each time sales begin to decrease in order to capture new segments of customers more sensitive to price. Price-cutting decisions are not determined by savings in economies of volume or scale, but by demand. All console producers have, so far, adopted this policy, and, in fact, PlayStation 2's strong sales justify the flat slope of its price curve.

Pricing policies: games

The console market is controlled by a small number of firms who have the copyright of the hardware. Their influence extends over the pricing policies of companies who produce games and this is a strong disincentive for games to compete on price. At the same time, the cost structure of games, and their sunk nature are incentives for publishers to drastically cut the price of older games and still retain a very high margin. Price reductions of older games can give a strong boost to software sales (the 'Platinum' edition, a collection of best selling games sold at a discounted price, of Sony *Gran Turismo 2* topped the UK games charts for months, despite the game being several months old. The success of the Platinum series encouraged other producers to adopt a strategy quite common in PC games. Of course, top-selling games do not require a price rebate, as well demonstrated by Rockstar's *Grand Theft Auto 3*, which became a budget title only after the launch of the equally successful prequel *GTA: Vice City*.

BREAKOUT BOX 4.2 ● ● ●

Market structures

Markets can be classified according to several dimensions: size, geographical location and so forth. One of the most famous classifications in economics distinguishes between three main structures: perfect competition, oligopoly and monopoly. In perfect competition firms are price-takers – they cannot influence the price at which its goods are sold. As consumers have perfect information, products are homogeneous and there are many firms in the market.

In the opposite case, monopoly, there is a single firm that sets the price in order to maximize its profit according to a downward-sloping demand curve (the higher the price, the lower quantity sold). Various kinds of barriers to entry are employed including legal, institutional, financial and other aspects to prevent other firms from entering the same market.

Both cases offer little, if any, element for strategic discussion, but the intermediate situation, the oligopoly, presents a different situation. In oligopoly a small number of firms interact with each other for the supremacy over the same market. Since firms are assumed to be similar in terms of bargaining power, size and cost structure, competition based on price is quite uncommon, since each reduction would be immediately replicated by competitors, taking their relative position back to the starting point, but at a lower price level for each firm.

Considerations concerning non price-based competition did not apply during the PlayStation versus Nintendo 64 era, when it was quite common to see a strong difference in price in favour of Sony's games. The two firms chose a different cost structure and this, in turn, affected their market performance: Sony adopted the CD-ROM as a medium, while Nintendo stuck with mask-ROM cartridges. Each support had both advantages and disadvantages such as capacity, access speed, protection against piracy. However, from an economic standpoint, the biggest difference relied on production costs: CDs were considerably cheaper than cartridges. With the adoption of optical media Sony was able to reduce the price of software, knowing that Nintendo could not adopt the same strategy without a noticeable reduction in profit.

● The demand side

● Consoles

The drive behind the decision to buy a games console is mainly determined by the will to play games. In the long run, the survival chances of a digital games system depend on the availability of quality titles, which, in turn, affects the installed consumer base. This creates a virtuous circle: the higher the installed base, the more attractive the platform becomes for independent developers and more games are likely to become available. While the two elements which determine the purchaser's decision are price and the games available, both in terms of quantity and quality, several other variables, such as backwards compatibility and accessory features can also effect this decision.

● Backwards compatibility

Several consoles in the past offered the possibility to play games released for previous systems via various kinds of adapters. The Atari 5200 and 7800, SEGA Megadrive, Super Nintendo Entertainment System, and PlayStation 2 all offered compatibility with their predecessors. Generally the compatibility is granted by physically integrating the old hardware into the new console: Sony PlayStation 2 and SEGA Megadrive installed respective predecessors' main chip as I/O controller (i.e. the functional unit that controls input-output channels). The effect of this feature is questionable: customers generally buy new systems if attracted to their superior graphic capabilities (considering that the lifespan of a games console is approximately five years, improvements are generally noticeable). Additionally, games designed to run on obsolete hardware do not fully exploit the potential of the new machine. Nevertheless, this option is often implemented because of its strong marketing potential and relative low cost.

● Accessory features

Following the introduction of optical support, games consoles started offering accessory features not strictly linked to games. Sony PlayStation and SEGA Saturn both offered the possibility to play Audio CDs. The latter went one step further, allowing Video CD support (MPEG-1 video) with a dedicated add-on. These features had little (if any) effect, due to the fact that the awkward game controller and the television-based interface were sub-optimal devices as opposed to a standard remote control and an LCD panel. Also, the Video CD standard was not very common outside Asia. Accessory features became a major factor in the launch of PlayStation 2 in Japan. Its ability to play DVDs was a strong sales point during its first year: according to Sony, PlayStation 2 shipments reached 3.52 million units on 25 October 2000. At the same time, software shipments amounted to 8 million units, resulting in a poor *tie-ratio* of 2.27 (source: www.scee.com). To make a rough comparison, the Xbox tie ratio was 3.8 four months after its North American launch (source: Gameplay, April 2002, GMK).

Despite accessory features boosting the commercial performance in the short run, a console's attractiveness is mainly determined by the quality and range of games available. Exclusive rights (both absolute and temporal) and/or superior versions (graphic or content wise) of successful games, strongly influence the decision to purchase. Sony's exclusive rights over the Konami soccer series *Winning Eleven* (dubbed *International Superstar Soccer* and *Pro Evolution Soccer* in its European incarnation) were a solid selling point in the European market, and UbiSoft's *Splinter Cell*'s temporal exclusivity contributed to Xbox's good performance at Christmas 2002. On the other hand, the lack of support from some key developers (Electronic Arts and SquareSoft) contributed to SEGA's Dreamcast failure.

Launch titles are the 'business card' of a system, having to justify the adoption of the console as it is released. A lacklustre line-up at launch may discourage early adopters, therefore working against the novelty factor represented by the superior technical capabilities of the console: there are no technical features advanced enough to represent an alternative to appealing games. In the 24 months following the launch of a system it is essential that one or more so called **killer applications** becomes available to convince customers to adopt the console in favour of the competitors' or to replace the one they already own. Great games at launch must be backed-up by a regular flow of attractive titles over time. In this respect, an extremely important role is played by expectations: games due for release in a foreseeable future are just as important as available games in influencing customer behaviour. Managing expectations is quite a delicate task. SEGA Dreamcast's failure was mainly determined by the looming shadow of the upcoming Sony PlayStation 2 with its missile-guidance capable Graphic Process Unit and its long list of successful franchises. At the time, the original PlayStation was stronger than ever and its hardware and software sales were rampant (PlayStation was the best selling console even in the first year following the launch of its successor). SEGA's acclaimed software library was not enough to resist the effect of Sony's marketing campaign and buyers did not jump on SEGA's bandwagon, doubting its long run survival potential.[4]

Games

In economic terms, games can be considered 'experience goods', that is goods whose quality can only be determined after their sale through their consumption. Brand new goods are typically experience goods as their novelty does not allow them to be compared to previous products. Some categories of goods maintain their experiential nature even though the product may not be new. Books, records, movies and magazines are perfect examples of experience goods. Firms selling these kinds of products have developed several strategies, and their effectiveness holds true for digital games as well. The most important thing is to inform customers of the quality of the product. To do so, several options are available.

One is the distribution of demonstration versions of the product. For console games this was not possible until the introduction of optical support, which dramatically lowered the cost to produce and distribute the demo. Recently, broadband Internet introduced in the current generation of consoles has the possibility of solving, or at least softening, many of these problems, allowing users to download partial demos of a game at nearly zero cost.

An alternative way to communicate the quality of the product prior to the actual purchase is to use a licence linked to a successful film, comic book, famous sportsperson, non-digital game, and so on. Even though this kind of game has often proven to be lacklustre according to games critics,[5] they often result in a commercial success. Despite low ratings in the specialized press, Atari's *Enter the Matrix* (a tie-in to the sequel of the blockbuster *The Matrix*) managed to sell over 2.5 million copies in less than a month after its release (source: Atari press release).

Huge investments in marketing campaigns may also facilitate the process of knowledge diffusion. Furthermore, the sunken nature of this kind of expenditure induces potential buyers to attach more value to the title, since in common knowledge 'a poor game is not worth a marketing campaign' (see Kotler [2003] for a discussion on the importance of signals in marketing.)

One of the most severe **barriers to entry** (Porter, 1980) a firm must overcome is the reputation of consolidated franchises or mascots.

Capcom's *Street Fighter*, SquareEnix's *Final Fantasy* or Rockstar Games's *Grand Theft Auto* are examples of franchises which, over time, have built up a reputation for their excellence in their respective category. A mascot is a character (generally, but not exclusively, cartoonish) starring in several games, which signals the quality of the game through consumers' previous experience with games. In the majority of cases, a mascot spans a franchise (such as Ubisoft's *Rayman* or Eidos's *Tomb Raider* series), but the presence of a mascot can be used to promote a completely different kind of game from its original series as with the extensive use of Nintendo's icon, Mario, in tennis, kart, golf and party games. The use of mascots to signal quality is no different from the use of other forms of branding.

Mascots and franchises represent an extremely valuable asset, subject to path-dependent processes and slow accumulation over time. From this point, franchises and mascots can be considered as firm resources and software houses are generally very careful in associating mediocre games with a franchise or a mascot (see Grant [1998] for a discussion on the role of resources in strategy formulation) given that a disappointing game could ruin, or at least severely compromise, the appeal of the series or of the mascot itself.[6]

Of course, these options are not self-excluding alternatives, but can rather be combined in a variety of ways. Electronic Arts' *FIFA* soccer offers games demos, a clear example of an extremely famous and long lasting franchise with a very important license, and are distributed with various magazines and backed-up by a massive marketing campaign in print, on air and on the web.

Digital games as a system ●

So far we have considered software and hardware separately. However, it is of limited use to make a distinction between consoles and games, since these two products are only valuable in conjunction with one another. In industrial economics the most famous instrument for analysis is Michael Porter's 5-Forces Framework (1980). Porter identifies the five forces which compete for the market: clients, suppliers, potential entrants, competitors and substitutes. Quite simply, in Porter's view, the profitability of a firm operating in a given industry is mainly determined by the intensity of the competitive forces that operate within it: the stronger the force, the higher the profit share it will capture. In Porter's framework, firms within the same industry are involved in a 'zero-sum game': higher profitability can only be obtained at the expense of other firms.

While this scheme proves to be extremely valuable in traditional industries, its usage is highly unsuccessful when applied to a number of others. The relationship between a firm that produces games and another that produces consoles cannot be explained using the Porterian framework: they clearly do not have a buyer–supplier relationship, since no part of a game is needed to build a console. At the same time, they are not competitors or substitutes (a console without games would be of little use, as would be games without a console) despite the fact that most console producers are developers and publishers of games, as well. As shown by the transition of SEGA into a software-only firm and Sony's success in the hardware industry, producers of games and consoles can, to some extent, consider each other potential entrants.

The Brandenburger and Nalebuff (1996) concept of complementors is a far more effective framework with which to analyse the systemic nature of consoles and digital games. For them, 'A complement to one product or service is any other product or service that makes the first one more attractive' (from Co-opetition homepage, mayet.som. yale.edu/coopetition/index2.html). By distinguishing between suppliers, clients, competitors and complementors, the Value Net model captures much of the richness of the relationships in the industry.

Considering digital games as a system means acknowledging that customers are attracted to the best combination of hardware and software (an extremely powerful hardware without games to exploit it is just as unattractive as a hardware with technical shortcomings so evident to limit games potential), and that for console manufacturers it is extremely important to build strong linkages with software *and* hardware producers. The relationships between console producers and third-party developers are equally important: all console producers are software developers and their own strategies have a direct influence on third-party developers. Microsoft's decision to build its own servers to back-up the LIVE project initially alienated the support of Electronic Arts, who preferred Sony's more customisable, manageable and less structured online plan, depriving 2004 versions of its popular sport franchises of network capabilities.

Digital games business model ●

As mentioned above, hardware is generally sold at a loss, with royalties on games being the main source of revenues for companies such as Sony, Nintendo and Microsoft. In this respect, the business model is strikingly similar to that found in razor blades or inkjet printers, where the main unit is almost given away for free and consumables are sold at a very high margin. The higher the tie-ratio, the more successful (in terms of revenues) a system is. For digital games companies to obtain a high tie-ratio, two conditions must be met:

(1)   a high number of attractive games must be available; and
(2)   it must be possible to discriminate between those who are valuable customers and those who are not.

Let's first examine the latter condition. A valuable customer is one willing to purchase several games during the console's life cycle. Pricing policies in the digital games industry are mainly driven not by economic considerations, but by the will to contribute to the diffusion of the hardware which is sold at a fraction of the production cost. So why don't hardware manufacturers give away the console for free in order to give maximum burst to the adoption process and to recover losses with software sales? Quite simply because this would not discriminate between customers. The purchase of the console represents some kind of long-term investment, a signal on the buyers' side of their intentions to support the hardware via the purchase of software to justify the expenditure. If consoles were given away for free the installed base would no longer represent a strong indicator of the revenue-generating potential for software developers. This brings us back to the first consideration: third-party developers' interest in a system is directly proportional to the diffusion of the system itself; the higher the installed base, the higher the profit potential.

Of course, it is possible to internally produce most of the software to back-up the console but this solution has recently proven less effective than relying on a strong line-up of external publishers. Nintendo is acclaimed as one of the best software companies in the history of digital games, yet its strict policy towards third parties alienated the sympathy of several long-time partners, who en masse decided to support Sony PlayStation rather than Nintendo 64.[7] Furthermore, the level of investments and the risks involved in internally producing games are considerably higher than relying on software produced by others. This decentralized model is less defendable than the integrated model, since the basis of the competitive advantage is not bound within the firm but rather is dependent on third-party behaviour (see Grant [1998] for a discussion on sustainability of competitive advantage).

Moreover, the digital games industry is strongly affected by **Metcalfe's Law** and by consequent network externalities: once a system reaches a certain level of diffusion compared to its competitors, it triggers a positive feedback which gets stronger and stronger. The Betamax versus VHS war in videocassette recorders was determined by network externalities. When the VHS system enrolled a number of software producers on its side (in this case, movie studios), the move granted it an edge the Betamax was never able to recover. Due to network effects and positive feedback VHS became the standard for home recording, while Betamax disappeared (Cusumano et al., 1992). This is particularly important in determining a system's launch date: the vast installed base of SNES, combined with Sony's scarce reputation in the industry, induced Nintendo to underestimate the success of PlayStation and to postpone the launch of Nintendo 64. Nintendo 64 did not hit Japanese shelves until 26 June 1996. Meanwhile, the PlayStation installed base had reached 7.2 million units, and Nintendo was never able to close the gap due to the positive feedback triggered by network externalities.

BREAKOUT BOX 4.3 ● ● ●

Metcalfe's Law

In an article first published in Forbes ASAP *on 13 September 1993, George Gilder discussed various network paradigms. One is Robert Metcalfe's, founder of 3Com Corporation and major designer of Ethernet Law, according to which a network becomes more useful as more users are connected. In more formal terms, the value of a network of size n is proportional to n^2, or $V(n) \cong n^2$.*

From this, the notion of network externality is derived: a product is subject to network externalities when its value to new customers is directly dependent on the number of other customers that already posses the product.

Noticeable examples are the fax machine, the telephone and, in our case, consoles.

The most critical aspect in the industry for success is still unclear, and its solution is no easy task: I showed that, once a considerable number of consoles are in the market, the leader's advantage becomes impossible to recover for competitors. I also claimed that a large number of quality games are necessary to favour the adoption process. At the same time, a solid installed base is necessary to induce third-party software companies to develop for the system.

But how is it possible to persuade developers to support a console *before* the console has reached the critical mass at which it will begin to self-sustain its own growth? There are a number of plausible explanations, such as lower or no royalties for early supporters, exclusive contracts or no-competition agreements; yet the first months of each new hardware generation sees a fierce competition for the supremacy in the industry. One can summarize a few guidelines to determine the success of a digital game system.

Time of entry ●

New generations of hardware are subject to cyclical patterns: launch, growth, consolidation and obsolescence. In recent years, overlapping cycles have resulted in a failure for laggards. The decisions as to when a new gaming console is launched must consider the market leader's situation: premature entry could face fierce opposition from a large portion of customers who wish to ensure getting their money's worth from the previous generation console. Postponing the launch of a system could result in an insurmountable installed base of the first-mover.

Technological performance ●

Andy Grove's '10X' rule of thumb states that a product must be ten times more powerful in order to shift customers from one system to another (Grove, 1996). At the same time, a manufacturer must provide hardware powerful enough not to suffer the same fate in a couple of years time.

Managing expectations ●

Investments in massive marketing campaigns can have two positive outcomes: building brand reputation and signalling commitment, and using forthcoming newly announced titles as killer applications. The latter could prove to be a two-edged sword, as postponed titles may let down customers.

Pricing policies

The launch price must not exceed the psychological threshold, even if per-unit losses may be relevant. Successive price reductions may occur each time sales slow down, possibly in proximity to holiday seasons, and must be adequately promoted. Price reductions must not be too quick, or too drastic, in order not to compromise the reputation of the console and of the manufacturer.

Software line-up

The game library must be as wide as possible in order to cover the most popular categories. Focusing too much on a single genre could turn the console into a niche product. Launch titles must be followed by a constant flow of games, with publishing peaks at holiday seasons.

Getting third parties on board

Internally developed games, albeit a solid base for building a successful line-up, cannot guarantee the variety and the sheer number of titles published by a plethora of independent developers. To encourage third parties, a manufacturer should pay particular attention to designing a not too severe royalties system, in order to give publishers the possibility to take risks with new brands instead of merely focusing on existing franchises.

Piracy trade-off

The effects of piracy on the diffusion of a system are not fully clear. Developing and adopting proprietary technology to minimize the risk of piracy often results in a trade-off between protection and manufacturing costs.

Following these guidelines will help the system in the early stages of its life cycle, favouring the rise of the installed base and attracting third-party developers and maximizing a console's chances to succeed (Alvisi et al., 2003).

Relevant web sites ● ● ●

Datamonitor www.datamonitor.com
DFC Intelligence www.dfcint.com
GameIndustry.biz www.gamesindustry.biz
GameInvestor www.gamesinvestor.com
Screen Digest www.screendigest.com
Strategy Analytics www.strategyanalytics.net

Notes ●

1 For example, Nintendo Entertainment System (NES) and Atari 7800 used a custom version of Motorola 6502. The Megadrive and the SNES both mounted a processor from the Motorola 68000 family; PlayStation and PlayStation 2 processors were co-developed by Sony and Toshiba; ATI supplies Nintendo with its graphic processor, and so does Nvidia with Microsoft's Xbox.

2 A Mask ROM is a type of Read Only Memory (ROM) that can only be programmed once during the semiconductor manufacturing process. For high volume productions, the Mask ROM is the cheapest ROM available. The chip has to be incorporated into some kind of physical support (i.e. cartridges) for safe handling. The first console to use the CD was the NEC PC-Engine CD-ROM (1988).

3 In marketing literature this kind of customer can assume several names (pioneers, leaders, trendsetters, innovators, etc.) yet maintain the same traits. For a description see Kotler (2003).

4 Of course, several other factors were involved in the Dreamcast's failure, including SEGA's poor marketing ability, it's financial weakness, the lack of support by several key game developers, and so on.

5 The website GameRankings (http://www.gamerankings.com) offers a database of reviews for most games published in the USA. Among the all-time worst rated 15 titles for console, ten are licences.

6 Despite the 500,000 copies shipped in a few weeks, Eidos Interactive was unsatisfied with *Tomb Raider: Angel of Darkness*'s overall quality. As a result, the publisher considered replacing the British developer Core Design (creators of the original game) with US-based Crystal Dynamics, authors of another successful franchise by Eidos, *Soul Reaver*.

7 Nintendo allowed third parties to develop a maximum of five games for its consoles, encouraging them to concentrate investments on few, quality titles. All games had to be approved by Nintendo before publishing, and game developers had to buy cartridges from Nintendo itself, with a minimum of 10,000 units (see Kerr, 2002; Schilling, 2003).

● References

Alvisi, A., Narduzzo, A. and Zamarian, M. (2003) 'PlayStation and the power of unexpected consequences', *Information, Communication & Society*, 6 (4): 608–27.

Brandenburger, A.M. and Nalebuff, B.J. (1996) *Co-opetition*. New York: Doubleday.

Cusumano, M.A., Mylonadis Y. and Rosenbloom, R.S. (1992) 'Strategic manoeuvring and mass-market dynamics: the triumph of VHS over Beta', *Business History Review*, Spring: 51–94.

Grant, R.M. (1998) *Contemporary Strategy Analysis*. Oxford: Blackwell.

Grove A.S. (1996) *Only the Paranoid Survive*. New York: Doubleday.

Kerr, A. (2002) 'Loading … please wait: Ireland and the global games industry', SteM working paper series No. 1.

Kotler, P. (2003) *A Framework for Marketing*, 2nd edn. Upper Saddle River, NJ: Prentice Hall.

Porter, M.E. (1980) *Competitive Strategy*. New York: Free Press.

Schilling, M.A. (2003) 'Technological leapfrogging: lessons for the US video game console industry', *California Management Review*, 45 (3): 6–32.

5   A player-centred approach to digital game design

Jonathan Sykes

Interactive digital games are but another chapter in the long history of gaming, and the process of game design is much the same, regardless of the actual medium in which the game is situated. Whether designing board games, role-playing games or video games, the five stages of game design, illustrated in Figure 5.1, are necessary (Bates, 2001; Crawford, 1984; Dunnigan, 2000; Pederson, 2003; Rollings and Morris, 2000; Rouse, 2001). The first four stages may be carried out by an individual, as in the design of many board games such as *Monopoly*, although digital games are more commonly developed in small teams (see Kerr, Chapter 3). The following chapter will discuss each stage in turn.

Concept identification

Every game begins with a concept – a proposal describing the game's principle direction and the kind of game experience being catered for (Crawford, 1984). Some game designers argue that a particular story-line, technology or a gaming genre can be a good place to begin the development of the game concept (Rollings and Morris, 2000; Rouse, 2001). However, Sid Meier, designer of the games *Railroad Tycoon* and *Civilization*, warns against this approach. Instead Meier recommends defining the theme of the game first, and then identifying applicable narratives, technology or genre (Rouse, 2001). Meier argues that the game's subject matter is of primary importance, and that any design decision made prior to the identification of the game's topic can provide unnecessary constraints.

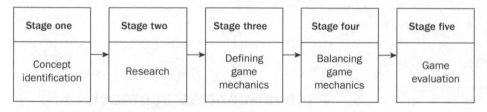

FIGURE 5.1   *The five stages of game design*

However, Meier's approach involves its own constraints. The choice of the game's subject matter has the potential to alienate key sectors of the game buying public. Building a railway, dancing with Britney Spears or shooting creatures from outer space does not appeal to everybody. To date, Meier has been fortunate that his interests are shared by a significant percentage of gamers around the world. For the rest of us it would be much safer to first identify regular purchasers of games and then consider *their* preference when choosing a topic.

● Audience identification

Designers would prefer to develop games for 'everybody': the bigger the game's market; the greater the potential profit. However, different audiences have very different requirements. Hardcore gamers expect a different experience to casual gamers (Rollings and Adams, 2003), games designed for an older audience are unlikely to contain content suitable for a younger audience, and games designed for a male market are not necessarily going to appeal to a female market. The problem with designing a game for everyone is epitomized by the car industry. The overall car buying market is huge, consisting of different people with different requirements. The tradesman needs a spacious vehicle that is also hard wearing, parents look for something economical and comfortable for the kids and the game designer does not care about cost, they just want something sleek and fast. Designing a car to satisfy all three is likely to involve such significant compromise that the final product would fail to please anybody. Rather than developing a product so diluted by the demands of different markets, it is much better to develop a car with a single audience in mind. The same is also true of video games, which is why game designers need to identify who they are designing their game for.

When choosing an audience, the development team will take into account the current state of the games market. They need to ensure that the audience they design for have access to a games machine and like to play digital games. At the moment console games are primarily aimed at a younger audience. This is because most console gamers (78 per cent) are below the age of 35 (IDSA, 2001). As the demographic of the gaming market changes, so will the content of games. To gain an objective insight into gaming markets it is better to rely on market research data than personal prejudice and there are many publicly available documents that offer detailed summaries of the game industry – at a cost.

There is little point in identifying the target audience if the designer then fails to take their requirements into account. There are a variety of techniques that place the user at the centre of the design process. Participatory design, for example, aims to include player opinion by having a representative of the target audience on the design team. However, while this can be very useful for the development of traditional application software, it can sometimes hinder the design of entertainment software – it is difficult for users to explicitly identify what constitutes a good game. Rapid prototyping, another user-centred design technique, differs from participatory design in that the user does not directly contribute to the design process. Instead, the user is asked to evaluate a series of prototypes; the result of which slowly shapes the final product. With respect to digital game design, prototyping is a powerful tool, which can be implemented during the later phases of the design process, but of limited use during the concept identification phase where there is little tangible for evaluation.

The use of *personae* is a technique that combines the strength of both participatory design and rapid prototyping and is also simple and cheap to apply. Rather than 'real' users, the design team create a 'persona' to represent the target population (Cooper, 1999). A persona is a fictitious character who embodies the desires and needs of the target audience. The persona is the archetypal player of the proposed game. The benefit of a persona is that they can be consulted during the design process and used to evaluate design proposals. When choosing a topic for a new game any suggestion can instantly be evaluated with regard to the persona. For instance, Samira, the primary persona for a game aimed at Indian teenagers, enjoys romantic novels and speaking with her friends, and is therefore unlikely to enjoy a violent action game based on the Gulf War. The more knowledge the team have of their personae, the greater the level of confidence they will have in their design decisions.

To build a believable persona requires detailed understanding of the intended audience. The analysis of market research will provide the customer demographics. The next step is to gather greater insight into their lives. This typically involves interviewing representatives of the target audience. Questions such as 'what are your likes/dislikes?', 'how do you spend your spare time?', 'what films do you enjoy?' and so forth are designed to determine audience preferences. It is important that the interviewer identifies and talks with people who are representative of the target audience but who differ from the rest of the group with respect to their play requirements. In the car design example above, three different groups of car buyers were identified (tradesmen, parents and game designers).

Once interviews have been collected and the different groups identified, the design team can begin to develop the personae. For each group, the most representative constituent should be taken as the persona. Based on the data collected, the design team should then provide the persona with an identity, a name, a personality, a career, pets, cars, hobbies, and so forth until they become a three-dimensional, believable entity. The provision of photographs can benefit members of the development team in their visualization of the persona and their lifestyle. Magazines can be a useful resource for images to represent the persona, their house, their car, pets and other details. The more detailed the identity, the easier it is to use the persona for day-to-day design decisions.

There are two main categories of personae: the *primary persona*, and the *secondary persona*. There is only ever one primary persona for each design. The primary persona is the character who cannot be satisfied if we design for someone else. However, a design that satisfies the primary persona should not ignore the needs of a secondary persona. The best way to identify the primary persona is to determine which of the personae cannot be primary (because designing for them would make others unhappy), and see who is left. If you have two personae that require drastically different design solutions, then you have identified two very different markets and no single product will satisfy both. In this scenario it must be decided which persona will remain and which will be excluded. Again, if we return to the car example, the parent wanted economical and spacious and the game designer wanted a car that was fast. In trying to satisfy each persona our design would be a product of compromise – a car that is neither as fast as alternative sports cars nor as economical nor as large as alternative people carriers. The best solution is to develop a different product for each primary persona.

Identifying the play experience ●

Having identified the personae, the design team can begin to create a game specifically tailored to their audience. The next task is to identify a play experience most suited to the personae. Some players prefer light hearted, fast action games, whereas others prefer a darker, slow paced, methodical experience. The play experience, as defined here, is a product of the *category of play*, the *formality of play*, and the *affective tone*. Several authors (Caillois, 2001; Huizinga, 1955; Miller, 1968) have tried to catalogue types of play, and the categories are discussed further in Box 5.1. The categories are elemental, which means that many games will often incorporate several categories of play. However, it is frequently the case that a single play category will be dominant. *Sonic the Hedgehog*, for example, competes against his evil nemesis and therefore incorporates **agon** into the play experience. However, the dominant play category is clearly **ilinx**. The definitive impression of *Sonic the Hedgehog* is speed. Sonic moves so quickly that it is not always possible to perceive the environment, and playing can leave you feeling dizzy. Identifying the dominant play category allows the design team to focus on techniques to emphasize the dominant category of play. The design team for *Daytona USA*, for example, increased the competitive element of their game by adding a feature which reduces the speed of the leading player, allowing others to catch up. This technique adds to the drama of the competition, reduces the possibility of any player having such a significant lead that the outcome is determined before the first car passes the finishing line.

BREAKOUT BOX 5.1 ● ● ●

Categories of play

Caillois (1958) divides play into four categories:

Agon *Play activities where competition is the primary focus. Here, enjoyment derives from competing with another person, whether directly (as in a competitive sport), or indirectly (such as through a crossword puzzle); from competing with oneself (for example when trying to improve on a previous performance); from competing with nature (such as climbing Everest), or from competing with a system (as in Solitaire or Mah Jong).*

(Continued)

(Continued)

Alea *Games of chance, where the outcome is independent of the player's actions. Such games are usually associated with gambling, where enjoyment stems from the player's potential winnings.*

Mimicry *Play involving make-believe, where the player takes on a new identity. Examples include the children's activity cops-and-robbers, and the more serious simulations such as Formula 1, or Championship Manager.*

Ilinx *Play activity centred on the quest for vertigo, where vertigo is characterized by the temporary destabilization of the perceptual system. Examples include fairground rides, where the rider is quickly spun or jolted until they feel dizzy, and Sonic the Hedgehog, where the movement of Sonic can become fast enough to disorient the player.*

Miller (1968) also includes:

Exploration *Miyamoto, the designer of the Mario and Zelda games is said to base much of the exploration found in his games on the fun experienced exploring the attic and the local caves as a child. However, play centred around exploration need not be about geographic discovery, it might also include the player's exploration of the game mechanics (that is, identification of the player's limits and boundaries of the play world) or even the games interface (when selecting player preferences).*

Social play *Activity where the player either cooperates or competes against at least one other player. Some activities require membership to a group or clan. Secret languages, nicknames, initiation rites and passwords can help to foster close social bonds, and add to the play experience.*

Play categories are mediated by the *formality scale*. The formality scale refers to different dimensions of formality that influence the play experience. The informal end of the spectrum represents the spontaneous expression of the animalistic impulse to play – referred to by Caillois (2001) as *paidia*. Such play is characterized by the lack of ritual and rules, and can be seen in activities where children spin themselves until they fall through dizziness or the kitten playing with a ball of wool. Digital games which are associated with the paidia end of the formality scale would include *House of the Dead*, or *Samba de Amigo*. The formal zone of the formality scale represents disciplined, ritualistic, rule-based play – referred to as *ludus* (Caillois, 2001). Ludus is exemplified by formal competition – such as the Olympics, or puzzles (crosswords and anagrams). Digital games found towards the ludus end of the formality scale would include *Silent Hill*, or *Microsoft Flight Simulator*.

The term *affective tone* is used here to refer to the emotion the game designer aims to evoke during play. The affective tone is the result of stimuli presented to the player during the game. The colours, the lighting, the artwork, the music, the plot development, the way characters move, they all leave an impression on the player. Other media, such as cinematography have developed theories for how to manipulate the audience and have found techniques to evoke a complex array of emotions (for example, see, Brown, 2002 and King and Krzywinska, Chapter 7). In comparison to film, the range of emotions produced through playing digital games is still very small (Rollings and Adams, 2003). Chris Crawford, author of *The Art of Computer Game Design*, finds most games emotionally sterile (Rouse, 2001). This is partly because games rely on stereotypical triggers of emotion. Games do not so much evoke new emotions, but trigger memories of a previous affective state. The opening scene of *Mario 64*, for example, portrays bright sunlight, trees, a gentle river, butterflies flying around the main character, Mario skipping on the grass. All of this imagery and symbolism makes the player feel good because implicit memories of their childhood are being subconsciously awoken. Although the memories are not necessarily explicit, they still produce the same biological response and the player feels happier (LeDoux, 1998).

The problem with this method of evoking emotions is that people have wide-ranging experiences and therefore differ in the associations they make. Although most of us have happy memories of eating an ice cream on a sunny day, common triggers for other emotions such as disgust or reverence are not as easy to identify. The end result is that games generally rely on a simplistic set of emotions that can be applied to a single dimension of light and dark emotions. Games that project a lighter affective tone include the Mario franchise, *Pokémon*, *Animal Crossing* and *Samba de Amigo*, each of which differ in their play category and in their position on the formality scale and yet share a very similar affective tone. Games with a light affective tone are usually very bright, dominated by primary colours, and have upbeat musical accompaniment. This is in contrast to games such as *Silent Hill*, *Deus Ex* or the *Doom* series, which implement lower light levels and subdued colours to reflect a darker affective tone.

To help define and communicate the affective tone of a game to other members of the design team, 'mood boards' can be a very valuable tool. Mood boards are large panels covered with images (often taken from books and magazines), blocks of colour and different textures, which convey a specific emotion. They can be used to indicate the feelings the game should invoke during play. Building the mood board can be a great way of focusing on the feelings you hope to engender, and as importantly, the aspects to be avoided.

● Situating the play experience

Having identified the target audience and the kind of play experience they prefer, the final ingredient needed for the game concept is the topic of the game. This is not a reference to the game's narrative but to the general subject area. Is the game to be about jet-skiing, railroads, scuba diving, archaeology, snowboarding or dancing? Or is it about being a hit-man, the best thief, the best space pilot, getaway driver or stuntman? A good method for developing ideas is to host a brain-storming session, where each guest is briefed on the personae prior to the meeting. This allows people to introduce topics that they feel would be suitable, and the remaining members can evaluate the idea with respect to each persona. Again, it is better to aim for primary persona satisfaction, and then see if the topic would be suitable for the secondary personae (Cooper, 1999).

● Research

The research phase of the design process is an essential component to game design. Research undertaken during the early stages of the design process is likely to inform decisions regarding the game mechanics at a later stage. For example, Casper Field, the producer of the jet-ski title *Carve*, discovered that professional jet-ski riders will use the wake created by their vehicle to slow down competitors behind them, and thus gain a tactical advantage (Edge, 2003). This provides a novel game mechanic which is very different to motor racing games where the car behind maintains a speed advantage caused by the slip-stream of the car in front. In this example, the research phase provided Field with a unique game mechanic, differentiating his product from the competition.

● Defining game mechanics

Much of the discussion so far has looked specifically at the play experience. However, the ultimate goal of game design is 'game' production. While the concepts of 'play' and 'game' are very similar, there are distinguishing factors which separate the two activities. Games are a type of play activity, but they are particular in that they have explicitly stated rules and goals. It is argued by Huizinga (1955) that games are a product of sharing a play experience with others. Rules are created to identify agreed boundaries of the play experience. They define what is, and what is not, allowed should people choose to participate.

Turning a play experience into a game can be simple. The play activity of jump can easily be turned into the game of high jump by the addition of a goal – in this example 'who can jump the highest?'. However, with just a goal and no rules, the game is open to abuse. What is to stop a participant from adding a huge spring to their shoes? Rules are therefore applied to create a level playing field for all and to ensure that it is just a participant's jumping ability that will determine the game's outcome.

When developing the game mechanics it is often easier to start with the topic on which the game is to be based. In reviewing the research data there are likely to be elements that naturally lend themselves to a game. Sid Meier finds that a topic will often point to a particular genre (Rouse, 2001). Running a railroad, for example, involves a lot of resource management and is therefore particularly suited to a strategy game – rather than a first person shooter. Soccer is a game where the action takes place both on and off the pitch – which lends itself to either an action or a club management game.

The difficulty when developing games is not in the development of rules but identifying which rules will generate an enjoyable experience. Unfortunately a predictive theory of game design is still some way off. Instead developers have provided a set of heuristics that they have found to be useful in game development.

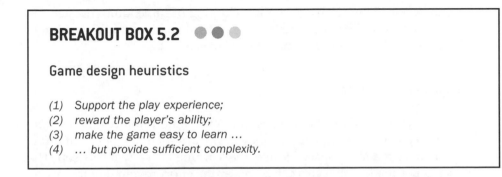

BREAKOUT BOX 5.2

Game design heuristics

(1) *Support the play experience;*
(2) *reward the player's ability;*
(3) *make the game easy to learn ...*
(4) *... but provide sufficient complexity.*

● Support the play experience

The *game concept* is fundamental to the development of game mechanics. It explicitly defines the target audience and details their requirements with respect to the play experience, and the topic of the game. Any decision regarding the introduction of a game mechanic should support, and be informed by, the play experience. If the game's primary focus is social interaction, then a mechanic supporting communication is necessary This is the case for many of the MMORPG (massive multiplayer online role-playing games, such as *Asheron's Call*, *Ultima Online*), whose longevity is directly related to their ability to foster a strong player community. In his book on online game design, Friedl (2003) argues that communities flourish when players find like-minded individuals with whom they can communicate, and suggests that designers should be 'facilitating and encouraging small-group formation by offering distinct gameplay styles … by implementing various character archetypes, races, or classes' (Friedl, 2003: 197).

● Reward the player's ability

When designing interactive games the designer has a duty to ensure that the player's input has some bearing on the final outcome. The mechanics of a game should be developed to reward the player's skill, rather than some factor outside of the player's influence (Rollings and Morris, 2000). Perhaps more importantly, the reverse is also true – failure should be a result of the player's action (or inaction). At no point should the player be punished for something over which they have no control. For example, a game with a door leading to certain doom should provide the player with ample clues and warnings so that the player can make the decision whether or not to pass through the door (Bates, 2001). Without a warning of impending disaster, the player's progress is determined via the outcome of an unpredictable event and the game becomes one of chance.

● Make the game easy to learn

A graphical plot of knowledge gain over time produces the *learning curve*. If a game requires the player to learn a large amount of information in a short space of time, the learning curve will be steep. The steeper the learning curve, the greater the effort required of the player and the longer it is before they get to grips with the game. As games become more complex it is becoming increasingly important to consider the gradient of the learning curve to ensure the player can quickly get going (Crawford, 1984; Sanchez-Crespo Dalmau, 1999). With hugely complex business applications, human–computer interaction (the field of computing that investigates ways to make computer software easier to use) has been tackling the problem of steep learning curves for some time and many of the techniques used in traditional software applications are also suitable for games. In their textbook, Dix et al. (1998) identify three principles for increasing learnability (the ease with which the novice can learn the system) that are applicable to interactive digital games:

Predictability

Giving your game elements of predictability does not imply that you cannot surprise your audience. It merely means that the player should be able to logically predict the outcome of a novel action. For example, in *The Legend of Zelda: Wind Waker* the main protagonist learns that a grappling hook can be attached to a branch to reach a higher position. Later in the game the player has to cross a chasm. Knowledge of how the grappling hook works and the presence of a branch half-way between the ledges provides the player with enough information to predict that the grappling hook can be used to swing the player from one side of the chasm to the other. Allowing the player to deduce new knowledge reduces the knowledge that the player must learn – and thereby reduces the gradient of the learning curve.

Consistency

It is much easier and quicker for people to learn something when the outcome of an action is consistent. For example, the learning of an association between switch and lamp illumination will be weaker, and take longer to learn, if the action is only occasionally accompanied by the onset of light (Pavlov, 1927). Consistency also supports predictability. If an action produces a specific result under a given set of conditions then as long as the conditions remain the same the action should always produce the same result. For example, if early in the game a beer-barrel is used as a makeshift raft to traverse a calm river, the beer-barrel should also float on a calm lake later in the same game. The attributes of the beer-barrel and the water are the same so the outcome should be the same.

- **Familiarity**

    The gradient of a game's learning curve can be reduced if the game designer considers the wealth of knowledge the player brings to their game. The player might already be familiar with games of a similar genre and will therefore have knowledge of how other systems work. Capitalizing on the player's familiarity and knowledge of similar games will reduce the amount of new information needed. For example, most first person shooter (FPS) games on the PC share the same basic controls for player movement. By applying a similar control method the game designer is reducing the amount of new information the player has to learn. The same is also true for gaming conventions. Supporting current gaming conventions, such as moving over objects to pick them up, the use of items to improve health and so forth, can also reduce the amount of new information the player must learn.

- **Provide sufficient complexity**

    '... the rules of Go can be learned in minutes, but ... it can take a lifetime to master. (American Go Association, www.usgo.org)

    While other games have been long forgotten, Go, a board game originating in China approximately 4000 years ago, is as popular today as at any other time in history (Kim and Soo-hyun, 1999). It is widely argued that games, such as Go, benefit hugely from the complexity that can emerge from the interaction of simple and easy to learn game mechanics (Bates, 2001; Rollings and Morris, 2001; Rollings and Adams, 2003; Rouse, 2001). Emergence is exemplified by the cellular automaton in the *Game of Life* (Gardner, 1970). Although not really a game, it is a simple example of how complexity arises from the interaction of simple rules.

BREAKOUT BOX 5.3 ● ● ●

An Example of Emergent Complexity

The Game of Life *has three rules (Gardner, 1970):*

(1) ***Survival*** *Every counter with two or three neighbouring counters survives for the next generation.*

(Continued)

(2) **Death** *Each counter with four or more neighbours dies (is removed) from over-population. Each counter with one neighbour or none dies from isolation.*

(3) **Birth** *Each empty cell adjacent to exactly three neighbours – no more, no fewer – is a birth cell. A counter is placed on it at the next move.*

Although not a game in the typical sense in that it has no players, goals, winners or losers, the game of life begins with a series of pieces on a grid. Complex patterns then emerge from the application of the three rules described above.

Many websites offer the chance to see The Game of Life in action: http://www.bitstorm.org/gameoflife; http://mathworld.wolfram.com/Life.html; http://lcs.www.media.mit.edu/groups/el/projects/emergence/index.html

---

Will Wright claims that his game, *SimCity*, is 'like a big three-dimensional cellular automata' (Rouse, 2000). *SimCity* is a game where the player takes on the role of city planner. The player makes decisions that affect the development of a small town. However, the rules are so tightly bound that any action performed on one aspect of the game affects related areas of the game world. For example, if in tackling the city's pollution problem the player reduces the number of industrial areas people are made unemployed which means less income through the tax system which means less money to pay for upkeep of the city and so the consequences go on.

To develop a game with emergent properties, it is important that the designer adopts a few generalizable rules, rather than numerous rules specific to previously identified scenarios (Garneau, 2002). For example, rather than having a rule that allows the explosion from a missile to blow up the door, the door can be given a strength property and weapons an attack property. This adds complexity to the gameplay, allowing the player to develop their own strategy for breaking down the door. If the player has run out of missiles, they might choose to pile and ignite several grenades by the door instead. This kind of game allows players to arrive at novel solutions perhaps not envisaged by the designer. However, Rollings and Adams (2003) warn that emergent gameplay can be a two edged sword in that the solution to a puzzle can be taken away from the design team. The player may well identify an easier method of puzzle solution than predicted by the designer, which makes it difficult to balance the difficulty level of a game.

● Balancing game mechanics

Player enjoyment is central to the process of game design. However, player satisfaction is almost always diminished when ambiguity surrounding goal accomplishment is determinable in advance (Huizinga, 1955). Noughts-and-crosses (known as Tic-Tac-Toe in the USA), for example, is a game widely disregarded by adults because it rarely ends in anything but a draw (exemplified in the finale of the film *War Games*). Some games, particularly older games like *Space Invaders* and *Pac Man*, are based upon an impossible quest to survive which seems initially contradictory to the above assertion. However, the player's goal in such games is not to win but to witness the next level and improve the score. Although the ultimate outcome of the level is not in doubt, mystery still remains around the player's goal – will they survive long enough to be rescued.

A *dominant strategy* is a strategy so beneficial to the outcome of a game that alternative strategies are unworthy of consideration (Rollings and Morris, 2000). There are two types of dominant strategies: strong and weak. The adoption of a strong dominant strategy will always place the player in a winning position, whereas adoption of a weak dominant strategy will ensure the player does not lose (Rollings and Adams, 2003). Games supporting dominant strategies are therefore weakened by the inevitable outcome of the game. It is therefore essential to ensure that games are free from dominant strategies. This can be accomplished by balancing of the game's mechanics.

There are two industry-wide techniques for balancing game mechanics. One involves the use of 'real' players to evaluate the game mechanics, and the other use of simulated players. Play-testing with real players can be one of the most informative evaluation methods for balancing a game. There are various ways to test the playability of a game. Some companies will employ the talents of professional play-testers. Although they can be very useful for the more regimented trawling for bugs, professional play-testers are rarely representative of the target audience. This is why companies such as Microsoft are approaching play-testing by recruiting players who are representative of the game's target audience (Pagulayan et al., 2003). Observing gamers at play with a product, and interviewing them afterwards can yield highly significant information about the strengths and weaknesses of a game. During the many hours of game testing it is common for most, if not all, dominant strategies to be documented. Several iterations of the prototype – evaluation – new prototype cycle will usually culminate in a well balanced game.

The benefit of play-testing is that the team are given an insight into how people actually play the game and can see if the game is supportive of their play experience. However, play-testing can be both expensive to administer and very time consuming. A cheaper alternative is to use Artificial Intelligence (AI) routines. Taking two AI players and putting them head-to-head will provide a quick indication of how balanced your game is. If one strategy always wins then further balancing is necessary. On the negative side, the number of issues raised is dependant upon the quality of the AI. Also, the actions of human players can be irrational and hard to simulate and sometimes an irrational move can reveal strategies that AI routines would never uncover.

Game evaluation ●

Continual player evaluation of design decisions is central to the process described here. However, at some point, real players need to evaluate the game. There are three different modes of evaluation appropriate to game design: usability testing, play-testing, and bug-testing. Play-testing has been discussed in some detail above, and will not be discussed further.

Usability-testing is different from play-testing in that the focus is on the usability of games rather than the enjoyability of games. Pagulayan et al. (2003) discuss the success of various case studies carried out at Microsoft Game Studio User-Testing Group. The work at Microsoft identifies a series of issues which are unlikely to be identified during play-testing. For example, observing user performance on various game oriented tasks while they think aloud, the Microsoft team was able to identify problems with the game shell screens for *Combat Flight Simulator*. The design team had not appreciated their advanced technical knowledge when designing the game's option screens. Usability tests established that the term 'AI level' and the available choices of 'low', 'medium' and 'hard' was not easily understood by players. However, simply changing 'AI level' to 'enemy level', and the options to 'rookie', 'veteran' and 'ace' quickly rectified the problem.

Bug-testing is a quality control procedure with more relevance to the development team than the design team. The procedure involves a regimented approach in search of bugs, such as graphical glitches, logic problems and software crashes. Whereas play-testing benefits from 'real' users, bug-testing is carried out by professionals. This is in part because they have the experience required to identify problems with the code, but also because it can be a laborious role unsuitable for volunteers.

● Conclusion

Hopefully this chapter has provided some insight into the design of interactive digital games. The approach presented here is the brief summation of the game design literature, carefully wrapped in relevant user-centred design principles. It is not the only approach, and many game designers have seen a healthy profit applying their own unique method. Will Wright developed a simulation and then discovered it was fun to play, and Sid Meier has found that games designed for himself also appeal to many game buyers (Rousse, 2000). However, not everybody is a Wright or a Meier, and it is for them that the player-centred approach described here is particularly suited.

● Acknowledgements

Sarah Haywood, Peter Lonsdale and Judy Robertson for their valued contribution.

Relevant web sites ● ● ●

Chris Crawford's Erasmatazz www.erasmatazz.com
Develop Magazine www.developmag.com
Gamasutra www.gamasutra.com
Game Developers Ireland www.gamedevelopers.ie
Independent Game Developers Association www.tiga.org.uk
International Games Developers Association www.igda.org
International Journal of Intelligent Games and Simulation www.scit.wlv.ac.uk/%7Ecm1822/ijigs.htm
Journal of Game Development www.jogd.com

References ●

Bates, B. (2001) *Game Design: The Art and Business of Creating Games*. Rocklin, CA: PrimaTech.

Brown, B. (2002) *Cinematography: Theory and Practice*. San Diego, CA: Focal Press.

Caillois, R. (1958) *Les jenx et les hommes.* Paris: Gallimard.

Caillois, R. (2001) *Man, Play and Games*. Chicago, IL: University of Illinois Press.

Cooper, A. (1999) *The Inmates Are Running the Asylum: Why High Tech Products Drive Us Crazy and How to Restore the Sanity*. Indianapolis, IN: SAMS.

Crawford, C. (1984) *The Art of Computer Game Design*. Berkeley, CA: McGraw-Hill Osborne Media. (Also available for download at http://www.erasmatazz.com)

Dix, A., Finlay, J., Abowd, G. and Beale, R. (1998) *Human–Computer Interaction: Second Edition*. London: Prentice Hall.

Dunnigan, F.D. (2000) *Wargames Handbook, Third Edition: How to Play and Design Commercial and Professional Wargames*. New York: Writers Club Press.

Edge (2003) 'Carve', *Edge,* 124: 43–5.

Friedl, M. (2003) *Online Game Interactivity Theory*. Hingham, Massachusetts: Charles River Media.

Gardner, M. (1970) 'Mathematical games', *Scientific American*, 223: 120–3.

Garneau, P. (2002, September) 'Emergence: making games deeper', retrieved 15 March 2005 from: www.pagtech.com/Articles/Emergence.html

Huizinga, J. (1955) *Homo Ludens: A Study of the Play Element in Culture*. London: Routledge and Kecgan Paul.

IDSA – Interactive Digital Software Association (2001) *State of the Industry Report 2000–2001*. Washington, DC: Interactive Digital Software Association.

Kim, J. and Soo-hyum, J. (1999) *Learn to Play Go: A Master's Guide to the Ultimate Game, Volume 1*. Corte Madera, CA: Good Move Press.

LeDoux, J. (1998) *The Emotional Brain: The Mysterious Underpinnings of Emotional Life*. London: Weidenfeld & Nicholson.

Miller, S. (1968) *The Psychology of Play*. London: Penguin Books.

Pagulayan, R.J., Keeker, K., Wixon, D., Romero, R. and Fuller, T. (2003) 'User-centred design in games', in J. Jacko and A. Sears (eds), *Human–Computer Interaction Handbook: Fundamentals, Evolving Technologies and Emerging Applications*. Mahwah, NJ: Lawrence Erlbaum Associate, Inc, 883–906.

Pagulayan, R.J., Steury, K.R., Fulton, B. and Romero, R.L. (2003) 'Designing for fun: user-testing case studies', in M.A. Blythe, K. Overbeeke, A.F. Monk and P.C. Wright (eds), *Funology: From Usability to Enjoyment*. Dordrecht: Kluwer Academic Publishers. pp. 137–50.

Pavlov, I. (1927) *Conditioned Reflexes*. Oxford: Oxford University Press.

Pedersen, R.E. (2003) *Game Design Foundations*. Plano, Texas: Wordware Publishing Inc.

Rouse, R. (2001) *Game Design in Theory and Practice*. Plano, Texas: Wordware Publishing Inc.

Rollings, A. and Adams, E. (2003) *Andrew Rollings and Ernest Adams on Game Design*. London: New Riders.

Rollings, A. and Morris, D. (2000) *Game Architecture and Design*. Scottsdall, Arizona: Coriolis Technology Press.

Sanchez-Crespo Dalmau, D. (1999) 'Learn faster to play better: how to shorten the learning curve', retrieved 15 March 2005 from: www.gamasutra.com/features/19991108/dalmau_01.htm

Part two

Theories and approaches

6 Literary theory and digital games ● ● ●

Julian Kücklich

Literary theory and criticism have played a significant role in the formation of digital game studies. Important works such as Espen Aarseth's (1997) *Cybertext* and Janet Murray's (1997) *Hamlet on the Holodeck* used the terminology of literary studies – terms such as 'text', 'narrative', 'protagonist' and so forth – to describe digital media. While other theorists have challenged this approach because of its 'theoretical imperialism', this terminology remains indispensable in the discussion of digital games today.

This chapter introduces these terms as they relate to digital games while at the same time pointing out the pitfalls of using this terminology. Digital games are a hybrid medium, a medium in which different traditions and different technologies converge. The literary tradition is one of those, but by no means the only one. To regard digital games as a storytelling device is not only an oversimplification but a distortion of the medium. However, literary theory can be a valuable tool for understanding the inner workings of digital games, the appeal they hold for players and the significance they have within their cultural context.

This chapter begins with the most basic similarity between digital games and literature: the fact that, in many cases, they are fiction. The many schools of literary theory can be seen as different answers to the question of how reality and fiction relate to one another. Generally speaking, these different schools try to answer this question by determining the rules of a certain literary genre, by studying the meaning of literary texts or by trying to assess literature's effect on the readers. These three approaches – known as poetics, hermeneutics and aesthetics, respectively – are introduced and discussed in three consecutive sections of this chapter, each highlighting the possibilities as well as the limitations of these approaches.

● Digital games as fiction

'At End of Road: You are standing at the end of a road before a small brick building. Around you is a forest. A small stream flows out of the building and down a gully.' These are the opening words of Will Crowther's and Don Woods' *Adventure* (1977), probably the first text adventure game in digital game history (see Montfort, 2003). At first glance, *Adventure* resembles a literary **text** quite closely, for example, in its use of capitalized chapter headings and descriptive language. Furthermore, our experience with novels and short stories tells us that this is the beginning of a story, and once the player starts to play, this suspicion is quickly confirmed.

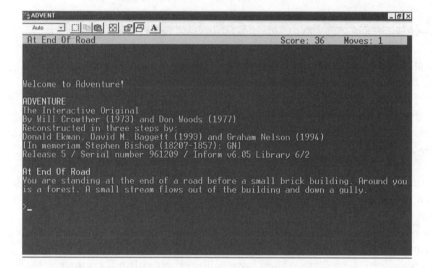

FIGURE 6.1 *Is it a story or is it a game? The 'storygame'* Adventure *(Crowther and Woods, 1997)*

BREAKOUT BOX 6.1 ●●●

Text *From Latin* texere *– 'to weave'. While this term usually refers to a coherent sequence of two or more sentences, it is often used in a different sense in literary theory. Due to the writings of the French literary theorists Jacques Derrida, Julia Kristeva, Roland Barthes and others, its meaning has expanded and has come to signify any cultural object. Thus, art, music and architecture, but also cities, fashion and rituals can be regarded as texts that can be read and interpreted.*

In contrast, there are some points in which *Adventure* differs from the vast majority of literary texts, for example, in its use of the second person singular and the present tense. Although there are texts that make use of these means to tell a story, such as Tom Robbins' novel *Half Asleep in Frog Pajamas*, it is a deviation from the conventions of storytelling. These rules of storytelling – or **narrative** – are studied by a branch of literary studies called narratology, and much narratological research has been directed at digital games.

BREAKOUT BOX 6.2 ● ● ●

Narrative From Latin narrare – 'to tell, relate, report, recount, set forth'. A narrative text is a text that tells a story. The most common narrative forms in literature are novels and short stories, but narrative is not limited to the written word. Films, television shows and comic books can also be narrative. Scholars of digital games generally agree that there is a narrative element in many games, but the significance ascribed to this element differs widely.

The most remarkable feature of *Adventure* when compared to a literary text is that it requires the player to type something into the command line that follows the paragraph quoted above. No literary text demands such a high degree of participation from its readers. While any text allows the reader to skip certain passages, or read the ending first, and some literary works even give the reader a choice of different endings (for example, John Fowles' *The French Lieutenant's Woman*), this form of participation is always voluntary. In *Adventure*, there is no choice: in order to read, the reader must participate in constructing the text and vice versa. Still, the player's progress in the game is dependent on literary conventions of plot development and description. While this apparent similarity between *Adventure* and, say, *The Adventures of Huckleberry Finn* seems to warrant a literary analysis of the game, the obvious differences between the two raise some doubts as to whether such an analysis would produce valid results.

The matter has become more complicated through the development from text adventure games to adventure games with graphics. The introduction of animated game characters was a step further away

FIGURE 6.2   *Can you read this?* Grand Theft Auto *3 (Rockstar, 2001)*

from a game-world represented by text, and towards the cinematic realism we find in contemporary digital games such as *Grand Theft Auto 3* (*GTA 3*).

If it seems questionable to subject the rather 'bookish' *Adventure* to literary analysis, it must seem even more dubious to do so with a game like *GTA 3*. However, looking at two games as diverse as *Adventure* and *GTA 3* allows us to see as their common denominator something so obvious that it is easily overlooked: both games create a **fictional** world, and playing these games allows us, however briefly, to inhabit these worlds. This has been recognized by theorists of digital games such as Barry Atkins, who argues that 'the computer game ... can also be a form of fiction making' (2003: 10). One of the advantages of literary theory is that it has a long history of studying the relationship between the real world and the fictional worlds of literature.

> **BREAKOUT BOX 6.3** ● ● ●
>
> *Fictionality* From Latin fingere – 'to shape, form, devise, feign'. Texts that do not claim to refer to reality are called fictional. Usually, the fictional character of a text is indicated by characteristics such as a formulaic beginning ('Once upon a time … '), the title (Great Expectations. A Novel) or other signals. The reader of a fictional text is expected to react differently to a fictional text than he or she would react to a true story ('willing suspension of disbelief').

What is literary theory? ●

Before we explore the possibilities of literary analysis in the study of digital games, we should be aware of the limitations of this approach. While literary theory might be useful in the analysis of some games; other games are best studied from a different perspective. A game like *Tetris* cannot be said to create a fictional world any more than does *Parcheesi* or a soccer game. In other games the fictional world is secondary to the gameplay and is ultimately nothing but a prop: the racing courses of *Gran Turismo* might be visually stunning, but they have no influence upon the player's interaction with the game.

We should also keep in mind that literary studies is by no means a homogenous discipline. In fact, much of what is known as literary theory has been borrowed from other disciplines, such as sociology, philosophy or psychoanalysis. As Jonathan Culler points out, the term literary theory refers mostly to 'writings from outside the field of literary studies … taken up by people in literary studies because their analyses of language, or mind, or history, or culture, offer new and persuasive accounts of textual and cultural matters' (1997: 3).

Here, the term literary theory is used in a different sense: it does not refer to theoretical imports from other disciplines but rather to the systematic study of literature and the methods for its analysis. In particular, there are three areas of literary theory that can be said to constitute the core of the discipline:

- Poetics: the study of literary conventions and rules.
- Hermeneutics: the study of literature's meaning.
- Aesthetics: the study of literature's effects.

Each of these areas of literary studies focuses on one element of the process of fiction-making: poetics is concerned with the act of creation of a literary work, hermeneutics' interest is in how the finished work creates meaning and literary aesthetics takes the role of the reader into account.

● Poetics: the rules of the game

Historically, there has been a shift from *normative poetics* to *descriptive poetics* in the field of literary theory. While the former were basically guides to writing literature that supplied the aspiring poet with all the knowledge necessary to write a ballad, a sonnet or an elegy, the latter are studies of a genre that attempt to extract its rules. An example of normative poetics is the *Poetics* of Aristotle in which he gives a detailed account of how a tragedy must be written and staged to achieve the desired effect of purifying the spectators' souls. Vladimir Propp's (1968) *Morphology of the Folk Tale*, on the other hand, can be regarded as a descriptive poetics, as the rules stated there are derived from comparing a large number of texts and noting their structural resemblances.

An important attempt to extract the intrinsic poetic rules of games by textual analysis is Espen Aarseth's (1997) study of adventure games in his book *Cybertext*. Here, Aarseth regards digital games as a subset of a larger textual category which he calls **ergodic text**, a term meant to signify that non-trivial effort is required to traverse the text. This definition includes most digital games, since they typically put up some form of resistance against the players' attempts to solve the game. Formulated as a rule, this means that digital games must resist the players' efforts to get to the end by presenting them with barriers against their progress which are increasingly difficult to overcome.

BREAKOUT BOX 6.4 ● ● ●

Ergodic text From Greek ergon – 'work', and hodos – 'path'. Espen Aarseth defines cybertext as a concept that focuses on the 'mechanical organization of the text' (1997: 1). This organization is such that the user of cybertext has to make an effort to traverse the text. This effort is not only directed at understanding the text, but also at constructing it, for example by making decisions, throwing dice, or engaging in some form of contest.

Books on game design can be seen as the normative poetics of digital gaming, as they inevitably prescribe rules for designing a good game. For example, in Chapter 6 of *The Art of Computer Game Design*, Chris Crawford writes: 'As a player works with a game, s/he should show steady and smooth improvement. Beginners should be able to make some progress, intermediate people should get intermediate scores, and experienced players should get high scores' (1982).

Genre

This rule is implemented in almost every digital game today. While this is not necessarily a result of Crawford's writing, it draws attention to the fact that normative poetics can amplify existing trends within a game *genre*. In all likelihood, Crawford's rule was derived from personal experience with games in which the player was given the opportunity for 'steady and smooth improvement.' By observing this trend in game design and stating it as an explicit rule, Crawford amplified this trend, which in turn gave rise to more and more games with a smooth learning curve. Thus, games with this feature gained an advantage over other games. (See Sykes, Chapter 5.)

What we can see at work here is the development of conventions within a genre. After all, a genre is nothing but a general term for a number of texts with similar characteristics. While these characteristics are not always explicitly formulated, we know what to expect from a first person shooter or a real-time strategy game, just as we know what to expect from a detective story or a romantic comedy. Aberrations from these conventions are tolerated to some degree, but if they go too far the game will not be accepted as a representative of its genre. That one of the weapons in the shooter-game *No-one Lives Forever 2* is a banana is a breach of the genre's rules; if a rather subtle one. If the banana were the only weapon, however, this would almost certainly exceed the tolerance of most players, and the game might fail commercially.

Mark J.P. Wolf suggests classifying digital game genres by their form of interactivity, since a 'classification by iconography ignores the fundamental differences and similarities which are to be found in the player's experience of the game, ... but interactivity will always be an important factor in the way games are experienced' (2001: 115). The 39 genres proposed by Wolf are based on an analysis of several examples in every category and can thus be termed a descriptive poetics.

FIGURE 6.3 *What if the banana was the only weapon?* No-one Lives Forever 2 (Monolith, 2002)

When analysing a digital game from a literary viewpoint, the question of genre is an important one. Usually, the game in question will be an adventure or role-playing game, rather than a sports or strategy game. If this is not the case, the choice of literary theory as an approach to the game in question requires explanation. Specifically, it is important to point out the specific features of the game that justify the application of literary theory and why this approach is chosen over others. It is crucial to the validity of the argument to address these questions. Otherwise, the analysis might be misconstrued as 'theoretical imperialism' (Aarseth, 1997: 16).

It can often prove fruitful to question the placement of a game within a certain genre. Popular genre classifications such as the ones found in gaming magazines are likely to be based on intuition rather than careful analysis. Furthermore, popular game criticism is prone to be influenced by the marketing departments of the games' publishers. As researchers, it is our obligation to question genre classifications, even if it seems obvious that a game belongs to a certain genre. As a rule, a game is rarely a 'pure' manifestation of a genre, but will differ from other games within the same genre in some points.

Conventions ●

Once the question of genre is clarified, one should be aware of the conventions within this genre. Specifically, we should try to determine which of these conventions are part of the genre's essence and which are merely accidental. For example, in an adventure game such as *Monkey Island*, we expect exploration and puzzles to be part of the gameplay. If one of these elements were missing it would be hard to place the games within its genre. However, adventure games have also come to be associated with a third-person view rather than the first-person view of many action games. We can ask ourselves whether this is part of the genre's definition or an arbitrary convention. How about a first person shooter that does not offer a range of different weapons or an adventure game in which the protagonist can carry only one item? By asking these questions, we can become aware of what is required in a genre and what is merely expected.

Deus Ex is a good example for a mix between genres as it is usually classified as an action-adventure game but it has some role-playing elements as well. It is, after all, a matter of personal style whether a player accomplishes the game's missions by brute force, or by stealth and agility. The game's rudimentary skill system is also reminiscent of the 'stats' in role-playing games (RPGs). While this is clearly an aberration from what is expected in an action-adventure game, it is in no way detrimental to the gameplay. *Deus Ex*'s rather complicated plot, on the other hand, would be more befitting for a classic adventure game and is arguably harder to follow because of the game's strong action elements.

Hermeneutics: making sense of software ●

In a game like *Deus Ex* the 'experience' of a player relying on stealth might differ dramatically from that of a player taking a brute-force approach. Thus, the question can be raised whether the fact that games are interactive means that there is no fixed meaning but rather a range of meanings depending on the way the game is played. Literary studies face a similar problem: the meaning of a literary text is not part of the text itself but rather something external to it. Hermeneutics is the branch of literary studies that tries to solve this problem by determining dominant aspects in a text that privilege one interpretation over another.

In digital games, hermeneutic interaction is embedded in the process of playing itself since the player has to interpret the signs on the screen in order to determine their meaning. Only thus can he or she extract the internal rules by which the game is governed and use this knowledge to solve the game. In his essay 'Making sense of software' (1995), Ted Friedman describes this as a process of 'demystification' since the solution of a game will typically reveal the world of the game as governed by a fixed set of rules. Once these rules are revealed the game is not challenging anymore.

This is a rather trivial form of hermeneutic activity, since it focuses exclusively on the meaning certain signs have within the fictional world of the game. However, like literary texts, digital games are not shut off from the world, but are cultural products with deep roots in the culture they stem from. This is where literary studies and cultural studies find their common ground – in the analysis of what cultural objects reveal about the world we live in (see Crawford and Rutter, Chapter 9). As mentioned before, this analysis can be done in various ways depending on the theoretical framework of the analysis. To put it simply, different schools of literary theory can be seen as different ways to put texts into context.

Games in Context

In his analysis of the real-time strategy game *Close Combat*, Barry Atkins regards the game within the context of historiography in order to study its relationship to historical truth on the one hand and historical fiction on the other. As he points out, '[t]his tension created between the fidelity it displays towards the historical field, and the liberties that are then taken with how a form of historical narrative may be constructed, can be seen to reflect wider changes in the way popular culture has approached questions of historical representation' (2003: 88). By taking the context of the game into account, Atkins not only makes a statement about the game's 'realism', but also arrives at a hypothesis about the status of history and its representation in Western culture.

Similarly, in their article 'Nintendo® and new world travel writing' Mary Fuller and Henry Jenkins (1995) study games such as *Super Mario Bros* in the context of the travelogues written during the colonization of America in the 16th and 17th centuries. They argue 'that the movement in space that the rescue plot seems to motivate is itself the point, the topic, and the goal and that this shift from narrativity to geography produces features that make Nintendo® and New World narratives in some ways strikingly similar to each other and different from many other texts' (1995: 58). For someone who grew up in Western culture, it is easy to see the superficial similarities between Pocahontas and Princess Toadstool ('the rescue plot') but through careful textual analysis the authors uncover a much deeper resemblance between these two cultural objects that seem to be so far removed from each other.

It should be clear from these two examples that it is indeed possible to make sense of game software as representative objects of the culture they are part of. In contrast, readings of computer games that do not take their contexts into account tend to produce rather meagre results.

Intertextuality

While hermeneutics was traditionally an activity that was concerned with the work of art as an autonomous object, it is now almost universally recognized that 'making sense' is a creative process that is necessarily influenced by the reader and the context in which the reading takes place.

If we want to make sense of digital games we must determine in which context they are supposed to make sense and in what way this meaning changes if they are removed from this context. For example, many games manufactured today are meant to make sense within the cultural context of Western society. Games such as *America's Army* or *Conflict: Desert Storm* is likely to be understood differently when played by an American or an Iraqi, respectively. From the perspective of literary studies, however, it is more interesting to focus on a game's contexts in a more literal sense, that is, the texts that the game in question refers to explicitly or implicitly. These contexts, often called **intertexts**, are not limited to literary texts, but might also include legal, scholarly and journalistic texts as well as films, song lyrics, urban legends and myths.

BREAKOUT BOX 6.5 ● ● ●

Intertextuality The sum of a text's explicit and implicit references to other texts constitutes its intertextual dimension. Depending on the definition of text and textuality, the notion of intertextuality varies in scope and extent. While Julia Kristeva, who coined the term in the 1960s, stressed the connectedness of all texts, whether they be fictional or non-fictional, printed or spoken, it is often used in a more limited sense in literary studies, that is, as a general term for quotations, allusions, parody and other means to refer to other literary texts.

For example, it is rather hard to understand many of the puns in a game such as *Space Quest* if one is not familiar with science fiction literature and films. Of course, it is possible to play the game without this cultural knowledge, but the game implicitly addresses a player that fulfils this requirement. Therefore, playing *Space Quest* with no prior experience of science fiction is bound to be a rather dull experience. In the literary analysis of a digital game it is often useful to think about the texts the game quotes from, alludes to or hints at because this will reveal a lot about the kind of player the game is targeted at. Specifically, it is useful to analyse what kinds of texts are referred to, what kind of person will be familiar with these kinds of texts and whether there are allusions that some players are bound to miss.

By investigating these questions we can learn a lot about the culture the game stems from. If the game refers to non-fictional texts such as advertisements, news or legal disclaimers, these texts might be either quoted as is or they might be parodied or distorted in some other fashion. The way other texts are quoted in a game reveals a lot about the game's implicit world view. Some games might even have several world views vying for dominance. While one should strive to avoid an argument based purely on the associations invoked by these references, they are valuable clues as to how a game is meant to be read.

Once we have determined how a game is supposed to be read, we can start thinking about whether there are other ways of reading it, and why such an alternative reading might or might not be more meaningful. Since the meaning of a cultural object is constructed by its recipients as well as its creators it is always a possibility that we find minor aspects of a game more meaningful than those that first meet the eye. Thus, we can arrive at an interpretation that is meaningful to us. Whether or not this is the 'meaning of the game' ultimately depends on the soundness of the argument more than anything else. If we can convince others that ours is a valid interpretation we have succeeded in making sense of the game. We should always bear in mind, however, that meaning is plural and heterogeneous and there are always other ways in which a game can be read.

Aesthetics: the pleasure of the game ●

One of the main reasons for literary studies' insistence on having a stake in the study of digital games is their fictionality, that is, their ability to create and sustain the illusion of a world distinct from our own. In asking questions about the specific qualities of these worlds and their effects on the player textual analysis goes beyond the realm of hermeneutics and enters the field of aesthetics. Literary aesthetics is concerned with the 'literariness' of certain texts, that is, the specific qualities that set a fictional text such as *Ulysses* apart from non-fictional texts such as a telephone directory or a computer manual.

By extending this perspective to the digital realm one might ask as well what differences there are between *Grand Theft Auto 3* and an electronic encyclopaedia. Obviously, at least part of the answer lies in the fact that *Grand Theft Auto* is set in Liberty City which might share a number of traits with New York but is nevertheless an entirely fictional place, while the encyclopaedia claims to make statements about the real world.

An aesthetics of control ●

However, fictional and non-fictional texts differ in at least one other respect: their effect on the reader. While a telephone directory might make its readers fume with rage if they cannot find the desired entry this is by no means the average response. Invoking the emotions of their readers is usually the domain of works of fiction such as novels, films and digital games. While it is an oft-repeated cliché of digital games criticism that, as of yet, no game has moved us to tears or made us cry with joy, this is neither backed by empirical fact nor would such a display of deep emotion prove digital games' worthiness of critical attention. The fact that they affect our emotions in any capacity is sufficient reason to study them from an aesthetic point of view.

In former times, literary aesthetics was predominantly occupied with determining how literature can be used to educate the readers or influence their opinions, in the twentieth century it has turned to the question how fictional texts please the reader. Roland Barthes' (1975) book *The Pleasure of the Text* has been very influential in this respect and Barthes' approach has been taken up in Janet Murray's *Hamlet on the Holodeck*, where she outlines three key pleasures that are provided by digital games: *immersion, agency* and *transformation*.

According to Murray, immersion is 'the sensation of being surrounded by a completely other reality' (1997: 98), '[a]gency is the satisfying power to take meaningful action and see the results of our decisions and choices' (1997: 126) and transformation refers to the computer's ability to create an environment for role playing: 'It makes us eager for masquerade, eager to pick up the joystick and become a cowboy or a space fighter' (1997: 154). While immersion is merely a technical term for what Samuel Taylor Coleridge has called 'the willing suspension of disbelief,' which is a pleasure provided by literary texts as well, albeit by different means, agency is another word for interactivity and transformation can be translated as identification.

In digital games, however, interactivity and identification are two sides of the same coin: players are able to identify with the **protagonist**, or **avatar**, of the game because they interact with the fictional world through him/her, and vice versa. An aesthetics of the digital game is therefore necessarily an aesthetics of control. In digital games, the player controls the game through the protagonist but the game also controls the player. Therefore, the pleasure of digital game can be said to derive from equilibrium between the player's control over the game and the game's control over the player.

BREAKOUT BOX 6.6 ● ● ●

Protagonist *From Greek* protagonistes *– 'first competitor'. The hero of a play or a novel, and often the focal point of the narrative. In many digital games, there is one central character which can be regarded as the game's protagonist. This game-protagonist is often called the* **avatar** *(from Sanskrit* avatara *– incarnation of a deity). This is a problematic term, however, due to its religious connotations, and should not be used without explanation.*

In studying digital games, we should strive to analyse how these control structures are created and maintained, and how these influence and shape the experience of the game. Espen Aarseth has suggested a concept called *'aporia* and *epiphany'* to understand the workings of such control structures: 'In ergodic works such as *Doom*, the aporias are formal figures, localizable 'roadblocks' that must be overcome by some unknown combination of actions. When an aporia is overcome, it is replaced by an epiphany: a sudden, often unexpected solution to the impasse in the event space' (1999: 38).

In other words, as long as the player's progress is impeded by the game the player is largely out of control. In order to regain the control equilibrium the obstacle must be removed which puts the player in control again. This gain of control is experienced as pleasant by the player, and the game is continued. Once a game has been mastered, however, it ceases to please the player, because then the player is always in control.

Advanced literary theory regards reading in similar terms: in a branch of literary studies called reader-response theory (see Fish, 1980; Iser, 1978), a text is regarded as the site of a playful struggle between the text itself and the reader. Just as the pleasure of digital games derives from losing and regaining control, in this model the pleasure of the text derives from maintaining a balance between the meaning embedded within the text and the reader's attempts to make sense of it. This seems to indicate that literary texts and games are not fundamentally different, but that there is, rather, a structural resemblance worth investigating.

Conclusion ●

As this chapter has demonstrated, a basic understanding of literary theory and terminology can be useful in analysing digital games. As fictional texts, games can be compared to other forms of fiction. Thus we can gain an understanding of how games relate to the real world – a question that has yet to be answered, despite the industry's obsession with 'realism'.

By employing textual analysis, we can determine the conventions and rules that apply within certain game genres. Analysing these conventions is an indispensable step to gain insight into the evolution of distinct genres and its effect on the players' expectations. As these expectations necessarily shape the experience of playing a game, understanding them better will allow us to comprehend the process of playing and the specific pleasures it entails.

Making sense of digital games is more than just an activity of the mind, but of intuition, reflexes and skill as well. The text actively resists our attempts to make sense of it, and in order to succeed, we have to reveal the rules that govern it. Once these rules are established, players might lose interest in the game, but researchers will not. For them a new game begins: the game of establishing the context of the game, and determining the elements that text and context have in common.

If we want to understand the enjoyment players derive from playing digital games, we must determine in what respect digital games differ from other forms of entertainment. There are some pleasures that are unique to digital games, while others are universal. Certainly, the pleasure of inhabiting someone else's persona is a pleasure that games share with literature. Most importantly, however, games and literature both provide the pleasure of immersing us in a world different from our own.

Relevant web sites ● ● ●

Barry Atkins http://uk.geocities.com/barry.atkins3@btopenworld.com
Games Studies http://www.gamestudies.org
Grand Text Auto http://grandtextauto.gatech.edu
Joystick 101 http://www.joystick101.org
The Ivory Tower http://www.igda.org/columns/ivorytower
Ludology.org http://www.ludology.org
Ludonauts http://www.ludonauts.com

● References

Aarseth, E. (1997) *Cybertext – Perspectives on Ergodic Literature*, Baltimore, MD and London: The Johns Hopkins University Press.

Aarseth, E. (1999) 'Aporia and epiphany in doom and the speaking clock: the temporality of ergodic art', in M.-L. Ryan (ed.), *Cyberspace Textuality*. Bloomington and Indianapolis, IN: Indianapolis University Press.

Aristotle (1967) *Poetics*. Trans. G.F. Else. Ann Arbor: University of Michigan Press.

Atkins, B. (2003) *More Than A Game. The Computer Game as Fictional Form.* Manchester and New York: Manchester University Press.

Barthes, R. (1975) *The Pleasure of the Text, trans.* R. Miller. New York: Hill and Wang. (Original work published 1965.)

Coleridge, S.T. (1817) *Biographia Literaria; or Biographical Sketches of my Literary Life and Opinions.* Vol II, Ch. 14. Retrieved from: www.english.upenn.edu/~mgamer/Etexts/biographia.html. Last accessed 14 February 2004.

Crawford, C. (1982) *The Art of Computer Game Design.* Retrieved from: www.vancouver.wsu.edu/fac/peabody/game-book/Coverpage. Last accessed 14 February 2004.

Culler, J. (1997) *Literary Theory: A Very Short Introduction.* Oxford and New York: Oxford University Press.

Fish, S. (1980) *Is There a Text in This Class? The Authority of Interpretive Communities.* Cambridge, MA: Harvard University Press.

Fowles, J. (1969) *The French Lieutenant's Woman.* London: Jonathan Cape.

Friedman, T. (1995) 'Making sense of software: computer games and interactive textuality', in S.G. Jones (ed.), *Cybersociety. Computer Mediated Communication and Community.* Thousand Oaks, CA: Sage, pp. 73–89.

Fuller, M. and Jenkins, H. (1995) 'Nintendo® and new world travel writing: a dialogue', in S.G. Jones (ed.), *Cybersociety. Computer Mediated Communication and Community.* Thousand Oaks, CA: Sage. pp. 57–72.

Joyce, J. (1922) *Ulysses.* Paris: Shakespeare & Company.

Iser, W. (1978) *The Act of Reading: A Theory of Aesthetic Response.* Baltimore, MD: The Johns Hopkins University Press).

Montfort, N. (2003) *Twisty Little Passages. An Approach to Interactive Fiction.* Cambridge, MA and London: MIT Press.

Murray, J. (1997) *Hamlet on the Holodeck: The Future of Narrative in Cyberspace.* New York: The Free Press.

Propp, V. (1968) *The Morphology of the Folk Tale*, 2nd English edn. Austin, TX: University of Texas Press.

Robbins, T. (1994) *Half Asleep in Frog Pyjamas.* New York: Bantam.

Twain, M. (1884) *The Adventures of Huckleberry Finn.* London: Chatto & Windus.

Wolf, M.J.P. (2001) 'Genre and the video game', in M.J.P. Wolf (ed.), *The Medium of the Video Game.* Austin, TX: University of Texas Press. pp. 113–34.

7 Film studies and digital games

Geoff King and Tanya Krzywinska

The use of perspectives taken from film studies in the analysis of digital games can be a contentious business. A number of games theorists have argued that games, as distinctive media forms, need to be approached in their own terms, rather than those drawn from other disciplines (see Eskelinen, 2001). To apply film studies approaches to games is sometimes seen as an act of academic colonization that fails to account for the specific qualities of games. Games are not films, or some form of interactive cinema, and should not be studied as if they were. A number of perspectives offered by film studies can profitably be brought to bear on the analysis of games, however, including a comparative analysis of the two media that helps to bring out some of the specific qualities of games.

As media consumed in the form of moving images on a screen, games share some qualities with films (and, in some cases, other screen media such as television). New media forms such as digital games do not exist in isolation. They offer distinctive characteristics of their own, but also draw on the qualities of existing media, a process encapsulated in David Bolter and Richard Grusin's (2000) concept of *remediation*. This, for Bolter and Grusin, is part of the normal pattern of similarities and differences that exists between one medium and another. It is largely for this reason that academic approaches pioneered in one medium often get translated across into others, although this is far from a straightforward approach and often leads to territorial struggles between theorists from rival subject areas.

Games studies is a particularly good example of this phenomenon, partly because of its recent arrival as a distinct field of analysis, and partly because of the range of other media or cultural phenomena on which games draw. Our argument is that perspectives from film studies offer a valuable set of tools with which to approach games, especially in getting to grips with close formal analysis of the onscreen game world, an aspect of game study that has traditionally been subject to neglect. Approaches from film studies can be used to highlight some points of similarity between films and games, but they can also serve as a useful way of drawing attention to a number of major differences.

Different modes of analysis ●

Film studies has developed a range of concepts designed to enable a close analysis of film form and content, and the contexts in which films are made and consumed. Film studies is itself an interdisciplinary creation, drawing on approaches developed in other fields of arts, cultural and media analysis. Three broad modes of analysis can be identified, each of which can be applied to games: formal, social-cultural-political and industrial-institutional analysis.

- Formal analysis: One of the primary building blocks of film studies that can be applied to games is the close analysis of *formal* characteristics: the precise manner in which sounds and images are organized on the screen. These are fundamental to the way we engage with any given film or game, orienting the viewer/player within the onscreen landscape. A formal approach to games, drawing in some cases on terms and concepts developed in the study of film, provides a vocabulary within which to understand the organization of audio-visual material and its potential effect on the experience and pleasure of gameplay. Particular aspects of game form to be considered in this chapter include the use of point-of-view structures, the framing of onscreen action, visual motifs and styles and the use of sound effects and music. Film studies also offers some ways to approach debates about the role of qualities such as narrative and spectacle or sensation in games.
- Social-cultural-political analysis: Formal qualities do not exist in isolation, and an important contribution of film studies is the consideration of how they are shaped by broader contextual factors. To be understood fully, the formal aspects of media such as films and games need to be understood in their social, cultural and political contexts. This opens up many issues in which film studies, along

with other areas of media studies, has drawn on disciplines such as sociology and cultural studies. (See Crawford and Rutter, Chapter 9; Hand and Moore, Chapter 10.)

- Industrial-institutional analysis: Films and games can also be analysed from an industrial-institutional perspective that considers the extent to which their qualities are shaped by the business strategies pursued by the organizations within which they are produced. Most mainstream films and games are the products of large media corporations or their affiliates. Their operations are usually governed by the need to maximize market share, a factor that has a strong influence on the nature of the product. (See Kerr, Chapter 3; Alvisi, Chapter 4.)

At its best, film studies mobilizes a combination of these different perspectives, a model that can also prove highly productive in the analysis of digital games. This chapter is organized primarily around issues raised by the formal qualities of games, into which considerations of social-cultural and industrial context are integrated. The reason for this approach is twofold. First, close formal analysis is the dimension most specifically associated with film studies as a distinct discipline. Second, it is the aspect of games studies that has been most conspicuous by its absence until relatively recently. Earlier generations of games research tended to be driven by social and psychological 'effects' agendas, focusing largely on the supposedly 'harmful' nature of games, rather than on close and detailed analysis of the qualities of games themselves. (For further discussion of this see Bryce and Rutter, Chapter 12.)

Formal aspects of digital games

Formal analysis similar to that developed in film studies can be applied to most games that create a world or space that can be traversed or explored by a player, even those that draw their visual style from two-dimensional cartoons. Many games have aspired to present such spaces (or aspects of them) in film-like ways. *Phantasmagoria* (1995) is an early example of a two-dimensional action-adventure game that overlaid filmed footage of human characters onto a computer-generated graphical environment through which the player moves. The aspiration was to create a game that operated like an interactive film, drawing on the conventions of horror cinema. The subsequent development of three-dimensional graphics and the technical capacity to create more complex game environments has led many games to aspire to a film-like quality of reproduction. Many also draw on narrative and generic frameworks familiar from the cinema. The games that most closely resemble films in these ways lend themselves most readily to analysis using tools from film studies, but they are not the only examples that can be understood in this way.

The impression of a coherent fictional game world onscreen is created through audio-visual features such as the framing of images, *mise-en-scène*, shifts in time and space, and the use of sound effects and music – all of which can be analysed in terms similar to those used in film studies. The manipulation of these qualities is what provides orientation for the player, establishes meaningful contexts and resonances within which gameplay occurs, and contributes to the creation of emotional states (fear and suspense in horror and some action-based games, for example).

The game feature that has the most apparent connection with film form is what has become known as the 'cut-scene', a short movie-like pre-rendered sequence during which the player performs the role of detached observer. Cut-scenes usually follow the framing and editing conventions of mainstream film – sometimes starting with longer, 'establishing' shots, for example, to provide initial orientation before moving to close-ups of important detail – and mark a break from moments of more active gameplay. As players do battle with the first 'boss' in *The Thing* (2002), for example, they are engaged in a battle with a large entity, seen from a perspective close to that of the avatar. After shooting at this entity for a few moments, the player is presented with a short cut-scene, operating as a cut in to a close-up, in which the entity sprouts the head and shoulders of a man. The fact that cut-scenes are the most film-like aspects of games, and that they intrude on active gameplay, has been taken by some to imply that film-related perspectives can be of relevance only to what is sometimes considered to be marginal aspects of games. We argue against this position, offering a number of tools of analysis developed in film studies that can be applied to many other aspects of games and to a comparative analysis of points of similarity and difference between the two media forms.

Point of view ●

An important dimension of gameplay that can be examined in formal terms similar to those used in film studies is the way point of view

FIGURE 7.1 *First-person view in* Halo

Source: http://www.picdump.jolt.co.uk/articles/031013/halo/07.jpg

structures operate to shape the player's experience of the onscreen world. In film, a variety of points of view are usually on offer. Generally, a smoothly orchestrated blend is used of seemingly objective, third-person perspectives that are not anchored to a particular character and more subjective viewpoints that approximate to the perspective of a particular character (see Bordwell and Thompson, 2001: 208–40, 247–8). Analysis of point of view helps to bring out some of the specific qualities of games. Games tend to divide into those that offer first or third person perspectives. In the former an illusion is created of experiencing the game through the eyes of an onscreen avatar. In the latter the avatar is viewed from a position behind, above, or a combination of the two (or from the side in some scrolling games). Some games also offer a choice between third- and first-person perspective depending on the specific in-game task undertaken.

Differences between third- and first-person perspectives have substantial ramifications for the player's subjective involvement with a game, much as they would in a film. The use of a first-person point of

FIGURE 7.2 *Third-person view in* Primal

Source: http://uk.playstation.com/games/gamesinfo04_game.jhtml?localeTitleId=
1037578&linktype=SSL

view, shot from the perspective of the killer, in films such as *Peeping Tom* (1960) and *Halloween* (1978), implicates the viewer in the actions performed, to some extent, precisely because of the coincidence of point of view. A third-person perspective would enable the viewer to be more distanced from the killer's actions (see Neale 1984; for more general consideration of issues of identification or allegiance with film characters, see Smith 1995). In a first person shooter such as *Doom* (1993) or *Quake* (1996), a strong impression is created of player immersion in the game space. In third-person games, in which the player's activity is represented in the form of an avatar visible to the player, issues relating to the form in which the avatar is represented become of more obvious relevance (for more on this see the discussion of gender representation below). A more objective-seeming point of view is offered in strategy games, such as *SimCity* (1989–2003), *Civilization* (1999–2003) and *Black and White* (2001), in which the third-person view is translated into a detached, God-like view from on high.

Comparative analysis of point of view in film and games is a way of highlighting the specific devices of visual orientation that operate in games because of the particular relationships established between players and the space–time co-ordinates of game worlds. Mainstream cinema has developed well-established systems of spatial orientation, especially the *continuity editing* system to avoid confusing the viewer during shifts from one camera position to another. Many first- or third-person games permit the player to look and move throughout 360 degrees (as far as obstacles permit). This is possible with less disorientation than would usually be expected in a cinematic context because the player/avatar moves through a particular virtual space in real time with the camera-view often seamlessly anchored to a single viewpoint.

Any game can be analysed in terms of its point of view structure, and how this shapes the player's experience. In third-person games, such as *Tomb Raider* (1996–2003), the player's point of view is anchored to a position behind that of the avatar. The player's view is restricted to the way the avatar's range of movements have been programmed. A similar constraint is present in first person games, although anchored to the player's point of view. In some third person games, such as *The Getaway* (2002) and *Enter the Matrix* (2003), the avatar can be made to lean around corners to see or attack what lies beyond. In others, such as *Tomb Raider* or *The Thing*, the player's view is more limited and other strategies have to be developed by the player to cope with potential threats lurking around corners. The first time a substantial threat is encountered the result is often the death of the avatar, the result of a form of attack for which the player is unprepared, largely as a result of a fixed point of view that leaves the player behind the point of action. On subsequent attempts, the player can take evasive action, knowing what to expect. A shift occurs here between the qualities of surprise (a sudden attack from an unexpected quarter) and suspense (the tension created by the player's awareness that the attack is about to be triggered).

Suspense can also be created more immediately in third-person games that use fixed, pre-set viewpoints rather than creating the illusion of a camera fixed always behind or above the avatar. Predetermined framing that is not directly anchored to the avatar, found in *Dino Crisis* (1999) and the *Resident Evil* series (1997–1999), functions more like that of a film, directing the attention of the player to upcoming events, such as imminent attacks, and using edits to move the player through the game space. This comes at the expense of player freedom and seamless continuity, however, and often feels like an intrusion on the ability of players to determine for themselves where to look. Point of view structures are constitutive of the experience offered by both games and films. They operate differently in the two media, however, most substantially in the fact that point of view in games is tied to modes of action by the player, a dimension absent from film.

Mise-en-scène, iconography, genre, sound ●

Much of the detailed quality of the fictional world created onscreen can also be analysed with the aid of concepts used in film studies, including *mise-en-scène*, iconography, genre and sound.

Mise-en-scène analysis focuses on how a particular environment is realized and arranged in the onscreen world. A game's *mise-en-scène* provides the setting in which gameplay takes place and objects with which the player can interact or that might act as barriers defining the limits of a particular space. The design of visual and auditory content is part of the meaning-creating apparatus of both films and games, and can be analysed in similar terms in both media. The environment of *The Thing*, for example, is hostile. Snow-bound arctic wastes and comfort-less interiors of military installations harbour an array of threats, a setting appropriate to the harsh nature of the conflict between human hero and polymorphic alien threat (imagine how different similar gameplay might seem if set in cosy, domestic interiors.)

The *mise-en-scène* of a game functions in much the same way as that of a film, creating context for the action, but it can also be interpreted in more game-specific terms. In many horror-based games, such as *Silent Hill* (1999–2003), *Resident Evil*, *Doom III* and *The Thing*, interiors are often splattered with scarlet gore. This horror based aspect of *mise-en-scène* contributes not just to background atmosphere, as would be the case in a film, but also to the *player's* sense of constant endangerment.

The term 'iconography' is used in film studies to describe particular sets of visual motifs that become associated over a period of time with one kind of film or another – another useful tool in the analysis of games. Many games draw on iconographies familiar from film genres such as horror and science fiction, including aspects of the settings of the horror-related games described above. Games also establish their own iconographies, such as the spaces littered with crates and boxes found in many first- and third-person shooter and action-adventure games.

Sound, an often neglected aspect of games, can also be analysed with the use of tools developed in film studies. A distinction can be made between what film studies terms 'diegetic' and 'non-diegetic' sound. Diegetic sounds are those which have their source in the onscreen world – the sounds of battle in a shooter, for example. Non-diegetic sound is added to the game-world from the outside, the most obvious example in games and films being the external imposition of

FIGURE 7.3   *Gory* mise-en-scène *in* The Thing

soundtrack music to create atmospheric or emotional effects (see http://www.filmsound.org, for more on the analysis of film music and sound). Games, like films, usually offer a blend of diegetic and non-diegetic sound. *Quake II* (1997), for example, deploys a multilay-ered, adrenaline-inducing soundscape composed of diegetic environ-mental and reactive sound (an intense battle takes place offscreen in the opening level, along with more local sound events) and non-diegetic industrial-sounding, fast-paced heavy metal music. The result contributes significantly to the generation of excitement and an impression of immersion. Non-diegetic music tends to accord with genre type: electronic for science-fiction related games, orchestral scores for medieval/fantasy role-playing games.

Analysis of *mise-en-scène*, iconography and sound of the kind per-formed in film studies can also be related to other more game-specific technical dimensions, such as issues that result from the management of limited processing resources in games. A trade-off has constantly to be made between the level of audio-visual detail and gameplay func-tionality: the higher the level of detail, the slower or more clumsy gameplay is likely to become without an increase in processing power. If the settings of *Silent Hill* draw on cinematic genre iconographies, for example, they are also relatively simple and undemanding to render – plain, unfussy interiors, fog-bound exteriors, which restrict views – factors that help to determine the kinds of properties likely to be converted into games. Iconographic features such as crate-littered interiors are both graphically economical and functional for gameplay, providing cover during battles and concealment for resources.

Narrative ●

The role of narrative, or story-structure, in games is one that has prompted much debate, including other contributions to this book (see, for example, Kücklich, Chapter 6). A problem for the use of perspectives from film studies here is that its most influential narrative model – that of 'classical' linear narrative structure – has only limited application to games. The classical model was developed by David Bordwell as an analysis of the form of narrative dominant in Hollywood. The model has a number of features, including an emphasis on forward-driving story-telling momentum built upon a series of tightly linked cause-and-effect relationships between the events of one scene and another. This version of narrative translates problematically into games, in which linear momentum – where present – tends to be halted for the performance of gameplay tasks.

The classical narrative model has also been challenged from within film studies, however. Some film theorists argue that recent and contemporary Hollywood cinema has abandoned the classical narrative model, in favour of a constant emphasis on periods of action and spectacle that break up the narrative flow. This has led in some cases to a comparison between cinema and digital games in which films are said to have become more like games, a comparison usually given negative connotations (a recent example being critical commentary on *The Matrix Reloaded* [2003]). Others have argued that Hollywood cinema has always used more flexible models of narrative, including more episodic structures (see, for example, Cowie, 1998). Models of narrative such as these have more purchase on the structure of some games, especially those described by Jesper Juul (2002) as 'games of progression'. Games of progression, usually action adventure games such as the *Tomb Raider* series, require the player to follow a pre-set course of narratively-framed action. These are contrasted by Juul with 'games of emergence', such as role-playing games, in which a number of initial rules lead to a more complex range of options.

The typical structure of a game of progression is to intersperse narrative elements amid the setting of gameplay tasks. An initial narrative situation is usually established at the start, including a back-story, often set out briefly in the game manual or in an opening cut-scene. Further narrative detail is then worked in, through various devices including the further use of cut-scenes and information supplied by non-player characters as the game proceeds. How exactly this process works can be considered in detail in any particular example, and can be compared with the equivalent process in films – how narrative information and development is mixed with the provision of qualities such as action and spectacle.

Narrative content in games, as in films, should be considered at both larger and smaller scales. Games of progression usually have an overarching story framework, a broad outline into which local detail is fitted. So do many games of emergence. In both cases, the story arc moves in and out of focus during the completion of game tasks. Narrative development may remain in the background, as far as gameplay tasks are concerned, but the two are often integrated. In *Halo* (2001), for example, a significant plot twist occurs part way through the game. This is important in terms of story development – a fresh twist in the narrative background – but it also means the player has to contend with two sets of enemies instead of one. The extent to which the larger story remains 'in play' varies from one game to another and from one type of game to another, and in some games according to the approach of the player. In role-playing games such as *EverQuest* (1999–present) or *The Elder Scrolls III: Morrowind* (2002), for example, players can advance whether or not they choose to pursue elements related to a larger plot.

Games also employ narrative strategies at a more local level, as do even the most action and spectacle orientated films. Cause–effect relationships and linear progression, of the kind described in the classical Hollywood narrative model, are found in much of the detail of gameplay (certain 'causes', such as being attacked by a monster, can have obvious 'effects' such as killing the player's avatar; in this case, the result is not progression, but regression, a requirement to restart at some point and try again).

The key difference between film and games is that narrative *progression* is shifted more to the sidelines in games, even those with the most developed narrative frameworks. Narrative usually provides a context within which more localized gameplay tasks occur, however. Moment-by-moment developments usually gain narrative resonance through their position in a wider frame that is largely pre-established, either in the individual game or through its relationship with other texts, including films and film genres. Many games draw on the pre-existing narrative worlds developed in other media – from the universe of the

Star Wars franchise to those of *Buffy the Vampire Slayer* or *The Matrix*. This reduces the extent to which they have to elaborate a large amount of narrative material themselves.

This does not mean that narrative or genre-based resonances are entirely absent from periods of gameplay in which narrative material is not explicitly offered. A question considered in film studies, especially in analysis of genres such as the musical or the special-effects oriented block-buster, is the extent to which narrative is still in operation during the big musical number or the special-effects extravaganza. In some cases, narrative might seem to halt, for a song-and-dance routine or for the attack of a dinosaur. Sequences such as these can also carry narrative resonances, however: the song-and-dance might mark the union of a couple, while the dinosaur attack might put into play a number of narrative elements (for an extended analysis of the latter in the case of *Jurassic Park*, see King, 2000).

The extent to which broader narrative resonances might still be in play during the attempted completion of game-tasks depends on a number of factors, including the rate at which progress is made through the game. Differences can be measured, then, between different games and between different ways of playing the same game. You might ask yourself, or others, how aware you remained of the narrative context during a particular gameplay action, but sub-conscious as well as conscious processes might be involved, which makes certainty hard to achieve. Analysis of the game text can establish what is *offered*, as is the case in film studies. Firm conclusions about the precise experience that results in any individual case are much harder to reach.

Spectacle and sensation

The production of qualities such as spectacle and sensation in games can also be analysed through approaches developed in film studies. A useful starting point here is to distinguish between two different modes in which spectacle is often generated in contemporary Hollywood action or special-effects oriented cinema (see King, 2000). Some forms of cinematic spectacle invite the viewer to sit back in a state of admiration/astonishment, contemplating the scale, detail, convincing texture or other impressive attributes of the image. Others seek to create a more aggressive, explosive and 'in your face' variety of spectacular or sensational effect. The more contemplative form tends to offer longer and more lingering spectacular vistas while the latter is more reliant on rapid montage-style editing and/or camera movement to create its visual effect.

A broad distinction can be made between the kind of experience offered to the viewer by these two forms of spectacular audio-visual effects, a distinction of relevance to the production of spectacle and sensation in games. The more 'contemplative' brand of spectacle emphasizes and invites the *look* of the viewer; it is designed to create a 'wow' reaction that entails a subtle dialectic between awareness of spectacle *as* impressive artifice and being 'taken in' by, and thus 'taken into', the fictional world of which the images is a part (for more on this, see Darley 2000: 104–5; King, 2000: 54–6, 2002). The 'impact aesthetic' created by the more explosive 'in your face' variety offers something closer to an assault on the sensations of the viewer, a vicarious impression of participation in the spectacular action/destruction on screen. The spectacular/sensational qualities of games share some of these qualities, but with a number of significant distinctions.

Spectacle of the contemplative variety is offered by many games, either in the provision of spectacular, larger-than-life imagery or marketing, packaging and reviews that emphasize the quality of resolution with which more mundane environments are produced with the latest in graphics-processing technologies. A pleasure based on delight in the quality of imagery, for its own sake, is offered by both the spectacular, hallucinogen-inspired world of *American McGee's Alice* (2000), for example, and the 'gritty' urban landscapes of *Max Payne* (2001) and *The Getaway* (2002).

New or unfolding spectacular vistas are frequently offered as reward and incentive for the completion of particular tasks or levels. The aesthetic qualities of digitally rendered environments are, generally, an important factor in games, in terms of both player enjoyment and industrial strategy. Improved graphics (along with improved gameplay options) is one of the lures with which the industry sells new titles and, especially, new generations of hardware, such as expensive graphics cards or platforms such as the PlayStation 2, the Xbox and their successors. In this sense the experience and underlying economics have a good deal in common with the production of cinematic spectacle, particularly that which involves the use of new generations of special effects technologies.

Spectacle and sensation of the 'impact aesthetic' variety is also offered by games. In some cases, this involves a mirroring of devices used in films, although more game-specific mechanisms also come into play. In the contemporary Hollywood action film, an impression of impact on the viewer is typically created through hyper-rapid editing, unstable, hand-held camerawork and the propelling of objects out towards the screen. Some of these effects are replicated in games, especially the widespread use of fireball explosions. Impact that remains vicarious in the cinema can also become more literally and physically

FIGURE 7.4 *Spectacle of scale in* American McGee's Alice

translated to the game-player, through the use of devices such as vibrating or pulsating console handsets. A sense of assaulting impact and sensation is also a central feature more generally of games that involve combat with assailants of one kind or another.

Similar questions can be asked in both film and games studies about the broader social context in which qualities such as spectacle and sensational impact are sought by viewers/players. In both cases, what is offered is an experience of audio-visual intensity that might be appealing in its contrast to the more mundane nature of everyday life (see Dyer, 1992). The intensity of engagement often involved in gameplay shares a number of characteristics with the concept of 'optimal experience' investigated as a more widespread cultural phenomenon by the psychologist Mihaly Csikszentmihalyi (2002), the creation of a state of 'flow' in which people become involved in demanding rule-bound activities to a point at which all other concerns disappear from consciousness. How exactly a desire for this kind of experience might be understood in any particular social context is a question too large to be pursued in detail here.

As in many other cases, however, a cinematic concept of spectacle or sensational impact only takes us so far in the analysis of games. Explosive-action based films and games both offer a form of vicarious impact on the viewer/player. The key difference, however, is that the player has to respond, a factor that leads us on to the biggest point of departure between films and games.

● Interactivity

The biggest challenge to approaches to games taken from film studies lies in confronting one of the most fundamental qualities of games: the fact that they are to be *played* rather than watched. A great deal of film theory is based on notions of spectatorship, the relationship that exists between the film on screen and the watching viewer. Put simply, arguments have ranged from theories of the spectator as in some way fixed or shaped by the image on screen to theories in which the spectator is seen as a much freer agent in terms of interpretation and personal investment, identification or allegiance, capable of a number of different relationships with the material onscreen.

Games, though, require something quite different. Watching and listening are important aspects of gameplay, but it also involves a great deal of *doing*. In a game such as *The Thing*, for example, we may be captivated by the spectacle of the transformation of what was formerly a helpful colleague into a horrific monster. The player is momentarily taken out of active gameplay to witness the spectacle – but not for long. Within seconds, the player has to respond, to fight back. Idle contemplation of spectacle on the part of the player, in the wrong place, is likely to lead to swift death for the avatar. From the point of view of sensation, in other words, this becomes a two-way process involving frenetic action on the part of the player.

The fact that the player is actively involved in the production of what occurs in the game space also has implications for the ways games are understood in their social context. In much the same way as films, games can be understood as both reflections of society and as playing some part in broader processes through which particular social attitudes are mediated, shaped or reinforced or undermined. Perspectives used in film studies can be a useful starting point for the consideration of some of these issues, but, again, they need to be supplemented by approaches that allow for the specific dimension of interactivity.

Much has been written in film studies about the representation of gender, for example, about the way the 'gaze' at the screen might be gendered (see Williams, 1994) or how particular role-models are enshrined onscreen – debates that have played into studies of gender in games. The key difference in games, however, is that whatever representations are on offer, they are available to be taken up more substantially by the player. Analysis of the meanings of films as part of their broader social-cultural context considers, among other things, the kinds of personal characteristics endorsed by being given glossy, shimmering embodiment on the big screen. The stakes might be raised in games by the fact that the player *takes part* in the act of embodiment. The figures of avatars and the kinds of actions open to them are pre-constructed by the game, as are movie characters. But it takes action by the player to mobilize them, which increases the stakes of any socio-cultural implications of the material on offer, extending the degree to which players are implicated in the actions of their avatars (exactly how these processes might work, however, and how they might ever be measured, is a complex and contentious issue).

Conclusion

Film studies offers a number of tools that can contribute to the analysis of digital games, as much to identify differences as similarities between the two media. Questions that might be asked, to summarize some of the issues covered in this chapter, include:

- How, in general, is the onscreen world presented to the viewer, and what implications does this have for the particular experience offered to the player?
- More specifically, what is the point of view structure, and how does this shape the way the game-world is encountered?
- What features of *mise-en-scène* or iconography can be identified? What about features recognizable from familiar genres? How do these encourage particular associations and meanings during gameplay? And how do they relate to the organization of gameplay tasks.
- How is sound used, both music and other sound effects. Which can be identified as diegetic and non-diegetic? What effect is created by each type of sound, on their own or in combination?
- What kind of narrative context is provided for gameplay? How exactly is narrative material supplied to the player? To what extent is narrative context a factor during different aspects of gameplay?
- What is offered in the way of visual spectacle? What seeks to impress through impressive imagery?
- What is offered in the way of sensation and impact on the player?
- How are avatars and characters represented, in terms such as gender? What is their appearance and how do they act – and how might these be related to broader social-cultural issues?

Questions such as these do not, of course, exhaust anything like all possible lines of enquiry. Film studies provides one among a range of frameworks that can be used to increase our understanding of games, although it includes some concepts that are of particular benefit to the analysis of the formal characteristics of the onscreen worlds in which we are invited to play.

Relevant web sites ● ● ●

FilmSound.org www.filmsound.org
Machinima www.machinima.com
Mihaly Csikszentmihalyi's Quality of Life Research Center qlrc.cgu.edu

● References

Bolter, J.D. and Grusin, R. (2000) *Remediation: Understanding New Media*. Cambridge, MA and London: MIT Press.

Bordwell, D. and Thompson, K. (2001) *Film Art: An Introduction*, 6th edn. New York: McGraw Hill.

Cowie, E. (1998) 'Storytelling: classical hollywood cinema and classical narrative', in S. Neale and M. Smith (eds), *Contemporary Hollywood Cinema*. London: BFI. pp. 178–90.

Csikszentmihalyi, M. (2002) *Flow*, 2nd edn. London: Rider.

Darley, A. (2000) *Visual Digital Culture: Surface Play and Spectacle in New Media Genres*. New York and London: Routledge.

Dyer, R. (1992) *Only Entertainment*. London: BFI.

Eskelinen, M. (2001) 'The gaming situation', *Game Studies*, retrieved 15 March 2005 from: http://www.gamestudies.org/0101/eskelinen/

Juul, J. (2002) 'The open and the closed: games of emergence and games of progression', in F. Mayra (ed.), *Computer Games and Digital Cultures: Conference Proceedings*. Tampere: Tampere University Press. Retrieved 15 March 2005 from: http://www.jesperjuul.dk/text/openandtheclosed.html

King, G. (2000) *Spectacular Narratives*. London: IB Tauris.

King, G. (2002) 'Die hard/try harder: narrative, spectacle and beyond, from Hollywood to Videogame', in G. King and T. Krzywinska (eds) *ScreenPlay: Cinema/Videogames/Interfaces*. London: Wallflower Press. pp. 50–65.

Neale, S. (1984) '*Halloween*: suspense, aggression and the look', in B.K. Grant (ed.), *Planks of Reason: Essays on the Horror Film*. Metuchen/London: Scarecrow Press. pp. 331–45.

Smith, M. (1995) *Engaging Characters: Fiction, Emotion and the Cinema*. Oxford: Clarendon Press.

Williams, L. (ed.) (1994) *Viewing Positions: Ways of Seeing Film*. New Brunswick, NJ: Rutgers University Press.

8 Digital games as new media ● ● ●

Seth Giddings and Helen W. Kennedy

Introduction ●

This chapter is about digital games as new, computer-based, media. Digital games are mass market commercial products, developed and distributed by established media corporations and often populated by characters and scenarios from television, cinema and comics. The playing of digital games is rooted in long-established patterns and practices of media consumption. As such, media studies as a discipline offers valuable theoretical resources to the study of digital games and new media. Yet we will argue that digital games are also a challenge to media studies, and require new concepts and theoretical resources to fully analyse these games as popular media artefacts, and their consumption in play as new media practices. We will concentrate on the newness of digital games: focusing in particular on key similarities with, and differences from, longer-established forms of screen-based popular media such as television and film.

The newness of new media is precisely their digital nature, their status as computer software and hardware, and the new forms of engagement and experience this computer basis facilitates. Digital games are a paradigmatic new medium in that they offer experiences and pleasures based in the interactive and immersive possibilities of computer technologies. This chapter will explore these experiences and pleasures, identifying new conceptual frameworks to analyse and account for them. We will look at:

- How digital technology facilitates new relationships between media consumers (game players) and media objects (digital games).
- Ways of understanding new media forms integral to the digital game: forms (such as interactivity and simulation) that have their origins in computer science rather than popular media.
- Ways of understanding the distinct pleasures of *immersion* in the dynamic virtual worlds of digital games.
- How digital gameplay raises questions of the meanings – and agency – of technology.
- How digital games have imaged and dramatized technology, providing a 'technological imaginary' of digital culture.
- How both the technological imaginary and the actual, real-world relationships and networks between players and digital games suggest new ways of theorising the subject in digital culture.

● Texts or machines?

If the study of digital games necessarily foregrounds technology as a key object of study, what then are the implications for media studies? Media studies has been rightly critical of notions of technological determinism, the assumption that technologies have inbuilt qualities or characteristics that absolutely determine their subsequent uses and effects (see in particular MacKenzie and Wacjman, 1999; Williams, 1974). In part to counter this technological determinism, media studies has used the metaphor of the 'text' to study the uses and meanings of media technologies. Manufacturers may attempt to build in, and articulate through promotion and advertising, particular uses for their products, but these meanings can never result in anything more than 'preferred readings'. For example, early home computers in the 1980s were often sold as 'respectable' information technologies, but were widely consumed as games machines by their purchasers. Media technologies (like all commodities or media content) then, are 'texts', 'encoded' products which may be 'decoded' in their consumption to reveal a quite different message (Mackay, 1997: 10). So, 'the effects of a technology … are not determined by its production, its physical form or its capability. Rather than being built into the technology, these depend on how they are consumed' (Mackay, 1997: 263).

However, this approach has its problems. Media technologies are not only decoded, they are *used*, they facilitate new uses and activities (for example, the various practices of domestic photography or texting on mobile phones). Computer media technologies in particular, whilst they carry media texts (games, essays, photographs) are also artefacts and machines. In important ways their effects *are* both limited and facilitated by their physical form and capabilities. Theorists in a wide range of disciplines have addressed this issue: how to study the effects or agencies of technologies (including digital technologies) without lapsing into over-simplistic versions of technological determinism. Marilyn Strathern sees domestic information and communication technologies as 'enabling'. In terms which seem to assign some agency to these technologies, she suggests '[t]hey appear to amplify people's experiences, options, choices. But at the same time they also amplify people's experiences, options and choices in relation to themselves. These media for communication compel people to communicate with them' (1992: xi).

Digital games, media consumption and production ●

In the late 1970s and early 1980s, home computer owners had to build their new computers themselves from a kit, and learn some programming to make them work. Home computers were rarely bought for any clearly perceived need or purpose, rather they were explored as new technology, to see 'what they could do' (Ceruzzi, 1999; Haddon, 1992). If nothing else, the purpose and pleasure of home computers lay in learning to program, exploring the machine and its system. Though computers were usually marketed as tools for home accounting and word processing, digital games would be bought, copied, or written by users to explore graphics, sound and interactivity in addition to the pleasures of gameplay itself (Haddon, 1992). As the market for home computers became more established, game-playing emerged as a dominant (though by no means the only) domestic computing practice. Digital games explored the aesthetic possibilities of computers as new media technologies.

By the late 1980s the dominance of the personal computer over the domestic information technology market saw the standardization of operating systems that removed the need for computer enthusiasts to learn how to program. However, digital games continue to encourage intervention with both software and hardware. The highly successful game *Doom* (1993) is a good example of the ways in which this characteristic of digital games facilitates new forms of creative consumption. The publishers, id, produced a game editor and made game file formats for the game's design freely available, encouraging players to modify levels, add new enemies or construct new levels (or 'maps') themselves. Lev Manovich argues that:

> hacking and adding to the game became its essential part, with new levels widely available on the Internet for anybody to download. Here was a new cultural economy which transcended the usual relationship between producers and consumers ... *the producers define the basic structure of an object, and release few examples and the tools to allow the consumers to build their own versions, shared with other consumers.* (Manovich, 1998, our emphasis)

This approach underlies some of the most popular contemporary games, for example the highly successful modification ('mod') of the PC first-person shooter game *Half-Life* into the multiplayer networked terrorist/counterterrorist game *Counter-Strike. Doom*'s modding legacy lives on, as we explore below, in the *Quake* (id Software) series.

● 'Skinning': from players to producers

Devoted fans and ardent enthusiasts exist for all kinds of cultural consumption. Academic studies of screen media fans have long since demonstrated the creativity and complexity of the reading strategies as well as the cultural practices that have emerged to support the dissemination of fan art and fan fiction. Penley (1992) provides a detailed psychoanalytic reading of slash art – the production of images and stories based on popular media characters, often featuring male/male romances or sexual images such as Captain Kirk and Mr Spock. Jenkins (1992, 1998; Jenkins and Tulloch, 1995) has written extensively on fan cultures and Hills (2002) has made a more recent contribution to the study of fandom which analyses the relationship between fan knowledge and academic knowledge. Digital games are no exception and a vast range of both official and unofficial fan sites filled with walkthroughs (descriptions or itineraries of games, written by fans, taking the reader through the game's virtual world and events, identifying hidden objects and solving puzzles), cheats, artwork and fan fiction can be found on the Internet. The walkthroughs themselves often include many opportunities for exploring the limitations and blind spots within the software as devoted players find glitches in the system or ways of bypassing specific obstacles.

BREAKOUT BOX 8.1 ● ● ●

Skinning

'Skinning is the art of creating the images that get wrapped around 3D player character models in 3D games. These images are what give the 'mesh' a solid, realistic look. A good analogy is if you think of the skin as the paper that goes around the bamboo frame (mesh) of a chinese lantern. You paint what you want on the paper and the game wraps it around the frame for you based on the mapping the model has with it'. (Chiq/Milla, female Quake player and skin artist, see http://www.chiq.net)

The practices of mod development and skinning belong on this continuum of fan activity but seem to enable new forms of relationship between producers and consumers where power relationships between them may become less fixed. There are clear economic benefits for the producers when using gamers to test the games prior to publication (beta-testing), which is not so different from screening a film to audiences before final edit, or piloting a television serial. What is distinct here is the ways in which the accessibility of the technology allows for specific competences to develop which enable movement between consumer–producer relationships. Not all games allow for this degree of code manipulation on the part of the player but *Quake* has been extraordinarily successful in gaining and maintaining a fairly devoted network of committed players. The producers of *Quake* have actively fostered this range of cultural practices and have sought to facilitate the development of the community and the space for the exchange of material. The modding community can help to secure the success of a game – '[d]isappointment tinged reviews of *Quake III*, while often nonplussed with the actual content of the game proper, insisted it was worth buying for the support it would inevitably receive from the mod community' (Edge, #126: 58). New media consumption generally, and digital games playing specifically, allows for the emergence of participatory cultures where there is a collapse of distinction between the dominant culture (the games industry) and the sub-culture (games players, modders and skinners) not typically associated with cinema-going or television viewing.

A particularly adept skinner may eventually see their skins being included in the range of characters on offer to other players through online communities and may receive prizes and acclaim for their art. Polycount is one site that monitors and nominates particular skins as well as providing guides and downloads of recommended skins and mods (www.planetquake.com/polycount/). Skinning is not an easy process – some taking as much as 60 hours to complete a skin. Like other art forms it is a process requiring a great deal of commitment and engagement.

BREAKOUT BOX 8.2 ● ● ●

The skinner

Camilla Bennett (Milla) is a skin artist whose leisure practices have developed into more professional activities. A self-taught skinner since 2000, Milla has developed a high degree of competence and has moved on from designing her own skins to a professional role as a texture artist in the development of the skin for the heroine of Betty Bad (WildTangent) a web-based game (see details of her involvement in this online at http://www.planetquake.com/polycount/articles/chiq_interview_012602/chiq_interview.shtml.) Milla has won a number of awards for her skins, going on to receive commissions for her work and has been featured in many interviews as a significant and influential skin-artist. (Links to these interviews are available through her website listed above.) Examples of Milla's work can be viewed online at http://www.chiq.net

Digital games as technological imaginary ●

The characteristics of digital games as new media identified so far are primarily technical or material. We have looked at how digital hardware and software as media technologies facilitate different kinds of media use and experience. However, it is difficult to separate these material characteristics from the sense of excitement (or fear) that computers have engendered. For example, the domestic computer has generated excitement and contemplation that mark it out as distinct from other consumer electronic devices. It has been seen as a machine within which we could see or create artificial 'microworlds' (Sudnow, 1983; Turkle, 1984). Many early home computer users felt a sense of participation in the wider economic and cultural forces of the information revolution (Haddon, 1992). To some theorists it heralded fundamental shifts in our relationship with technology, in particular inviting comparisons with the human brain, informing popular ideas of artificial intelligence (Pryor, 1991). Sherry Turkle evokes both these aspects in her study of the culture of programming. When programming, the computer is a 'projection of part of the self, a mirror of the mind' (Turkle, 1984: 15). Drawing on her ethnographic studies of computer users in the 1980s, she addresses the unique fascination of computing and its implications for media culture and its subjects:

> When you create a programmed world, you work in it, you experiment in it, you live in it. The computer's chameleonlike quality, the fact that when you program it, it becomes your creature, makes it an ideal medium for the construction of a wide variety of private worlds and through them, for self-exploration ... computers enter into the development of personality, of identity, and even of sexuality. (1984: 6)

For Turkle, digital games should not be regarded as a distraction from other, more practical, forms of computer use, rather they should be seen as the paradigmatic example of the attraction or fascination of interaction with computer-based media in general:

> Video games are a window onto a new kind of intimacy with machines that is characteristic of the nascent computer culture. The special relationship that players form with video games has elements that are common to interactions with other kinds of computers. The holding power of video games, their almost hypnotic fascination, is computer holding power. (1984: 60)

BREAKOUT BOX 8.3 ● ● ●

The technological imaginary

In the sense we are using it here, the concept of 'imaginary' originates in psycho-analytical theory and has migrated to the study of media and technology via film theory. On its most general level the technological imaginary refers to a popular or collective imagination about technologies: 'a realm of images, representations, ideas and intuitions of fulfilment, of wholeness and completeness that human beings, in their fragmented and incomplete selves, desire to become' (Lister et al., 2003: 60). The technological imaginary often takes the form of visions of an ideal technologized future, superseding all that is imperfect and unsatisfactory in the contemporary world. Popular and commercial visions in the first half of the 20th century of a technological future of monorails and domestic robots is one example, the widespread predictions for virtual reality in the early 1990s is another. Howard Rheingold for example saw virtual reality as bringing about a new world of free communication in direct opposition to what he saw as the alienated and violent aspects of the contemporary 'real world'. The technological imaginary is not reducible to fantasy or illusion in any straightforward way though. At the very least it shapes consumers' expectations of, and producers' research into, new technologies. Indeed, though we should beware of the hype surrounding new technologies (not least from manufacturers and advertisers), in this chapter we argue that the imaginary of digital games and their materiality as both computer hardware and software and as games played in everyday life are closely bound together.

Take for example the term, 'cyberspace'. Originating in cyberpunk science fiction literature, it was an attempt to conceptualize and dramatize the kinds of communicative experiences made possible by computers as media technologies (Gibson, 1986). It is now applied very generally to cover virtual reality technologies and various Internet media (Benedikt, 1991; Featherstone and Burrows, 1995). However, we would argue that popular digital games can be seen as a specific and highly established form of cyberspace pre-dating the World Wide Web by some 15 years. From *Space Invaders* and *Defender* to the cyberpunk imagery of *Deus Ex*, digital games have represented a technologized future. However – and for the discussion in this chapter more importantly – regardless of the symbolic content (space ships, cyborgs, or other technologies) of any particular game, digital games *are* cyberspace: actual computer-generated dynamic spaces.

Games as interactive media ●

Films such as *Tron* (1982) or *The Matrix* (1999) merely represent computer-generated worlds. All digital games are cyberspace because the player interacts with the games' computer-generated worlds.

BREAKOUT BOX 8.4 ● ● ●

Interactivity

Interactivity is a broad term, often vaguely applied. It is used to sell new consumer media services (interactive television for example), the interactive experience of which may well be of limited scope, while for cybercultural theorists such as Mark Poster it heralds a new 'media age' (Poster, 1995). Interactivity can be understood first as a technical mode of digital media use, 'the ability for the user to intervene in computing processes and see the effects of the intervention in real time' (Lister et al., 2003: 388). In these terms interactivity is not unique to digital media – changing television channels is a limited form of interactivity – however with digital media interactivity becomes the central mode of engagement with screen information, images and worlds.

Media studies theorists have argued that any act of media consumption is an active process (Fiske, 1987, 1992). Audience studies demonstrate that watching television, for example, is not a passive activity, the viewer or viewers actively interpret programmes in relation to their knowledge of particular codes and genres (Morley, 1980). So the interactive playing of a digital game is not necessarily a more active practice than the interpretive engagement with non-interactive media consumption, but it *is* distinct:

> the problems which face us in understanding the processes of mediation are multiplied by new media: the acts of multiple interpretation of traditional media are not made irrelevant by digital and technological forms of interactivity but are actually made more numerous and complex by them. The more text choices available to the reader the greater the possible interpretative responses. (Lister et al., 2003: 43)

In fact, 'decoding' or learning is foregrounded in the playing of digital games. Playing requires this decoding of structures or systems (of levels, of architectural organization, of points, timing of events, of non-player characters' AI and so forth). This process must take place with each genre of game as each has its own mode of interaction, its own conventions and controls – and each game within the genre invents its own variations, different combinations of buttons to press or peripherals to add. Mastering the controls of each game is a fundamental pleasure in its own right. Video games are, as Provenzo says, 'literally teaching machines that instruct the player ... in the rules ... as it is being played' (1991: 34).

Players or viewers?

Films based on games and games based on films bring into focus the distinctiveness of the act of playing a game from other forms of screen media consumption (see King and Krzywinska, Chapter 7). A sense of 'being in' the game is central to understanding the nature of player–game interaction and potentially therefore a key element in the pleasure of digital gaming. Sony's *EyeToy* literalizes this through the use of a camera which projects the players image into the game.

Tomb Raider as film and game

Hunt (2002) writes of how films based on games are often experienced as disappointing through comparison with playing the game, the example being discussed here is the film adaptation of *Mortal Kombat* (1995), but also the ways in which these games 'refashion' traditional media texts. Hunt points to how fight scenes in the film were described by one critic as 'like "watching someone playing the game badly rather than feeling as if you are in the game itself" (Felperin, 1995: 48), ... fight games refashion kung fu movies while simultaneously distinguishing themselves by their heightened *immersiveness* (being 'in the game itself')' (Hunt, 2002: 196, original emphasis). Yet if cinema is also considered immersive, how are we to understand this distinction between immersion in a game and immersion in a film?

In the film *Lara Croft: Tomb Raider* (2001) – based on the Tomb Raider series of digital games (Core/Eidos 1996–2003) – Lara's spectacular balletic athleticism is not dependent upon the skill and virtuosity of the player: it is not the player's interpretation, manipulation and actions which determine the flow of events on the cinema screen. There is the opportunity to interrupt the sequence of events when choosing from the scene selection menu on a DVD version of the film but Lara's performance within the film *does not* depend on any action on the part of the viewer. The landscape is traversed for us, the obstacles are overcome without death, repetition or frustration on the part of the player. The enthusiast cannot develop a patch or a cheat that increases Lara's endurance or allows us to alter certain events and outcomes. For all the potential for identification with the screen protagonist and immersion in the film's events, Lara's successes and failures do not belong to or depend upon the viewer in the way that Lara's game successes depend upon our skill in using the game controls. The game signals its dependence on the player as (except during cut scenes) the avatar – in this case Lara – will not move without some action on the part of the player. Conventional cinema tends not to acknowledge the viewer and, when it does, risks interrupting the sense of immersion in the onscreen events. 'Whereas cinematic immersion involves denying our containment by a frame, the options offered by *Tomb Raider* centralise the issue of choice ... Interactivity makes a point of access, and thus the terms of access are never neutralised' (Carr, 2002: 173). It is the interdependency between the player and the game that signals a fundamental aspect of the specificity of games.

Simulation versus representation in *The Sims* ●

All digital games are computer programs and as such have been 'written'. Thinking of *Tomb Raider* or *The Sims* as textual serves to remind us that these games are still cultural products despite the sense they generate of alternative worlds or artificial life. Though they may initially look on screen like cinematic or televisual texts, these gameworlds may be more productively conceptualized (along with all other computer applications) as 'code' rather than 'text'. Digital games are computer software, constructed through a logical, procedural, mathematical sets of parameters with which the player intervenes and responds.

BREAKOUT BOX 8.5 ● ● ●

Simulation

The word 'simulation' has a number of meanings within the study of media and culture. Here we are using it to refer to a particular kind of digital software, 'a mathematical or algorithmic model, combined with a set of initial conditions, that allows prediction and visualisation as time unfolds' (Prensky, 2001: 211). Computer simulations are used in many different contexts, for example by economists to predict market fluctuations and geographers to analyse demographic change. The processes of simulation are foregrounded in a popular series of games designed by Will Wright including SimCity *and* The Sims, *though most digital games are simulations to some extent (Frasca, 2001).*

This distinction between representation and simulation is highly significant and an implicit understanding of it is essential to play many, if not all, games. For example: watch someone who is unfamiliar with simulation games playing *The Sims* for the first time. Building houses and naming characters is straightforward enough, but as the characters go about their daily artificial lives the tendency is to treat them as if they were real people, or at least as fictional characters who behave according to established conventions of narrative, and try to intervene accordingly. However, the game's dynamics are driven by algorithms which rarely map directly onto any sense of actual (or fictional) human behaviour. The mathematical or economic foundation of the gameplay is made clear in the game's instruction manual: the key to success lies in managing the characters' lives as an 'economy' rather than looking for the conventions of psychological depth and narrative coherence familiar from television or film drama. The manual advises that *time* is the player's most precious resource, and:

> can be converted to anything else in this game either directly or indirectly. The efficiency of the conversion will determine your success. Time can be converted into money through work … . Time can also be converted into hunger satisfaction: the efficiency in this case will depend on the furnishings of your kitchen, the layout of these furnishings, the cooking skill of your Sim as well as their energy level (they move slower when tired).

So one path to increasing hunger satisfaction over time would be to first convert time into money (through work), then take some of that money and buy a better equipped kitchen. ... This same idea applies to the social side of the game. As your Sims spend time developing better relationships in the game you will notice that they are able to fulfill their social needs in less time. (Electronic Arts, 2000: 11)

The Sims is representational on one level: its onscreen images of houses, human figures and ornaments are familiar from the universe of popular media culture. But to play the game is to interact with a profoundly different kind of environment to that of a film or a television programme. The gameworld, its dynamics, relationships and processes, is mathematically structured and determined. *The Sims* adds a 'highly intuitive, fun interface' to a cultural form rooted in science and mathematics, and traditionally presented only as numbers on the screen (Prensky, 2001: 210).

Moreover, thinking of digital games as simulations also returns us to the position of the player – the player is not only interacting with onscreen images and making choices from menus, but collaborating with the game, manipulating its system and parameters to bring virtual worlds and characters into being and action.

Playing the game: interactivity and/or immersion ●

The concepts outlined so far (interactivity, simulation, technological imaginary) will now be brought to bear on a discussion of the distinctiveness of digital game play as a media experience. Intense digital game play is often described in terms of a loss of a sense of time, place or self, of immersion. While a loss of sense of self is evident in a range of media consumption (being immersed in a film at a cinema for example), immersion in a game world is something different. Thrills and spectacle familiar from science fiction, action and horror films are experienced also as challenges and threats, a mode of experience that is distinct because of the player's intimate mental and physical engagement by, and a level of *control* of, the game and the game technology. The player has a level of agency in the game's world and events that is quite distinct from other popular screen media consumption. This sense of immersion or engagement within the game world may account for the ways in which sense of time and physical discomfort may recede as the player's skill develops. The state of consciousness achieved during this period can be related to Czikszentmihalyi's description of 'deep flow' – a total absorption in an activity which is both challenging and emotionally rewarding (Czikszentmihalyi, 1993, 1996, 1997). What is specific to digital games play, as opposed to other forms of popular media consumption, is the ways in which this engagement or absorption is brought about through interacting with digital media. As the player becomes increasingly proficient at working the controls and understanding the limitations of the software, the sense of the game or game character as separate to the player is suspended.

Game player as cybernetic organism

The analysis of digital games needs to take into account the inter-dependency of player and game. Games, from *Minesweeper* to *Halo*, come into existence through a feedback loop between hardware, software, screen and player. Terms such as 'feedback loop' derive, like simulation, from the language of computing, and suggest that we might think of the relationship between player and digital game as not only 'interactive' but also 'cybernetic'.

BREAKOUT BOX 8.6 ● ● ●

Cybernetics

The term cybernetics and in particular the prefix 'cyber-' from which it springs, are often used loosely to dramatize all things technological and computer-related (particularly when referring to human–machine relationships). The term's particular history and meaning is relevant here though: according to Norbert Wiener (1962 [1948]), cybernetics is the science of 'control and communication in the animal and the machine'. So, although the 'cybernetic' is most frequently used to refer to cyborgs ('cybernetic organisms'), it also refers to any kind of complex system (including political, economic, animal nervous systems) in terms of information and its regulation. A useful (though not very futuristic) example is the 'negative feedback' that thermostats use to control temperature – feedback is the process by which a system is changed by its own results. Digital games, like most computer applications, work through feedback between user and software.

This notion of digital game playing as cybernetic takes us beyond notions of the interactive and has far-reaching consequences. In these terms interactivity can be seen as players choosing pathways or objects via interfaces and menus, perhaps not so far removed from other forms of media consumption. To describe digital gameplay as cybernetic though is to suggest a much more intense and intimate relationship between the human and the machine, and a relationship in which neither partner is dominant: player and software become part of the same circuit, they become a cyborg (see Haraway [1990] and Gray [1995] on theorizing the cyborg, Hayles [1999] on cybernetics, culture and subjectivity and Lahti [2003] on the video game player as cyborg). The term cyborg is most often used to refer to human beings with mechanical or electronic prostheses (from fictional characters such as Robocop to actual examples such as people with heart pacemakers.

On the one hand this idea of the cybernetic loop seems to account for the sense players have of being 'lost' in a game:

> the perpetual feedback between a player's choice, the computer's almost-instantaneous response, the player's response to that response, and so on – is a cybernetic loop, in which the line demarcating the end of the player's consciousness and the beginning of the computer's world blurs. (Friedman, 1999)

While on the other we might argue that digital gameplay is paradigmatic of the relationships between people, computers and a computerized world:

> [Digital] games offer a singular opportunity to think through what it means to be a cyborg. [They] aestheticize our cybernetic connection to technology. They turn it into a source of enjoyment and an object for contemplation. They give us a chance to luxuriate in the unfamiliar pleasures of rote computation and depersonalized perspective, and grasp the emotional contours of this worldview. ... Through the language of play, they teach you what it feels like to be a cyborg. (Friedman, 1999)

However, the digital game as interactive artefact and play practice cannot be reduced to this circuit of screen images, algorithms and players' reflexes. These 'circuits' need to be understood as themselves nodes in the larger circuits of games and game cultures.

● Online games and cyborg subjectivity

Quake (and its sequels) is an enduringly popular example of the 3D first–person shooter (FPS) genre that like many others has multiplayer capabilities and can also be played online. Online players and their communities make visible new relationships between subjects and media technologies (Taylor, 1999). Wright et al. (2002) argue that:

> When you play a multiplayer FPS video game, like *Counter-Strike*, you enter a complex social world, a subculture, bringing together all of the problems and possibilities of power relationships dominant in the non-virtual world. Understanding these innovations requires examining player in-game behavior, specifically the types of *textual* (in-game chats) and *nonverbal* (including logo design, avatar design and movement, map making) actions.

As we have seen, *Quake* allows players to choose from a range of different avatars so there is already a degree of flexibility around how the player chooses to express their subjectivity within the game. Skinning extends this malleability. The online capability of these games has allowed for the emergence of 'clans' (teams of players who compete against other teams in tournaments) who may also develop their own particular clan 'skins'. This process of skinning and playing with your own skin further destabilizes the sense of boundary between player and game and exemplifies what Friedman describes as the aestheticization of our cyborg embodiment.

A number of communities have formed through these play practices, some are clan specific, others are more open. (Planet Quake, www.planetquake.com, is perhaps the most important example of the latter.) Playing as a clan in multiplayer mode with shared skins developed to provide a collective in-game identity is a compelling example of the 'circuit' described above. The complexity of this human–machine circuit is startling; the individual players respond to each other's actions within the game and the process of feedback through which play advances. During the game itself there is no separation of individuals and machines, only a collective process of engagement where action and reaction flow in a circuit of technologized bodies and their pleasures.

Conclusion ●

Digital games have brought computer forms such as simulation, artificial intelligence and interactivity into homes through popular entertainment. They are virtual reality and cyberspace in the here-and-now and the everyday. Colliding with established media forms and cultural economies they have generated new forms, new modes of consumption, muddying commonly accepted boundaries between media consumers and producers, between the subjects and objects of new media. The study of digital games illuminates not only the specific forms, practices and cybernetic pleasures of digital game play, but also offers a unique insight into the nature of contemporary media culture and subjectivity more generally, asking profound questions about the material, political and libidinal relationships between the human and the technological.

Relevant web sites ● ● ●

Buzzcut: Critical Videogame Theory http://www.buzzcut.com
Skins by Milla http://www.chiq.net
Lev Manovich http://www.manovich.net
Ludology.org: Videogame Theory http://www.ludology.org
Planet Quake http://www.planetquake.com
Television Without Pity http://www.televisionwithoutpity.com
The Matrix Trilogy http://www.whatisthematrix.com
Polycount http://www.planetquake.com/polycount

References ●

Benedikt, M. (ed.) (1991) *Cyberspace: First Steps*. Cambridge, MA: MIT Press.
Carr, D. (2002) 'Playing with Lara', in G. King and T. Krzywinska (eds), *Screenplay: Cinema/Videogames/Interfaces*. London: Wallflower Press. pp. 171–80.
Ceruzzi, P. (1999) 'Inventing personal computing', in D. MacKenzie and J. Wajcman (eds), *The Social Shaping of Technology*. Milton Keynes: Open University Press.
Czikszentmihalyi, M. (1993) *The Evolving Self: A Psychology for the Third Millennium*. New York: Harper Perennial.

Czikszentmihalyi, M. (1996) *Creativity: Flow and the Psychology of Discovery and Invention*. New York: Harper Perennial.

Csikszentmihalyi, M. (1997) *Finding Flow*. New York: Basic Books.

Edge (2003) Magazine number 126, August.

Electronic Arts (2000) manual for *The Sims*. Redwood City, CA: Electronic Arts.

Featherstone, M. and Burrows, R. (1995) *Cyberspace, Cyberbodies, Cyberpunk: Cultures of Technological Embodiment*. London: Sage.

Felperin, L. (1995) 'Mortal combat', *Sight and Sound*, 10 (7): 20–3.

Fiske, J. (1987) *Television Culture*. London: Methuen.

Fiske, J. (1992) *Understanding Popular Culture*. London: Routledge.

Frasca, G. (2001) 'Simulation 101: simulation versus representation', Retrieved 15 March 2005 from: www.jacaranda.org/frasca/weblog/articles/sim1/simulation101.html

Friedman, T. (1999) 'Civilisation and its discontents: simulation, subjectivity, and space', retreived 15 March 2005 from: web.mit.edu/21w.780/Materials/friedman.htm

Gibson, W. (1986) *Neuromancer*. London: Grafton.

Gray, C.H. (ed.) (1995) *The Cyborg Handbook*. London: Routledge.

Haddon, L. (1992) 'Explaining ICT consumption: the case of the home computer', in R. Silverstone and E. Hirsch (eds), *Consuming Technologies – Media and Information in Domestic Spaces*. London: Routledge, pp. 82–96.

Haraway, D. (1990) 'A manifesto for cyborgs: science, technology, and socialist feminism in the 1980s', in L.J. Nicholson (ed.) *Feminism/Postmodernism*. London: Routledge. pp. 190–233.

Hayles, N.K. (1999) *How We Became PostHuman: Virtual Bodies in Cybernetics, Literature and Informatics*. London: University of Chicago Press.

Hills, M. (2002) *Fan Cultures*. London: Routledge.

Hunt, L. (2002) '"I know kung fu!": the martial arts in the age of digital reproduction', in G. King and T. Krzywinska (eds), *ScreenPlay: Cinema/Videogame Interfaces*, London: Wallflower Press. pp. 194–205.

Jenkins, H. (1992) *Textual Poachers: Television Fans and Participatory Cultures*. London: Routledge.

Jenkins, H. (1998) 'The poachers and the stormtroopers: cultural convergence in the digital age'; retrieved 15 March 2005 from: http://web.mit.edu/21fms/www/faculty/henry3/pub/stormtroopers.htm

Jenkins, H. and Tulloch, J. (1995) *Science Fiction Audiences: Watching 'Doctor Who' and 'Star Trek'*. London: Routledge.

Lahti, M. (2003) 'As we become machines: corporealized pleasures in video games', in M.J.P. Wolf and B. Perron (eds), *The Video Game Theory Reader*. London: Routledge. pp. 157–70.

Lister, M., Dovey, J., Giddings, S., Grant, I. and Kelly, K. (2003) *New Media: A Critical Introduction*. London: Routledge.

Mackay, H. (ed.) (1997) *Consumption and Everyday Life: Culture, Media and Identities*. London: Sage.

MacKenzie, D.A. and Wacjman, J. (eds) (1999) *The Social Shaping of Technology*. Buckingham: Open University Press.

Manovich, L. (1998) 'Navigable space' retrieved 15 March 2005 from: www.manovich.net

Morley, D. (1980) *The Nationwide Audience*. London: BFI.

Penley C. (1992) 'Feminism, Psychoanalysis and the study of popular culture', in L. Grassberg, C. Nelson and P.A. Treichler (eds), *Cultural Studies*, New York: Routledge, pp. 479–500.

Penley, C. (1997) *NASA/TREK: Popular Science and Sex in America*. London: Verso.

Poster, M. (1995) The *Second Media Age*. Cambridge: Polity Press.

Prensky, M. (2001) *Digital Game-Based Learning*. Columbus, OM: McGraw Hill Education.

Provenzo, E.F., Jr. (1991) *Video Kids – Making Sense of Nintendo*. Cambridge, MA: Harvard University Press.

Pryor, S. (1991) 'Thinking of oneself as a computer', *Leonardo*, 24 (5): 585–90.

Robins, K. (1996) 'Cyberspace and the worlds we live in', in J. Dovey (ed.), *Fractal Dreams: New Media in Social Context*. London: Lawrence & Wishart, pp. 1–30.

Strathern, M. (1992) 'Foreword: the mirror of technology', in R. Silverstone and E. Hirsch (eds), *Consuming Technologies – Media and Information in Domestic Spaces*. London: Routledge. pp. vii–xiii.

Sudnow, D. (1983) *Pilgrim in the Microworld: Eye, Mind and the Essence of Video Skill*. London: Heinemann.

Taylor, T.L. (1999) 'Life in virtual worlds: plural existence, multimodalities, and other online research challenges', *American Behavioral Scientist*, 43 (3), 436–49.

Turkle, S. (1984) *The Second Self: Computers & the Human Spirit*. London: Granada.

Turkle, S. (1995) *Life on the Screen: Identity in the Age of the Internet*. New York: Simon and Schuster.

Wiener, N. (1962 [1948]) *Cybernetics: Control and Communication in Animal and Machine*. Cambridge, MA: MIT Press.

Williams, R. (1974) *Television: Technology and Cultural Form*. London: Fontana.

Wright, T., Boria, E. and Breidenbach P. (2002) 'Creative player actions in FPS online video games playing counter-strike', *Game Studies*, 2 (2), retrieved 15 March 2005 from: http://www.gamestudies.org/0202/wright

9   Digital games and cultural studies

Garry Crawford and Jason Rutter

In *Keywords*, the Welsh cultural analyst Raymond Williams suggests '[c]ulture is one of the two or three most complicated words in the English language' (1983: 87). Considering the development of 'culture' from its original association with 'husbandry, the tending of natural growth ... the tending *of* something, basically crops or animals' Williams offers the following understandings of the term:

> (i) the independent and abstract noun which describes a general process of intellectual, spiritual and aesthetic development, from C18 [the 18th century]; (ii) the independent noun, whether used generally or specifically, which indicates a particular way of life, whether of a people, a period, a group, or humanity in general ... . But we have also to recognize (iii) the independent and abstract noun which describes the works and practices of intellectual and especially artistic activity. This seems often now the most widespread use: culture is music, literature, painting and sculpture, theatre and film. (1983: 90)

More recently the understanding of culture has broadened to describe the production of symbolic meanings as well as material production and processes of development. For digital games, this means that not only is the digital games industry and its production of hardware and software part of a late 20th and early 21st century industrial culture, so too is *Tomb Raider*'s Lara Croft and our understanding of her as either a 'Feminist Icon or Cyberbimbo' (Kennedy, 2002).

Cultural theorists from the UK, Europe and North America have built upon Williams in an attempt to understand our own societies through the production and consumption of cultural products. This tradition has produced work which has explored the relationship between production, text (the form or structure of the item itself whether literary, visual, auditory or otherwise) and audience for media including television (Abercrombie, 1996; Glasgow University Media Group, 1976, 1980; Hall, 1980; Hall et al., 1978; Morley, 1980, 1992); magazines (Hermes, 1995; Jackson et al., 2001; McRobbie and Garber, 1976) and advertisements (Goffman, 1979; Jhally, 1987; Williamson, 1978). Such approaches opened up the possibility to investigate not only the texts themselves but different readers' approaches and understanding of them, the way power is encoded or resisted within the texts and how they portray members of a society within and outside it. It allows us to investigate the various ways in which culture is not just something which is 'out there' for us to passively absorb, but instead is something which we learn, manufacture and do within our own social networks including family, friends, workplace, school, and leisure practices and enthusiasms. This construction of meaning, its link to everyday practice and its role in managing relationships of power, are central concerns of the field we can now recognize as cultural studies.

Baldwin et al. (1999: 3) see cultural studies 'as a new way of engaging in the study of culture'. It is a growing field of research which has developed over the past few decades through taking a conspicuously cross-disciplinary approach. Drawing on many existing academic disciplines including anthropology, geography, history, literature studies, psychology and sociology (to name but a few) it has synthesized each of these discipline's own analyses and understanding of the concept of 'culture' and fused this with a specific 'political commitment' (Baetens, 2005). Writing in 1990, Graeme Turner offered the following observations on cultural studies:

> The term *cultural studies* is now well known as the title for an important set of theories and practices within the humanities and social sciences. As its international journal, *Cultural Studies*, put it, the field is 'dedicated to the notion that the study of cultural processes, and especially of popular culture, is important, complex and both theoretically and politically rewarding.' While the field is now achieving recognition it is not a discrete or homogeneous formation, nor is it easy to define. (Turner, 1990: 1)

This chapter draws upon the various perspectives, theorists and researchers who have contributed to the rich complexity that cultural studies offers in order to demonstrate how their approaches might be used to question and understand digital games. It argues that digital games can be understood not only as texts but also as cultural artefacts, which are given value, meaning and position through their production and use.

The Frankfurt School

A central theme that has run through many studies of culture (even long before the emergence of 'cultural studies') has been the concern with the role and location of culture (in its many forms) within power relations in societies. In particular, a group of academics, including Theodor Adorno, Max Horkheimer and Herbert Marcuse, working initially at the *Institut für Sozialforschung* (The Frankfurt Institute for Social Research), or the Frankfurt School as it is most commonly known, were among the first scholars to take the study of popular culture seriously. Their central thesis was that popular culture had a particular role to play in maintaining capitalism and helping oppress and exploit the working masses.

The argument of the Frankfurt School is complicated, however, because they offer a criticism of traditional Marxist theory, though it is evident that they themselves are offering a variation of Marxism. Where they differ most notably from Marxism, is in attempting to move away from an economic deterministic model, which sees the economy as the major factor shaping the nature of society. In particular, they develop a consideration and critique of contemporary culture and the cultural industry.

On arriving in the USA – having left Germany after the Nazi rise to power in 1933 – Adorno wrote extensively on popular music and the cultural industry he saw operating in the USA. He suggested that cultural goods 'are produced for the market and aimed at the market' (1991: 34). That is to say, for Adorno, what dominates and dictates the production of cultural goods (of which digital games are a contemporary example) is the production of economic capital (profit). What primarily drives and shapes popular cultural industries is not artistic freedom and creativity, but rather profit margins and exploiting the market. The Frankfurt School suggests that cultural products, therefore, become formulaic and standardized, as the industry continues to churn out carbon copies of what has gone before and has proven sales success, but involve minimal innovation:

Movies and radio need no longer pretend to be art. The truth that they are just business is made into an ideology in order to justify the rubbish they deliberately produce. They call themselves industries; and when their directors' incomes are published, any doubt about the social utility of the finished products is removed. (Adorno and Horkheimer, 1972 [1999]: 121)

Evidence could certainly be found to support this argument within the digital games industry when we look at the level of standardization evident in many markets. For example, a limited number of game genres, such as first person shooters and sport-related games dominate the North American and European markets. Moreover, the industry is increasingly dominated by a limited number of large companies and numerous games will share the same or similar gaming engines, reducing the need and cost of innovation and so maximizing the risk to profit ratio of titles. Further, sport games such as EA Sport's *FIFA* get minimal updates and are repackaged and resold each year, while classic games such as *Doom* and *Quake* are simply updated and remade (as in *Doom III* and *Quake III*) rather than creating new games and titles. Thus, from a Frankfurst School perspective, there is little evidence of real innovation or avant-garde artistry within the commercial digital games industry – rather standardized and formulaic games are sold at high prices compared to other cultural content such as music CDs, and this hard-nosed capitalism profiteering 'disguises itself as the object of enjoyment' (Adorno, 1991: 34). It is the entertainment and enjoyment that popular culture offers which Adorno suggests provides a release and escape for people; taking their minds off their exploitation and allowing capitalism to run smoothly.

In this system of cultural production, differences in films or music were not so much a reflection of creativity or expression but a method of ensuring that no section of the market was under exploited in an attempt to ensure that '[s]omething is provided for all so that none may escape' (Adorno and Horkheimer, 1972 [1999]: 123). While the Marxist influence of Adorno's work generally lacks current favour it is worth considering moves within the games industry to attract 'girl gamers', 'casual gamers', 'grey gamers' or other categorizations outside the nominally 'hardcore gamers'. These can be seen as a method of further developing a market growing exponentially in value rather than ensuring representation from categories of society previously excluded from game play and purchase.

The Frankfurt School's reading of popular culture has been extensively criticized (see Longhurst, 1995), most notably as a form of cultural elitism, where high culture (such as 'serious' art and music) is seen to be valued over more 'popular' forms (such as pop music and digital gaming). However, it is vital to realize that Adorno and his colleagues were not cultural snobs but rather neo-Marxists. What Adorno is advocating is that art and culture can potentially be liberating, freeing and an expression of human creativity, but the opportunities for this are stripped away by the capitalist pursuit for profit. However, the (occasional) contributor to the Frankfurt School, Walter Benjamin argues that Adorno overlooked the opportunities for popular culture to be liberating. For example, although the digital games market may be dominated by titles such as *Doom*, *FIFA*, and *Gran Turismo*, there is also a place for more innovative games such as *Animal Crossing*, *Rez* and *Wario Ware Touched*.

The Birmingham School

The use of culture as a form of capitalist exploitation and oppression was developed further by a series of scholars at the Centre for Contemporary Cultural Studies at Birmingham University (or the 'Birmingham School'). The Birmingham School utilized the ideas of the Italian Marxist Antonio Gramsci on hegemony, which suggest that class oppression exists by consent and is legitimated within society. That is to say, the shared values and culture of a society are those based largely on dominant (that is, ruling class) values and ideologies. Hence, culture is used to maintain the existing status quo and promote dominant capitalist values. Again, we do not have to look too hard at the games industry to find evidence to support this thesis. For instance, numerous games are based upon the principle of capital accumulation where the central aim and theme is to make more money to improve your character's or avatar's skills or possessions. This is a point clearly illustrated by Nutt and Railton (2003) in their consideration of the game *The Sims*. A central theme (if not *the* central theme) within *The Sims* is the occupational career development of your character and the acquisition of more and increasingly better consumer items. This is also evident in many motor racing games such as *Need for*

Speed Underground, where wining races earns you more money which is used to improve your vehicle.

However, what authors at the Birmingham School such as Richard Hoggart, Dick Hebdige and Stuart Hall developed further was the power and possibility of certain groups and individuals to subvert or resist dominant power relations. In particular, many authors at Birmingham paid a great deal of attention to 'sub-cultures' – groups which form around particular activities, values or concerns. These groups, particularly youth sub-cultures such as the Mods, Skinheads and Teddy Boys considered by Phil Cohen (1980), can exhibit values that go against the dominant ideology of society and can sometimes resist the dominant social order. Though sub-cultural theories have been criticized for exaggerating the homogeneity and structural nature of what are often little more than casual friendship networks (see Bennett, 1999), exaggerating levels of resistance (see Abercrombie and Longhurst, 1998) and for overlooking the role of women in youth cultures (see McRobbie and Garber, 1976), sub-cultural theories have continued to hold some influence in contemporary Cultural Studies, such as Paul Hodkinson's (2002) application of this to 'Goth' culture.

Certainly hackers, game modders and artists such as Tom Betts (whose *QQQ* project modified the *Quake* game environment) could be theorized as a loose and contemporary form of sub-cultures. These individuals may indeed subvert and change the 'intended' nature of the games that they and others play and will often share and exchange knowledge and game adaptation with others, such as friends or over the Internet. However, a more profitable theorization of gamer communities may be to adopt the concept of 'neo-tribes' (or 'tribus') from the Italian author Michel Maffesoli (1996). For Maffesoli, tribus constitute the multiple, loose and informal communities that have replaced those of extended family and neighbourhood communities and through which individuals move in and out of their everyday lives.

Probably the most important legacy of the Birmingham School for the study of digital gaming is Stuart Hall's paper on encoding/decoding. Here, Hall (1980) suggests that cultural products (such as television programmes, popular music and digital games) may be 'encoded' with dominant values, ideas and beliefs. He argues that audiences engages in a process of 'decoding' these texts, which is more than a process of translation but one where individuals provide their own readings and interpretations of the cultural products. Though some audiences may accept and 'incorporate' the dominant values inherent in texts, others may negotiate (accepting or rejecting certain aspects and locating these within their own existing ideas and lives) or even resist them altogether. This is important for the study of digital studies as it recognizes that media audiences are not necessarily passive consumers but may actively engage and (re)interpret the mass media. This then helps shift focus away from simplistic media effects debates that have often sought to establish links between digital gaming and aggressive behaviour (see Bryce and Rutter, Chapter 11).

Kline et al. (2003) highlight the importance of an active audiences model in considering digital game players. For instance, they cite examples of how gamers will subvert the preferred readings of games such as *Civilization* and *SimCity*. Indeed, digital games often provide the gamer with multiple opportunities to (some degree) change and adapt the game to fit their personal tastes and interests either via options built into the game, or via more 'illegitimate' methods, such as 'hacking' or modifying games. However, Kline et al. caution that it is important that we do not simply celebrate audiences, irrespective of the qualities of the media they use, and do not underplay the commercial structuring of the games industry and the audience's primary role as economic consumers. Certainly numerous authors (such as Gansing, 2003; Palmer, 2003) suggest that levels of 'user control' and the 'interactivity' of games is something that has been largely overestimated, and that the level of control audiences have to influence or subvert games is often very limited.

Palmer (2003: 160) suggests that new technologies are frequently introduced and sold to the market using the rhetoric of their increased 'user-control' as in the case of Sony's video cassette recorder, which promised the ability to 'master time, memory and circumstance' or *Microsoft's* advertising slogan of 'where do you want to go today?'. However, the user's control is still severely restricted by the limitations of technology, the aims of the designers and manufacturers, and their associated ideologies. Gamers only have certain limited options and possibilities within any particular game and the game's possible responses to their actions will likewise be restricted. However, games also involve other limits on their scope and possible interactivity. For instance, most digital games tend to be constructed from the perspective of the 'male gaze' and objectify and sexualize women, offering little opportunity to challenge this central ideology within the game (see Bryce and Rutter, 2003; Yates and Littleton, 2001).

Bourdieu and practice ●

Another important contribution to the study of culture and social class is offered by Pierre Bourdieu (1984). Unlike Karl Marx, and many of those influenced by his work, who see social class as shaped solely by economic capital, Bourdieu suggested that a person's class is also shaped by their social and cultural capital. Social capital refers to factors such as social prestige, status and authority. Cultural capital offers a theoretical understanding of the role of taste and consumption in patterns of social distinction. That is to say, how command and understanding of certain forms of culture (such as an understanding of art and literature) can be used by social groups to express their good taste and mark themselves as distinctive from others. Significantly for Bourdieu, taste is not an innate ability but rather something we are taught and which is used by communities to make value judgments about what is acceptable and desired culture (such as 'serious' forms of art and music) and to trivialize 'popular' forms of culture (such as pop music and digital gaming). However, the work of Bourdieu could also be employed to explore social distinctions and codes of 'authenticity' within gaming, such as how male gamers may utilize their under-standing of gaming practices and cultures to exclude females.

Significant in understanding the mechanisms of social distinction is Bourdieu's use of the concept of *habitus*. Habitus is similar to what other authors have described as the 'culture' of a particular group or society. For Bourdieu, habitus only exists 'inside the heads of actors' (for instance, ways of behaving and modes of practice are learnt and internalized by individuals). It is a residue of the past which shapes actions in the present and is evident through the regular knowledge and assumptions unconsciously built in to the practice and actions of social actors.

As an ex-rugby player, using games as a metaphor for social practice came easily to Bourdieu. He argued that playing sport was not just a matter of knowing and acting upon the rules, but having a sense of the larger context both of the team and the game itself. For example, part of being a successful player of a deathmatch in *Quake* is not just a matter of being an accurate shot, but having a feeling for the games' development and different strategies that inform when to shoot and how to get into the right position to do this. The experienced player uses the know-how of their previous games to develop a sense of their own strengths and weaknesses and can improvise their play in order to manage risk and influence the game's outcome depending on what is at stake.

Habitus is also dependent upon the *field* in which it is located. Fields are specific areas of cultural life such as sport, art, family life and so forth, which each have their own practices and habitus. This is important as Bourdieu highlights how culture is dependent upon specific physical and social locations that influence not only practice but create a framework for what is recognized as important (or seen) and what is considered irrelevant (or unseen). For example, in the habitus of an old-fashioned English gentlemen's club, the exclusion of women is not regarded as important as their absence is unseen as part of the culture. Digital gaming can be seen to have its own practices and culture (or habitus) distinct from other leisure forms where issues such as competition, conflict, technology, baiting of competitors, control, game statistics and rapid consumption of new game titles typically shape the practice of being a digital gamer.

● The postmodern turn

A significant development or 'turn' in cultural theory has been offered by the notion of 'postmodernism'. Modern society (or modernity) is often seen to have developed out of the industrial revolution. Here there was a shift away from agricultural-based societies toward industrial and Fordist production, a massive urban growth and a rise in rational-scientific thought. However, many theorists suggest that numerous (and in particular 'Western') societies no longer conform to this kind of societal model. Hence, at its simplest, postmodernity means a shift away from what was deemed 'modern' life.

We can distinguish between those writers who draw on and use postmodern theories to explore aspects of contemporary culture, and those who seek to define and explain postmodern society more generally. Obviously these trajectories can intersect, but they are not always the same. However, here are some of the basic elements of postmodern culture and/or society (though these are not the focus or concern of all writers on postmodernity). First, that there has been a significant rise in power and influence of the mass media leading to a media saturated society. Second, that there has been a shift away from social and economic life based around production to that based upon consumption. Hence, third, that social and physical lives (such as in the cities that we live in) become increasingly shaped around consumption (such as the rise of shopping malls). Fourth, a questioning of what is 'real' and 'reality', as history and narrative are replaced by image as the main organizing principle of social and cultural life – surface over depth. Finally, there is a rise in parody, irony, pastiche, eclecticism and hybridity where cultures and ideas are joined together in new perverse ways to explore meaning and knowledge.

An author often associated with 'postmodernity' (though he now prefers his own term of 'liquid modernity') is Zygmunt Bauman. Bauman suggests the consumption has become the primary defining influence in shaping that nature of contemporary society. As Bauman (1998: 22) states 'ours is a consumer society'. To a certain degree, he argues, all societies are consumer societies, but there is something 'profound and fundamental' about the nature of contemporary consumer society that makes it distinct from all other societies (1998: 24). Most significantly, Bauman argues that all prior societies have been primarily producer societies. Before an individual could fully participate in society, they had to be producers or at least part of the production process. In 'our' (consumer) society, an individual 'needs to be a consumer first, before one can think of becoming anything in particular' (1998: 26).

Bauman (1997) suggests that contemporary living is characterized by uncertainty and uncontrollability. There has emerged a 'new world disorder' devoid of visible structure and logic. The mass media conveys the essential image of the 'softness of the world' where anything and everything is possible and nothing is final (1997: 24). Identities become flexible and fluid. Rarely can a permanent identity be achieved through employment as assured life careers (apart for a few privileged professions) become less common. Hence, our identities become defined and constructed through our consumer and leisure activities. Bauman draws on the idea of neo-tribes from Maffesoli, but rather than seeing these as new forms of community, Bauman takes these as evidence of the loss of community and the individualization of society. Digital gaming could be seen (and has been seen by many) as a clear illustration of the individualization of society. Certainly, in recent years there has been evident a general fear within the popular press, and some sectors of academia, that the rise in popularity of digital gaming has helped create a generation of isolated and passive 'mouse potatoes' (Kline et al., 2003), whose only contact with other more 'healthy' activities, such as sport, is via their digital screens; such as O'Connor (2002: 2) wrote in *The Times* newspaper in respect of soccer related games:

The rate at which these games are flying off the shelves would suggest more football is being played on home computers than local fields. Which raises the question, 'could it be possible that virtual football is even bigger than the real thing?'

As Kline et al. argues, 'sport video games invite kids to sit in front of a screen rather than go out and kick a ball around (or even cheer in the stands)' (2003: 36). However, recent data does not seem to bear out the assertion that those who play digital games are less likely to play sport (see Crawford, 2005; Fromme, 2001), likewise Colwell and Payne (2000) found no evidence to suggest that those who regularly played digital games had fewer friends than those who did not. However, as already suggested, there is certainly evidence within the digital gaming industry to support the assertion that what dominates this is consumer culture. Not only do games such as *The Sims* revolve around consumerist values, but the whole industry is built around creating and selling high priced leisure goods that have a relatively short shelf life before they are replaced by updated versions or newer technology. As Bauman suggests, consumer society is built on desire, but not a desire that can ever be fulfilled but rather 'desire desires desire' (1998: 25).

Probably the most famous (and most controversial) postmodern theorist is Jean Baudrillard. As early as the late 1960s Baudrillard was arguing that we no longer lived in a society based upon the exchange of material goods with a 'real' use value (as Marx argued), but rather society was increasingly based around the exchange and consumptions of 'signs' or images. That is to say, what matters in our contemporary (postmodern) world, is no longer what is 'real' or has depth, but rather surface and image. For instance, celebrity figures such as footballers, pop stars or, taking Rehak's (2003) analytical lead, Lara Croft, primarily exist as media images which are bought, sold and consumed as symbolic and cultural meaning is written onto them:

> The fan movement surrounding Lara Croft – one of the most recognizable, globally popular and lucrative media stars working today – is all the more remarkable given than its object does not, in any localized or unitary sense, exist. Croft, a fixture of the pop-culture landscape since 1996, who has appeared in computer games, comic books, men's magazines, promotional tours, music videos, calendars, action figures, board games and a motion picture franchise, is an *artefact*: a software-generated character without human referent. (Rehak, 2003: 477–8, emphasis in original)

This blurring of the 'real' and the 'unreal' where no preference is given to the real or original item, what Baudrillard refers to as a 'hyperreality', could be seen to have a seemingly obvious application to gaming. Numerous films, such as *eXistenZ*, have explored the shifting boundaries between gameplay and real life, while other films and games (such as *The Matrix* and *Enter the Matrix*, respectively) draw directly on the work of Baudrillard to question 'what is real?'. Indeed, Murray and Jenkins write of gamers being deeply immersed in games and being 'transported to another place, of losing our sense of reality and extending ourselves into a seemingly limitless, enclosing, other realm ¼' (n.d.: 2).

As part of a postmodern turn questions about what is real, virtual or fictional become irrelevant as experience becomes a matter of consuming and producing texts each of which have no greater authority to truth than each other. In such a view, history is not about facts concerning the past but one of many stories available to us. Where Shakespeare, *National Enquirer* magazine, *The Simpsons*, Norse folklore, Lara Croft and Madonna all have equal standing, and we can only know their shallow top surface, there is little to stop us treating world culture as a supermarket where, in contrast to Bourdieu's view, we can chose things off the shelf and combine them at will.

In contrast to the authorial crafting of modernist films, in digital games such as the *Gran Turismo* series the soundtrack is not crafted in bespoke fashion but, like many television advertisements, appropriates existing hit tracks. Similarly in *Carmageddon 2* there is little to stop us drawing other cultural texts so that we exchange our car for a Dalek and replace pedestrians with the Spice Girls. A broad understanding of postmodern theory points to a potential for individuals to create not only their own texts but self and geographies. Whereas for Bourdieu our past was what structures our present actions, postmodernity argues that '[a]ppearance *substitutes* for past and present action and, at the same time, conveys an *incipience* permitting others to anticipate what is about to occur' (Stone, cited in Glassner, 1990: 227).

However, postmodern theory has been criticized for emphasizing social change over continuity, and neglecting that despite a potentially infinite range of cultural combinations, social life continues to be very real for most people. For instance, gamers are not actually 'transported to another place' or managing their football team to league supremacy but are physically and socially located within a very real world, which will shape their (and others) gameplay, which in turn has real world consequences. Hence, finally, we wish to consider the study of everyday life.

● Popular culture as resistance

Although sociological engagement with everyday activities and routines has a rich history that has focused most strongly on authors from a broadly interactionist (and North American) tradition such as Herbert Blumer, Harold Garfinkel and Erving Goffman, in recent years many cultural studies scholars have began to pay more attention to how culture is experienced and located at a micro-social level, or in other words, in our everyday lives. However, while the interactionist tradition has tended to emphasize the accomplishment of routine, stability of interaction and 'doing being ordinary' (Sacks, 1984), cultural studies has often focused on the oppositional aspects of everyday life.

This is the idea of everyday life offered by Michel de Certeau (1984; de Certeau et al., 1998) as he explores the everyday as a site for social resistance. It is possible to see overt examples of everyday 'resistance' and creativity in the work of de Certeau, and to interpret this as a straightforward celebration of an individual's capacity for 'oppositional' readings or their ability to disrupt a system of power in obvious ways. For instance, a much cited example is that of 'la perrugue' (or 'the wig'), which is '… the worker's own work disguised as work for his employer' (de Certeau, 1984: 25). That is to say, de Certeau uses this term to describe ways in which workers can use time and facilities at work to their own advantage, such as producing objects for themselves. These overt forms of resistance and creativity have been drawn on by numerous other authors, such as John Fiske (1989) and Henry Jenkins (1992). For example, Jenkins considered how *Star Trek* and *Doctor Who* fans will frequently 'poach' story lines and characters from these existing texts, and use these to create their own stories, songs, artwork or fantasies. Likewise, de Certeau could be applied to game modders who take the resources which capitalism gives (or more accurately, sells) them and use these creatively, subverting their 'intended' meanings, making their own games, adaptations or levels or even sometimes for deviant ends, such as illegally 'cracking', copying and distributing software.

De Certeau sees social life as constraining and oppressive, where individuals are largely marginalized and have little say or control over factors such as market forces, which dictate what individuals are given, or more commonly, sold. However, for de Certeau everyday life is extremely complex and multifaceted, and this allows room for manoeuvre and individuality. For example, he suggests that when an individual reads a text, such as a book, though the words on a page are set (in black and white) the reader frequently provides their own images and interpretations. This is not a misreading of the text, but rather that the reader provides their own understanding and derives their own pleasures from it. However, we must warn against exaggerating the ambition of de Certeau's work, in that he is not suggesting that texts are open to any number of endless readings, as language and social life will always place limitations on what is possible. In particular, de Certeau criticizes semiologists such as Saussure for failing to account for the role of social power relations in structuring interpretation. However, how individual meanings and understandings are applied to language provides an important metaphor for considering how individuals 'make do' (faire-avec) with the resources that society gives them.

This theorization is particularly useful, as for audiences (such as readers of a book or digital gamers) to be seen as 'active' does not necessarily need to involve overt or even conscious examples of 'resistance' that have measurable and visible consequences. Indeed, the enthusiasm of many of de Certeau's followers to apply his work has often led to his work being dismissed as excessively optimistic. However, Buchanan suggests that de Certeau is 'not nearly so frivolous as some of his followers' (2000: 87). In particular, Highmore (2002) suggests (and we would concur) that focus upon more exceptional forms of creativity often overlooks the importance of more common and mundane practices, which are more prominent and significant in the work of de Certeau.

De Certeau highlights that all audiences are active and creative, in that it is they who bring cultural objects alive in their imagination and give these specific and individual meanings, by locating them in their everyday lives. This is a similar line of argument taken by Abercrombie and Longhurst in their book *Audiences* (1998). Here they argue that consideration of audiences needs to move away from focusing on examples of incorporation and/or resistance of dominant values (such as those of capitalism), to rather understanding how media resources are located and drawn on as resources in individuals' everyday lives. For instance, it is possible to see gamers as a 'knowledge community' (Levy, 1997) where individuals will exchange information about games via websites, online forums and face-to-face conversations. Likewise, gaming will be drawn on as a resource for conversation, social interactions, and even for some, as a component in their identity construction, identifying themselves as a 'modder', 'LANner', 'game-head' or simply a 'gamer'.

Conclusion

Utility in applying a cultural studies approach is to be found in the manner in which it allows digital games to be seen as more than just objects existing as non-social artefacts waiting for use or analysis. It moves away from any basic assumption that digital games have a meaning or form which can be discovered through applying the right analytical cipher to the appropriate game code in a manner removed from social, economic and political contexts. As a broad field, cultural studies encourages the exploration of digital games as part of a process of continual cultural production and the management of social meaning. What cultural studies allows us as digital game researchers to do is observe the way in which games fit into established modes of practice, as well as being part of the development of new and evolving ones. It emphasizes how cultural products such as digital games have meaning placed on them through their context and use, and that these meanings are often negotiated or resisted in order to benefit specific groups of communities.

Unlike many areas of research, taking a cultural studies approach to understanding digital games does not mean that top-down and bottom-up approaches are incompatible. That is, it is possible to see cultural texts as 'encoded' in such a way as to embody the values of the powerful and ruling segments of society and act towards exploiting and pacifying other members of society (top-down), and that also these texts can be read creatively and even subverted or resisted by everyday consumers, readers or gamers, which can associate these with alternative cultures and struggle against power asymmetries.

This then provides a rich source for understanding contemporary digital gaming, not only as a cultural industry, involved in the production and sale of leisure and consumer items, but also how these are experienced and located in gamers everyday lives and culture.

In this chapter we have explored how the concept of 'culture' is a complex and contested one which has been variously used to encompass the rare and great offering of a society's artists; ways of living and the beliefs of a society; the practices of everyday life; and the patterns of production and consumption of a society, as well as their processes of development.

A central theme within cultural studies, and within this chapter, has been that of social power. Early studies of popular culture offered by Adorno and his colleagues saw popular culture as a source of exploitation and oppression, driven by capitalist ends. However, their contemporary Benjamin recognized the potential for freedom and liberation in popular culture. We have discussed how more recently, these themes have been explored further by the Birmingham School scholars who saw popular culture as a source of exploitation, but recognized the potential to subvert or negotiate preferred readings or authorial intention.

The discussion of Bourdieu added to our understanding of how culture is important in shaping our lives – a theme further developed by postmodern theorists, such as Bauman and Baudrillard, who argued that popular culture and consumption become of central importance in contemporary society, where these lead to a blurring between what is real and what is not. Another useful strand within cultural studies is the theoretical consideration of practices of everyday life which Fiske sees as a site of resistance and rebellion. For writers such as de Certeau the importance is understanding how individuals adapt, locate and personalize what society gives them into their everyday lives.

Relevant web sites ● ● ●

Media and Communication Studies Site http://www.aber.ac.uk/media
Tom Betts http://www.nullpointer.co.uk
Social and Cultural Theory http://www.theory.org.uk
Terra Nova http://terranova.blogs.com
Tony Fitzgerald's Sociology Online http://www.sociologyonline.co.uk

References ●

Abercrombie, N. (1996) *Television and Society*. Cambridge: Polity.
Abercrombie, N. and Longhurst, B. (1998) *Audiences*. London: Sage.
Adorno, T. (1991) *The Culture Industry*. London: Routledge.
Adorno, T.W. and Horkheimer, M. (1972 [1999]) *Dialectic of Enlightenment*. London: Verso.
Baetens, J. (2005) 'Cultural studies after the cultural studies paradigm', *Cultural Studies*, 19 (1): 1–13.
Baldwin, E., Longhurst, B., McKracken, S., Ogborn, M. and Smith, G. (1999) *Introducing Cultural Studies*. London: Prentice Hall Europe.

Bauman, Z. (1997) *Postmodernity and its Discontents*. Cambridge: Polity Press.

Bauman, Z. (1998) *Work, Consumerism and the New Poor*. Buckingham: Open University Press.

Bennett, A. (1999) 'Subcultures or neo-tribes? Rethinking the relationship between youth, style and musical taste', *Sociology*, 33 (3): 599–617.

Bourdieu, P. (1984) *Distinction: A Critique of the Judgement of Taste*. London: Routledge.

Buchanan, I. (2000) *Michel de Certeau: Cultural Theorist*. London: Sage.

Bryce, J. and Rutter, J. (2003) 'Gender dynamics and the social and spatial organization of computer gaming', *Leisure Studies*, 22: 1–15.

Cohen, P. (1980) 'Subcultural conflict and working-class community', in S. Hall, D. Hobson, A. Lowe and P. Willis (eds), *Culture, Media, Language: Working Papers in Cultural Studies, 1972–1979*. London: Hutchinson. pp. 78–87.

Colwell, J. and Payne, J. (2000) 'Negative correlates of computer game play in adolescents', *British Journal of Psychology*, 91: 295–310.

Crawford, G. (2005) 'Digital gaming, sport and gender', *Leisure Studies*, in press.

de Certeau, M. (1984) *The Practice of Everyday Life*. Berkeley, CA: University of California Press.

de Certeau, M., Giard, L, and Mayol, P. (1998) *The Practice of Everyday Life, Volume II: Living and Cooking*. Minneapolis, MN: University of Minneapolis Press.

Fiske, J. (1989) *Understanding Popular Culture*. London: Unwin Hyman.

Fromme, J. (2003) 'Computer games as a part of children's culture', *Game Studies*, 3 (1) retrieved from: http://www.gamestudies.org/0301/fromme/ Accessed 16 November 2005.

Gansing, K. (2003) 'The myth of interactivity? Interactive films as an imaginary genre', paper presented at MelbourneDAC2003 conference, retrieved from: http://hypertext.rmit.edu.au/dac/papers/Gansing.pdf Accessed 16 November 2005.

Glasgow University Media Group (1976) *Bad News*. London: Routledge & Kegan Paul.

Glasgow University Media Group (1980) *More Bad News*. London: Routledge.

Glassner, B. (1990) 'Fit for postmodern selfhood', in H.S. Becker and M.M. McCall (eds), *Symbolic Interaction and Cultural Studies*. Chicago, IL: University of Chicago Press. pp. 215–43.

Goffman, E. (1979) *Gender Advertisements*. Basingstoke and London: Macmillan.

Hall, S. (1980) 'Encoding/decoding', in S. Hall, D. Hobson, A Lowe and P. Willis (eds), *Culture, Media, Language: Working Papers in Cultural Studies, 1972–79*. London: Hutchinson. pp. 128–38.

Hall, S., Critcher, C., Jefferson, T., Clarke, J. and Roberts, B. (1978) *Policing the Crisis: Mugging, the State and Law and Order*. London: Macmillan.

Hermes, J. (1995) *Reading Women's Magazines: An Analysis of Everyday Media Use*. Cambridge: Polity.

Highmore, B. (2002) *Everyday Life and Cultural Theory: An Introduction*. London: Routledge.

Hodkinson, P. (2002) *Goth: Identity, Style and Subculture*. Oxford: Berg.

Jackson, P., Stevenson, N. and Brooks, K. (2001) *Making Sense of Men's Magazines*. Cambridge: Polity.

Jenkins, H. (1992) *Textual Poachers*. London: Routledge.

Jhally, S. (1987) *The Codes of Advertising: Fetishism and The Political Economy of Meaning in The Consumer Society*. New York: St. Martin's Press.

Kennedy, H.W. (2002) 'Lara Croft: Feminist icon or cyberbimbo? On the Limits of textual analysis', *Game Studies* 2 (2). Retrieved 16 November from: www.gamestudies.org/0202/kennedy/

Kline, S. Dyer-Witherford, N. and De Peuter, G. (2003) *Digital Play: The Interaction of Technology, Culture, and Marketing*. London: McGill-Queen's University Press.

Levy, P. (1997) *Collective Intelligence: Mankind's Emerging World in Cyberspace*. Cambridge: Perseus.

Longhurst, B. (1995) *Popular Music and Society*. Cambridge: Polity Press.

Maffesoli, M. (1996) *The Time of the Tribes: The Decline of Individualism in Mass Society*. London: Sage.

McRobbie, A. and Garber, J. (1976) 'Girls and subcultures', in A. McRobbie (ed.), *Feminism and Youth Culture,* 2nd edn. London: Macmillan. pp. 12–25.

Morley, D. (1980) *The 'Nationwide' Audience: Structure and Decoding*. London: BFI.

Morley, D. (1992) *Television Audiences and Cultural Studies*. London: Routledge.

Murray, J. and Jenkins, H. (n.d.) *Before the Holodeck: Translating Star Trek into Digital Media*. Available online at web.mit.edu/cms/People/Henry3/holodeck.html Last accessed 16 November 2005.

Nutt, D. and Railton, N. (2003) '*The Sims*: real life as genre', *Information, Communication & Society*, 6 (4): 577–607.

O'Connor, A. (2002) 'Even better than the real thing?', *The Times, The Game* supplement, 9 December. pp. 2–3.

Palmer, D. (2003) 'The paradox of user control', paper presented to the Melbourne DAC 2003 conference, 19–25 May, retrieved from: http://hypertext.rmit.edu.au/dac/papers/Palmer.pdf. Accessed 16 November 2005.

Rehak, B. (2003) 'Mapping the bit girl: Lara Croft and new media fandom', *Information, Communication & Society*, 6 (4): 477–96.

Sacks, H. (1984) 'On doing "being ordinary"', in J.M. Atkinson and J. Heritage (eds), *Structures of Social Action: Studies in Conversation Analysis*. Cambridge: Cambridge University Press. pp. 413–29.

Turner, G. (1990) *British Cultural Studies: An Introduction*. London: Unwin Hyman.

Yates, S.J. and Littleton, K.L. (2001) 'Understanding computer game culture: a situated approach', in E. Green and A. Adams (eds), *Virtual Gender: Technology, Consumption and Identity*. London: Routledge. pp. 103–23.

Williams, R. (1983) *Keywords: A Vocabulary of Culture and Society*. Oxford: Oxford University Press.

Williamson, J. (1978) *Decoding Advertisements: Ideology and Meaning in Advertising*. London: Marion Boyars.

10 Community, identity and digital games

Martin Hand and Karenza Moore

This chapter situates digital gaming within debates about community and identity in contemporary culture. This involves looking at the multitude of activities and artefacts implicated in digital gaming and how they contribute to the construction of gaming communities and identities. It has been suggested, often in the popular media, that digital gaming is an anti-social activity divorced from the routine and 'normal' contexts of everyday life. However, recent ethnographic research suggests that, on the contrary, gaming is performed in the context of existing social and cultural networks, friendships and relationships while at the same time producing novel forms of cultural activity (Bryce and Rutter, 2003; Yates and Littleton, 1999). In taking this latter perspective, we explore debates around the idea that such activities constitute or reconstitute different forms of community and identity. We illustrate how different concepts of community and identity provide us with a series of vantage points for illuminating emergent *multiple* cultures of digital gaming.

The terms *community* and *identity* have a diverse range of meanings in sociology, philosophy and cultural studies, reflecting their complex histories and variety of applications (Anderson, 1991; Bauman, 1990; Crow and Allan, 1994; Delanty, 2003; Lash, 1994; Maffesoli, 1996; Nancy, 1991; Poster, 1995). They are often used in reference to the *decline* of particular ways of life or social institutions (such as the family, religion and class-based affiliations) and also the emergence of new social and cultural formations (such as virtual, post-traditional and global forms of communication and experience). Most recently, debates about the emergence of information and communication technologies, computer-mediated communication, and 'cyberculture' have often looked toward ideas around community and identity in trying to explain apparently novel forms of interaction and representation (Jones, 1995; Poster, 1995; Rheingold, 1994; Stone, 1991; Turkle, 1997). Digital gaming can therefore be seen as one example of such phenomena.

This chapter will begin by looking at how different forms of digital gaming can be understood through theories of community, and will then move on to consider how this is related to the identities of digital gamers. In reality, these are inextricably interrelated, but we choose to artificially separate them here for the purpose of outlining key concepts and approaches. We suggest that they can provide us with a set of analytical tools for exploring the many phenomena of digital gaming as forms of techno-mediated *collective* and *embedded* cultural activity. The key aims of this chapter are to discuss digital gaming as a collective activity and to look at how differing theories of community and identity can help us understand the nature of these activities and their practitioners.

Gaming communities ●

What do we mean by community? ●

Digital gamers form common associations or friendships with other gamers. They communicate with each other, build networks, exchange ideas, swap 'cheats' and so on. However, to say that these kinds of associations and friendship can be understood as forms of *community* requires further exploration. We need to take a step backwards here and think about what we mean by community. There are three key concepts of community which can help us: communities of presence; imagined communities; and virtual communities. Each of these can provide ways of understanding different forms of digital gaming in their broader sociocultural contexts.

Communities of presence ●

The German sociologist Ferdinand Tonnies (1855–1936) distinguished between two ideal types of social relations: *Gemeinschaft* (community) – organic and informal social ties found in families or local neighbourhoods; *Gesellschaft* (society) – instrumental and impersonal ties found in urban developments and large-scale organizations. Gemeinschaft emerges 'naturally' through the geographical proximity, kinship, trust and mutual reliance found in small-scale localities. In contrast, Gesellschaft describes more abstract social relations where interactions between individuals are 'mechanical', reflecting the individual self-interest, private property and impersonal relations found in modern cities. Gesellschaft indicates a *decline* (rather than a replacement) of community during modernity, particularly within the *metropolis* (see also Simmel, 1950). While historically specific, this dichotomy continues to inform many debates about the nature of community, particularly where the members of such a community meet face-to-face. Whether particular social relations are judged as constituting a community or not is often discussed in terms of whether they are based upon traditional cultural values which are reproduced over time. While many forms of digital gaming do not involve or require face-to-face interaction, it has been noted that digital gamers often actually meet in conjunction with gaming over dispersed networks. In these cases, what kind of social relations are enacted? Let us take the example of LAN parties.

BREAKOUT BOX 10.1 ● ● ●

LAN parties

'Lanning' involves gamers meeting face-to-face to play against each other over a temporary local area network (LAN). This is a key example of how 'online' gaming occurs within an 'offline' context. LAN parties are not solely about competitive gaming. They are also attempts to demonstrate membership of a 'gaming community'. The physical presence of gamers is central to the gaming experience as a whole here, emphasizing the collective nature of the gaming experience. Such offline events have increased in tandem with online and networked facilities for digital gaming.

In the case of 'LAN parties', gamers come together face-to-face in a specific locality, forming sets of rules, norms or conventions, which shape emergent social relations. Gamers seem to have sets of shared values, while the gaming event itself seems to be an expression of the creative life of the group. Such characteristics seem to conform to the kinds of 'organic' relations sketched earlier. However, these relations are also *transient*. After the event, the gamers disperse, only coming together again for *lanning* events. As such, communality is based upon fleeting common interests rather than ongoing mutual need or kinship, and the development of long-standing social relations. In Tonnies' and others' terms, these relations could not be described as a community. Rather, they are indicative of the kind of fleeting social relations thought to be inherent to modernity, where 'tradition' is gradually eroded.

However, others within this sociological tradition have stressed the inherently symbolic nature of communities – where it is through the changing symbolic rituals of members that communities are formed and maintained, rather than simply through static traditional cultural values (see Cohen, 1985). In this sense, the ways in which the *lanners* organize their 'parties', how they decide who is included, how clans are formed, what 'rules' apply to the event, and so on, are all symbolic mechanisms for the construction and maintenance of a *sense of community*. According to this view, communities are not simply expressions of mutual reliance and shared cultural values which need to be reproduced over long durations. Instead they can emerge in a strong form through fleeting 'moments' where a social group asserts its collective identity by establishing its boundaries and its conditions of membership (see Delanty, 2003). This makes sense where collectives of digital gamers are in each others' presence, but how does this work when digital gamers *never* meet?

Imagined communities

The concept of community proposed by Tonnies and others is all about the geographical proximity of the community members and the 'organic' emergence of social relations. However, others have stressed that communities are not necessarily based upon presence. For example, if we think of 'national communities' it is immediately clear that not all members of such a community will know each other, or have even seen each other. To identify oneself as part of a 'British', 'European', or 'American' community, does not (indeed cannot) require all members to have strong social ties with one another. There are certain moments when such a community emerges through displays of apparent unity and common purpose, despite the necessarily dispersed nature of the membership. For example, such communities often appear to materialize during sporting events and national conflicts. Benedict Anderson's (1991) concept of *imagined communities*, in reference to how the idea of the nation as a community spread, is important in drawing our attention toward how all communities have employed *material symbolic* devices (such as flags, emblems, images, texts) to construct and maintain their status as communities. Anderson states that: 'all communities larger than primordial villages (and perhaps even these) are imagined' (1991: 6). The dynamics of inclusion and exclusion, belonging and membership are then not simply tied to mutual presence, but also to the symbolic construction of community as a dispersed *imaginary* entity.

In terms of digital gaming, we can look at the ways in which gamers actively construct images of community through the use of material artefacts and symbolic devices, especially where the members of the community never actually meet. In contrast to communities of presence, we would take the idea of a gaming community to describe the *imaginary* processes of community formation mediated by the objects of gaming. For Anderson (1991), it is the technology of print which enables the symbolic construction of the 'nation' as a community to emerge. In this way, we should also consider how material artefacts and new technologies mediate community formation: the assorted gaming 'paraphernalia' which reinforce ideas, values and symbols of inclusion in and exclusion from a community. These include digital artefacts – levels, maps, scenarios and stories – as well as physical objects such as digital gaming magazines, strategy guides or gaming-related clothing that operates as an explicit symbol of membership.

In thinking about digital gaming in terms of community formation and maintenance we are looking at gaming as a form of *collective activity*: an activity that involves interaction between individuals, the effect of which is to produce the experience of belonging to a community of one sort or another. What the precise nature of such communities is depends upon the actual activities of gamers, the nature of the games, and the social and cultural conditions within which games and gamers are situated. Both the senses we have outlined so far – communities of presence and imagined communities – rely upon the existence of specific boundaries, whether of a geographical, gendered, national or ethnic nature. In the next section, we consider in more detail the idea that some forms of digital gaming constitute a form of entirely boundless and non-territorial community – *virtual communities*.

Virtual communities

The concepts of community looked at so far have been premised upon either face-to-face contact between individuals or have been territorially limited in some way. But what about gaming practices which appear to involve no 'sense of place'? Are digital (online) gamers at their screens embedded within a wider social network which we could characterize as a *community*? In looking at the notion of virtual community, we focus in particular upon the work of Rheingold (1994) and Jones (1997), in characterizing computer-mediated communication (in this case online gaming) as producing radical opportunities for community construction. Howard Rheingold offers us the simplest definition or what we might mean by 'virtual community':

> Virtual communities are social aggregations that emerge from the Net when enough people carry on those public discussions long enough, with sufficient human feeling, to form webs of personal relationships in cyberspace. (1993: 5)

BREAKOUT BOX 10.2 ● ● ●

The virtual (or virtuality)

Anything 'that is so in essence or effect, although not formally or actually; admitted of being called by the name so far as the effect or the result is concerned' (OED).

'The virtual is real but not concrete' (Shields, 2003: 2).

'The virtual is precisely not the real; that's why 'postmoderns' like 'virtual reality' (Haraway, 1992: 325).

For Rheingold, it is not a matter of 'where' individuals might be, but whether the interactions between them are sufficient to form 'webs of personal relationships'. While Rheingold and others are primarily talking about discussion forums on the net, we might use this idea to characterize online gaming as constituting virtual communities through the web of interactions formed by the practice of gaming. In particular, the role-playing virtual worlds of MMORPG's (massively multiplayer online role-playing games) and MUD's (multi-user dungeons) can be thought of as forms of communication involving participants who have never met which may generate meaningful social ties. Squire and Steinkuehler describe such online games as 'persistent social and material worlds, loosely structured by open-ended (fantasy) narratives' (in press: 2). As such, MMORPGs such as *Star Wars Galaxies* and *Ultima*

Online are important sites for research on the relationship between technical and design elements of gaming worlds, and the social and cultural elements of gamer participation such as the use of currencies in virtual economies (Dibbell, 2003), the regulation of player behaviour (Squire and Steinkuehler, in press), language use (Wright et al., 2002), popular culture references (Kolo and Baur, 2004) and so on.

BREAKOUT BOX 10.3 ● ● ●

Multi-user dungeon (MUD)

A computer program that accepts connections from a number of simultaneous users over a computer network and provides them with access to a shared 'adventure game'; that is a shared virtual environment where players can move between rooms, interact with each other and manipulate virtual objects.

Massively multiplayer online role-playing games (MMORPGs)

A graphic environment that resembles the 'real world' in functionality and appearance. Players control their online personae via various modes of human–computer interface, confined by technical restrictions and 'community' rules, enabling social interactions amongst gameworld characters (Kolo and Baur, 2004).

In relation to MUDs and MMORPGs, Kolo and Baur (2004) highlight that online computer playing can create social and cultural spaces for the creation and stimulation of personal relations in the game as well as around it. Participants in online games often have different levels of commitment to these games, with some being 'super-users', devoting hour upon hour of their time to immerse themselves in the virtual world. In Kolo and Baur's (2004) study of *Ultima Online*, the average duration of a gaming session was four hours, with the typical player being online for an average of 5.7 sessions per week (2004: 9). However, other players are more casual in their use. For many, MMORPGs are 'just a game', or 'just another form of communication', while for some they offer the possibility of the exploration of alternative identities, connectivity with others and membership of a 'community' (however that may be conceived). Kolo and Baur (2004) found that the players they interviewed saw 'the social experience of gaming' as one of the most important aspects of their participation in *Ultima Online*. Two thirds of those surveyed mentioned the potential to interact with thousands of fellow players and participating in a 'virtual society' as one of their key motivations for gaming (Kolo and Baur, 2004: 12).

However, there are limitations to conceptualizing the social relations surrounding online digital gaming in terms of *community*. Critics of the virtual community idea point out that it is actually underpinned by problematic assumptions about what community is; it suggests that community is simply a matter of *communication*. Jones (1995) and Sardar (2000) argue that the term community is misused in this way – online virtual worlds do not constitute community just because their participants believe this to be the case. Where are the social bonds or ties, the webs of mutual obligation, the embeddedness within wider social frameworks? For example, Ziauddin Sardar argues that:

> Belonging and posting to a Usenet group, or logging on to a bulletin board community, conforms no more an identity than belonging to a stamp collecting club or a Morris dancing society. (2000: 743)

For the critics of 'virtual community', community has been stripped of its ethical dimensions. The very fact that they are formed through bonds of transient mutual interest rather than mutual obligation or proximity, makes them something other than communities. Rather, to think of online gaming as forming communities is to confuse *community* with the *simulation of community*. First, this means that 'authentic' communities are replaced with something that has the appearance, but not the substance, of 'real' community. Second, many of these accounts of community take online interactions to be undifferentiated. In reality, there are many different reasons why individuals participate in gaming, whether offline or online. Similarly, there are all kinds of interactions taking place – some hostile; some friendly – but they are not all necessary *communal* in nature.

Gaming identities ●

What do we mean by identity? ●

Having discussed the affinities between forms of digital gaming and theories of community in contemporary culture, we now turn to the ways in which the *identities* of gamers might be approached. In the same way as for community, we need to take a step backwards here and think about what we mean by identity in the first place. In simple terms, our identities are shaped by social structures and norms (such as social class, gender and ethnicity) but we also participate in constructing our own identities through, for example, the way we consume material and symbolic goods and services such as cars, holidays and clothes. On the one hand, then, identity is seen as primarily *ascribed* or given in terms of the socio-economic constraints, and national, ethnic and gendered aspects of identity which shape the ways in which we and others 'know who we are'. On the other hand, individuals are able to be cognitively *reflexive* about their 'given' identity. That is, they are able to participate in developing their outward identity and their sense of self (see Crawford and Rutter, Chapter 8). In terms of digital gaming, what we are interested in is how gaming involves the confirmation, negotiation and/or re-construction of identities. There are three key approaches to the question of identity which can help us here: social identity; reflexive self-identity; and virtual identity.

Social identities

In thinking about who we are, and who other people think we are, the idea of our identity as *socially defined* is central in understanding that our identities are negotiable and contested. The nature of the social world is open to change and interpretation and as such our identities are always subject to disagreement and possible re-shaping. Jenkins maintains that, 'Social identity is our understanding of who we are and who other people are, and, reciprocally, other people's understanding of themselves and of others' (1996: 8).

One of the ways in which digital gaming has been understood in terms of social identity is in the context of a person's everyday life. Here ethnography, the study of people's everyday routines, often in naturalistic settings such as the home, is useful in that it demonstrates the ways in which gaming, digital or otherwise, plays an important role in social life. Digital gaming forms part of people's joint leisure activities in pre-existing social networks, with the majority of computer games being played with family or friends (Bryce and Rutter, 2003; Griffiths and Hunt, 1995). While some argue that digital gaming causes adolescents to become withdrawn and uncommunicative (Grossman, 1995; Povenzo, 1991), research by Flynn (2003) highlights that social competition, drinking, conversation and wagers are a significant part of 'ordinary' domestic gameplay sessions.

Flynn (2003) notes how writers such as Baudrillard (1993) and Mitchell (1998) conceptualize home-based wired technologies and/or gaming consoles within a cyber utopian framework, viewing them as portals to a fantastical world of speed, danger and freedom. In contrast, we can also think of digital gaming technologies as relatively 'ordinary' technologies, which inhabit domestic spaces such as the living room. Flynn (2003) argues that research has to look at the ways in which digital gaming technologies are actually used in people's homes (or in public spaces) if we are to understand their relation to people's social identities. Exploring how the practices of digital gaming emerge in the home allows us to see the process of construction of social identity: the identities of gamers are positioned in relation to existing class, gender, ethnic and national interests, and constraints. In her study of domestic technologies, Flynn (2003) found that young people are subject to surveillance from parents (particularly mothers) within the domestic spaces in which digital gaming now increasingly takes place. Horrell and Schott (2000) show that although there are now a significant number of female game players, there is little evidence of female-based social networks in relation to gaming. Females tend to be excluded from social aspects of gaming culture. Where gamers gather together to demonstrate their membership of a 'gaming community', membership of which forms part of an individual's identity, females are noticeably absent (Horrell and Schott, 2000). To be a female gamer then may be a substantively different experience to being a male gamer given the differences in community links and identity-forming practices between the genders in relation to digital gaming (see also Bryce and Rutter, Chapter 11).

Reflexive self-identity

It has been argued that the previous account of identity is too static in the context of late modern culture, particularly as new forms of 'global' and non-territorial identity are said to be emerging (Poster, 1995; Urry, 2000). For some commentators, it is the notion of self-identity that is dominant in late modern culture, having become a 'reflexive project' (Giddens, 1991). Self-identity is not a set of traits or observable characteristics, but rather a person's own reflexive understanding of their biography. In this way, identity is an endeavour that we continuously work at and reflexively reconstruct. What this means for us is that we should be looking at how digital gamers self-consciously develop different self-identities through the consumption and playing of digital games. In other words, digital gamers do not simply follow the 'rules' or conventions of gaming; they also appropriate games for their own ends. The ways in which digital games are 'consumed' is an important one here, particularly as self-identity is thought to be increasingly tied to patterns of consumption (Bauman, 1990; Featherstone, 1995; Lury, 1997).

One example of digital gaming and the role of consumption in identity formation is the phenomenon of *Snake*, a simple game embedded in Nokia mobile phones that enjoyed immense popularity for a time, particularly among young people. The public visibility of mobile phones lends itself well to the notion that digital gaming is a profoundly social and cultural activity, and that consumption (and use) of new technologies is intimately linked to identity formation. Young people keenly swapped *Snake* scores with one another, sometimes with friends who were not co-present at the time. Rather than being a solitary activity, using the mobile phone to text and play games constituted a profoundly social interaction (Taylor and Harper, 2003). Consuming the mobile becomes part of an individual's identity (Fortunati, 2001).

From this perspective, digital gaming is indicative of how identity formation is increasingly centred upon *self*-identity, and that this has become a 'reflexive project' through consumption activity. A focus on the ways in which digital gaming is made possible through the consumption of other artefacts (such as mobile phones), which carry their own meanings for identity formation, is important in addressing the acquisition and use of consoles, phones, computers and other technologies as well as the playing of games.

● Virtual identity and disembodiment

When the former conceptions of gaming identity involve examining the wider contexts of gaming – how gaming is embedded within late modern consumer culture – the notion of *virtual identity* (like virtual community) reflects how digital technologies enable people to *transcend* those contexts. Where the notion of social identity would position gamers as 'players' embedded within sets of social and cultural constraints, the idea of virtual identity suggests that we should think of gamers as 'authors' as much as they are 'players'. In other words, they do not simply *enact* their given identity through gaming, but are able to *re-write* their identity through it. This kind of identity has been conceived in a number of different ways, from 'post-social' identities (Hayles, 1999) to 'multiple selves' (Stone, 1991; Turkle, 1997) to 'cyborgs' (Haraway, 1998). All these conceptions agree that 'identity' is not a given phenomenon – that the individual is not a pre-given entity – but that individuals (and their identities) are always in process, being formed through ongoing interaction with others and with material artefacts. Online gaming can be seen as one activity whereby inter-action with others through digital technology offers the opportunity to rewrite one's own identity *outside* of traditional constraints. Wright et al. note that games such as *Counter-Strike* (a first-person shooter) offer players 'a context in which to exercise safe ritual license with behaviours that would not be tolerated in the 'real' world or everyday life' (2002: 11). Wright et al. further argue that *Counter-Strike* resembles a youth subculture that can 'promote a temporary limbo of statusless-ness, flow and movement, as well as a refashioning of time and commu-nity' (2002: 11). It is in this sense then that virtual gaming environments such as *Counter-Strike* may allow users to 'transcend' the 'real-world' through becoming embedded in a virtual world, which has its own rules and norms nonetheless, creating a virtual (gaming and gamer) identity.

For Sherry Turkle (1997), players (in MUDs) are 'authors' as well as 'players'. MUDs offer the opportunity for players not only to create the text (or graphics) of the game but also to construct '... new selves through social interaction' (Turkle, 1997: 12). It is argued that when gaming in cyberspace, identities become so fluid that the traditional boundary between the real and the artificial breaks down as gamers are able to perform a range of different identities. What this means is that digital gamers may experiment with who they are, and who others think they are, by giving themselves alternative 'characteristics' in online text or 'avatars'.

In *Life on the Screen*, Turkle (1997) explores the nature of this kind of identity 'performance' in cyberspace. She suggests that through our interactions with networked machines we are encouraged to perform a *multiplicity* of selves, and that our performance in these environ-ments is enhanced when we recognize the possibility of non-linear identities and a 'distributed presence' (1997: 12–13). This means that traditional identities (such as those characterized by class, gender, ethnic and sexual orientation dimensions) may be rewritten through the presentation of a range of 'selves' in the game. We can think of online digital gaming as one such 'virtual system', allowing gamers to participate in the construction of the gaming environment itself (Wright et al., 2002), and their own 'virtual identities'. Of course, contained within these statements is the implicit notion that the body (and the forms of identity associated within bodies) are somehow 'left behind' when one enters the virtual world.

What might these 'multiplicity of selves' entail in terms of digital gaming? In virtual gaming worlds a 'real life' female gamer may choose to perform a male character, or vice versa, although this would seem to depend on game genre (Kolo and Baur, 2004; McKenna and Lee, 1996). Players may also take up the 'identity' of an animal, or an inanimate object. This exemplifies the so-called mutability of (post-) modern identities, in that one can pick and choose who, or what, one wants to be. Relating the digital gaming experience, particularly online gaming, to postmodern theories about identity and performativity, Turkle (1997) maintains that without the restraints of the body, gender and other identity 'markers', such as ethnicity, become *fluid*.

The story goes that use of digital (networked) technologies, including digital gaming, provides a less hierarchical and less formal freedom of expression than is possible in 'real life'. This in turn leads to identity becoming more ephemeral, with people choosing how they are represented (Chandler, 1998) and thus choosing who they are. Rutter and Smith (1999), for example, looked at the ways in which people presented themselves within an internet service provider (ISP) specific newsgroup. They maintain that people employed a number of different techniques to manage computer-mediated communication and 'present a commonly accepted self to those co-present in the newsgroup and to blur distinctions between on- and off-line selves' (1999: 11). However, in this online community enacted identities were taken as 'real, due to the level of trust participants had with one another. However, it is difficult to completely accept the idea that online identities are entirely separate from offline identities. Logging on to the Internet and/or playing a digital game does not immobilize a person's body and suspend their pre-existing consciousness. We do not 'have' bodies, but live life *through* our bodies. As Stone notes:

> It is important to remember that virtual community originates in, and must return to, the physical. No reconfigured virtual body, no matter how beautiful, will slow the death of a cyberpunk with AIDS. Even in the age of the technosocial subject, life is lived through bodies. (1991: 19)

Indeed, we can question whether, or to what extent, these virtual identities are novel; that is, increasingly 'free' from socio-cultural relations. One criticism of the notion of multiple identities is that it ignores the ways in which 'real life' identities are reproduced online and within the gaming experience. Gender for example can be reproduced mimetically, meaning through repetition, in cyberspace. This means that the performance of masculinity or femininity in cyberspace *reproduces* gender roles rather than transcends them.

In terms of digital gaming it is hard to argue that the player's identity is wholly malleable and fluid. The player cannot take on an identity *completely* of their own choice. The medium through which the player is playing the game necessarily restrains what the player can do while in the virtual environment. Just as it is important to remember that we cannot transcend our physical bodies in cyberspace, digital gamers cannot wholly transcend the rules of a game's programming, since 'the fact remains that the player still cannot do something that the game is not prepared to allow' (Poole, 2000: 117), although hackers may attempt to change the rules and cheats give the impression that the player is overcoming the deterministic nature of the digital game.

Conclusion: digital gaming as communication ●

In this chapter we have looked at the possibility that digital gaming has implications for our understandings of *community* in both online and offline settings. We have also explored the ways in which we can understand digital gaming practices through traditional and possibly 'novel' notions of community. Using three quite different notions of community, namely communities of presence, imagined communities and virtual communities, we have used examples such as *lanning* to suggest that communities may not necessarily have to be based on *presence* but maybe *imagined*, or even, in the digital gaming context, *virtual*. The exact nature of such forms of community depends on the gamers who participate, the nature of the games, the agreed but sometimes disputed 'rules' of play and player interaction, and more generally the socio-cultural context.

In this chapter we have also explored the idea that digital gaming has consequences for our notions of identity in contemporary times. Community and identity can be seen as related given that our identities are profoundly shaped by our socio-cultural environment and our social practices (such as consumption). Digital gaming, for example, plays a central role in some players' lives, and it is in this sense that we can think of identities as being socially defined and produced within the contexts of our everyday lives and 'ordinary' mundane practices.

Finally, we have discussed the possibility that digital gaming can enable players to 'transcend' their *socially ascribed identities* (in terms of gender, ethnicity, sexual orientation and so on), leaving their bodies behind as they perform a multiplicity of selves in cyberspace environments. We highlighted problems with this utopian vision of participation in digital gaming worlds through fluid *virtual identities*. The main difficulty is that we cannot ever transcend our bodies, as with Stone's (1991) example of a cyberpunk with AIDS. All experiences are mediated through our bodies. In addition, playing digital games involves working with, but never wholly transcending, the rules of the game's programming and the norms of particular gaming 'communities'.

Digital gaming may be seen as both embedded within existing sociocultural frameworks (as 'cultural artefacts'), and as enabling novel articulations of community and identity to emerge (as forms of 'culture'). Digital gaming represents a distinct cultural form which at once problematizes current understandings of community and identity, and allows us to explore emerging patterns of community and identity formation.

Relevant web sites ● ● ●

Cyberathlete Professional League www.thecpl.com/league
Daedalus Project www.nickyee.com/daedalus
Howard Rheingold www.rheingold.com
Smart Mobs www.smartmobs.com
Virtual Worlds Review www.virtualworldsreview.com

● References

Anderson, B. (1991) *Imagined Communities: Reflections on the Origin and Spread of Nationalism.* London: Verso.

Baudrillard, J. (1993) 'Hyperreal America', *Economy and Society*, 22 (2): 243–52.

Bauman, Z. (1990) *Thinking Sociologically.* Oxford: Basil Blackwell.

Bryce, J. and Rutter, J. (2003) 'Gender dynamics and the social and spatial organisation of computer gaming', *Leisure Studies*, 22 (1): 1–15.

Chandler, D. (1998) 'Personal homepages and the construction of identities on the web', paper presented at Aberystwyth Post-International Group Conference on

Linking Theory and Practice: Issues In the Politics of Identity, 9–11 September 1998, University of Wales, Aberystwyth.

Cohen, A. (1985) *The Symbolic Construction of Identity.* London: Tavistock.

Crow, G. and Allan, G. (1994) *Community Life: An Introduction to Local Social Relations.* Hemel Hempstead: Harvester Wheatsheaf.

Delanty, G. (2003) *Community.* London: Routledge.

Dibbell, J. (2003) 'Owned?: Intellectual property in the age of dupers, gold farmers, eBayers, and other enemies of the virtual state', paper presented at The State of Play: Law, Games, and Virtual Worlds, Institute for Information Law and Policy at New York Law School and Information Society Project at Yale Law School, 13–15 November 2003, retrieved from: http://www.nyls.edu/docs/dibbell.pdf. Accessed 13 July 2004.

Featherstone, M. (1995) *Undoing Culture: Globalization, Postmodernism and Identity.* London: Sage.

Flynn, B. (2003) 'Geography of the digital hearth', *Information, Communication & Society*, 6 (4): 551–76.

Fortunati, L. (2001) 'The mobile phone: an identity on the move', *Personal and Ubiquitous Computing*, 5 (2): 85–98.

Giddens (1991) *Modernity and Self-Identity: Self and Society in the Late Modern Age.* Cambridge: Polity.

Griffiths, M. and Hunt, N. (1995) 'Computer game playing in adolescence – prevalence and demographic indicators, *Journal of Community and Applied Social Psychology*, 5 (3): 189–93.

Grossman, D. (1995) *On Killing: The Psychological Cost of Learning to Kill in War and Society.* Boston, MA: Little, Brown.

Haraway, D. (1998) *Modest_Witness@Second_Millenium.FemaleMan©_Meets_OncoMouse®.* New York: Routledge.

Haraway, D. (1992) 'The promises of monsters: A regenerative politics for inappropriated others', in L., Grossberg, C. Nelson, and P.A. Treichler, (eds), *Cultural Studies.* New York: Routledge. pp. 295–337.

Hayles, N. Katherine (1999) *How We Became Post-Human.* Chicago, IL: University of Chicago Press.

Horrell, K. and Schott, G. (2000) 'Girl gamers and their relationship with the gaming culture', *Convergence*, 6 (4): 36–53.

Jenkins, R. (1996) *Social Identity.* London: Routledge.

Jones, S.G. (1997) *Virtual Culture: Identity and Communication in Cyberspace.* London: Sage.

Jones, S.G. (ed.) (1995) *Cybersociety: Computer-mediated Communication and Community.* London: Sage.

Kolo, C. and Baur, T. (2004) 'Living a virtual life: social dynamics of online gaming', *Game Studies,* 4 (1), retrieved 21 March 2005 from: http://www.gamestudies.org/0401/kolo/

Lash, S. (1994) 'Reflexivity and its doubles: structures, aesthetics, community', in U. Beck, A. Giddens and S. Lash (eds), *Reflexive Modernization: Politics, Tradition and Aesthetics in the Modern Social Order.* Cambridge: Polity Press. pp. 110–73.

Lury, C. (1997) *Consumer Culture.* Cambridge: Polity.

Maffesoli, M. (1996) *The Time of the Tribes: The Decline of Individualism in Mass Society*. London: Sage.

McKenna, K. and Lee, S. (1996) A love affair with MUDs: flow and social interaction in multi-user dungeons retrieved 16 September 2004 from: http://www.unikoeln.de/~am040/muds/ipages/mud.htm

Mitchell, W.J. (1998) *City of Bits: Space, Place and the Infobahn*. Cambridge, MA: MIT Press.

Nancy, J.-L. (1991) *The Inoperative Community*. Minneapolis, MN: University of Minnesota Press.

Poole, S. (2000) *Trigger Happy: The Inner Life of Video Games*. London: Fourth Estate.

Poster, M. (1995) *The Second Media Age*. Cambridge: Polity Press.

Povenzo, E.F. (1991) *Video Kids: Making Sense of Nintendo*. Cambridge, MA: Harvard University Press.

Rheingold, H. (1994) *The Virtual Community*. London: Secker and Warburg.

Rutter, J. and Smith, G.W.H. (1999) 'Presenting the offline self in an everyday, online environment', paper presented at Identities in Action, University of Wales, 10–12 December 1999, Retrieved 15 March 2005 from: http://les1.man.ac.uk/cric/Jason_Rutter/papers/Self.pdf

Sardar, Z. (2000) 'alt.civilizations.faq: Cyberspace as the darker side of the west', in Bell, D. and Kennedy, B. (eds) The Cybercultures Reader. London. Routledge, pp. 732–752.

Shields, R. *The Virtual*. London: Routledge.

Simmel, G. (1950) 'The metropolis and mental life', in K. Wolff (ed.), *The Sociology of Georg Simmel*. New York: The Free Press. pp. 409–24.

Squire, K.D. and Steinkuehler, C.A. (in press) 'The genesis of "CyberCulture": The case of Star Wars galaxies', in *Cyberlines: Languages and Cultures of the Internet*, 2nd edn. Albert Park: James Nicholas Publishers, retrieved from: website. education.wisc.edu/kdsquire/manuscripts/squire-steinkuehler-final.rtf

Stone, A.R. (1991) 'Will the real body please stand up? Boundary stories about virtual cultures', in M. Benedikt (ed.), *Cyberspace: First Steps*. Cambridge: MIT Press. pp. 81–118.

Stone, A.R. (1995) *The War of Desire and Technology at the Close of the Mechanical Age*. Cambridge, MA: MIT Press.

Taylor, A. and Harper, R. (2003) 'The gift of the gab: a design oriented sociology of young people's use of mobiles', *Journal of Computer Supported Cooperative Work* (*CSCW*), 12 (3): 267–96.

Turkle, S. (1997) *Life on the Screen: Identity in the Age of the Internet*. London: Phoenix.

Urry, J. (2000) *Sociology Beyond Societies*. London: Routledge.

Wright, T., Boria, E. and Bridenbach, P. (2002) 'Creative player actions in FPS online video games', *Games Studies*, 2 (2), retrieved 21 March 2005 from: www.gamestudies.org/0202/wright/

Yates, S.J. and Littleton, K. (1999) 'Understanding computer game cultures: a situated approach', *Information, Communication and Society*, 2: 566–83.

Part three

Key debates

11 Digital games and gender ● ● ●

Jo Bryce, Jason Rutter and Cath Sullivan

This chapter examines the gender dynamics of computer gaming, its identification as a masculine activity and the ways in which female gaming is routinely marginalized through a range of practices. It examines how theoretical perspectives from gender studies, sociology and leisure theory can contribute to understanding the conceptualization and experience of gaming as a masculine activity. This is achieved through an examination of the gendering of access to digital gaming, the spaces in which games are played and game content in determining female access and participation. Finally, the chapter questions the extent to which the gender dynamics of gaming are changing, and the possibilities of female participation for resisting traditional societal notions of femininity and the gender appropriateness of different leisure activities.

After reading this chapter the reader should understand the following:

- That there is a contradiction between societal conceptions of gaming as a masculine leisure activity and the number of females who engage in this activity on a regular basis.
- That the gender dynamics of computer gaming are consistent with wider societal conceptualizations and representations of masculinity and femininity.
- That gender dynamics should be understood in the context of the spaces in which game content is experienced and given meaning.
- That female participation in gaming has both the possibility to reinforce and allow resistance towards traditional conceptualizations of masculinity and femininity, and their respective technological competencies.

● Approaches to sex and gender

Before examining the gender dynamics of computer gaming in greater detail, it is necessary to outline theoretical perspectives on the development and maintenance of gendered identities, gender stereotypes and the distinction between the concepts of sex and gender.

Traditional approaches to sex and gender in the first half of the 20th century tended to be marked by 'biological essentialism' and 'determinism'. That is, the view that men and women have different biologically determined natures and, as a consequence of these differences, it is inevitable and appropriate for them to have different attributes, skills and areas of interest, as well as to take different roles within society (Korabik, 1999). For many years, this biological essentialism has formed one half of a crucial debate within studies of sex and gender – the 'nature–nurture' debate. Although research has demonstrated unequivocally that biological essentialism is unable to represent and explain the patterns, diversity and range of male and female behaviour (Korabik, 1999; Maccoby, 1998), it continues to be a strong component of many everyday beliefs about the relationship between sex and gender (Cockburn, 1991).

BREAKOUT BOX 11.1 ● ● ●

What do we mean by 'sex' and 'gender'?

*The differences between the terms 'sex' and 'gender' are complex and there is a large body of theoretical and empirical research examining such differences and their utility (see Brannon [2002] for an introduction to the debates surrounding this issue). Despite these definitional difficulties a basic distinction between the two terms is that **sex** refers to the biological and physiological characteristics that define men and women. For example:*

- *Women can menstruate while men cannot.*
- *Men have testicles while women do not.*
- *Women have developed breasts that are usually capable of lactating, while men do not.*

***Gender** refers to the socially constructed roles, behaviours, activities and attributes that a given society considers appropriate for men and women.*

(Continued)

(Continued)

This distinction between the biological (sex) and social (gender) indicate that sex characteristics will not vary substantially between different human societies, while gender roles, stereotypes and concepts of masculinity and femininity may vary greatly. For example, in some cultures it is considered inappropriate for females to work outside the home, that females are responsible for child-rearing, and that males and females should dress and behave in specific and different ways.

Adapted from: World Health Organization, see_www.who.int/gender/whatisgender/en/

Approaches to sex and gender which form parts of the 'nurture' side of the debate do, at times, still have something in common with those of the 'nature' side. That is, approaches that rejected biological essentialism (which became increasingly common in the latter half of the 20th century) did not necessarily reject a focus on biological differences between men and women. These approaches, irrespective of whether they saw sex-typed male and female behaviour and roles as resulting primarily from social or biological factors, still tended towards 'gender polarization'. That is, they still saw differences between men and women as an organizing principle for identity and social relations and assumed that gender differences were socially constructed around biological ones. These models also assume that the various components of gender are congruent in that women have feminine personality traits, values, attitudes and behaviours while men have masculine ones (Ashmore, 1993). The problem with such an approach is that although it adds social factors to biological ones it still reproduces a male–female opposition which allows no room for change, negotiation or resistance.

The current wave of research and scholarship on sex and gender has led to increased criticism and rejection of many aspects of traditional approaches, and a new perspective on sex and gender has emerged.[1] In this framework, rather than focusing almost exclusively on childhood socialization as an explanatory mechanism for the operation and effects of gender, gender has been understood as a contested phenomenon that is negotiated and constructed on a daily basis by both men and women. The sociologist Myra Marx Ferree has argued, 'gender is continuously being constructed and used to further a variety of individual and group goals' (1990: 124). These constructive processes have been referred to as 'doing gender' (West and Zimmerman, 1991) or 'gender performance' (Butler, 1990) as roles, relationships, institutions, objects and artefacts – in addition to people – come to have gendered meanings or identities and are in a constant state of flux and creation of meaning. As such Judith Butler has argued that 'there is no gender behind the expressions of gender; that identity is performatively constituted by the very "expression" that are said to be its results' (1990: 25).

These theoretical perspectives can contribute to a deeper understanding of the gender dynamics of computer gaming in the following areas:

- Gender differences in gaming preferences and behaviours.
- The gendering of gaming technologies and virtual gaming spaces, and their role in the creation and manipulation of gendered identities.
- The gendered representations of game characters and their implications for the development of gendered identities.

In the subsequent sections of this chapter, these issues are examined in relation to the gendered nature of game content and the spaces in which that content is experienced and given meaning.

● Doing gaming, doing gender

A number of studies have argued that a significant number of school aged females play digital games on a regular basis. For example, Funk (1993) found that 75 per cent of females, contrasting with 90 per cent of males, played computer games in the home. Colwell and Payne (2000) showed that 88 per cent of the 12–14-year-old females surveyed played computer games on a regular basis. Recent commercial research has suggested the significant involvement of females in digital gaming. For example, the Entertainment Software Association (ESA) suggests that approximately 39 per cent of US computer gamers are female and that females make up 40 per cent of online gamers (Entertainment Software Association, 2004). In several European countries females account for approximately a quarter of all players whereas in Korea the figure is closer to 70 per cent (Krotoski, 2004).

Recent academic research in the UK suggested that female undergraduate students were half as likely as their male colleagues to have played any digital games in the previous three months, and approximately a third as likely to play more than once a week (Crawford and

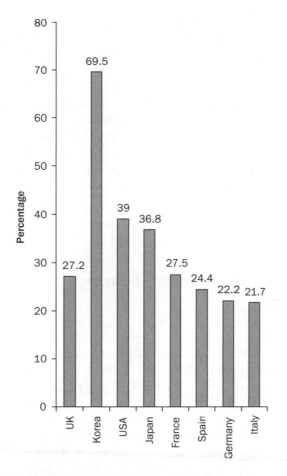

FIGURE 11.1 *Active female gamers by country (Krotoski, 2004)*

Gosling, 2005). They also point to the important issue of a digital gaming 'career' where involvement changes over time by suggesting that the level and frequency of female gaming decreases as they leave the childhood home and take on additional roles and responsibilities.

Such research suggests that a significant number of females play computer games on a regular basis, however it is useful to consider how the everyday spaces and practices of doing gender help us understand what the above figures mean. To do so we must supplement demographic snapshots of digital gaming participation with an examination of the ways in which gender dynamics, from access to technology to the management of spaces within the home, affects how digital games are played, experienced and given meaning.

Looking at the ways in which general societal gender dynamics interact with digital gaming allows us to understand how many females do or do not play games, and also to ask questions about whether there are differences in gaming experiences, the motivations and constraints which influence gaming participation, and the social, content-based and technological issues relevant to gendering of gaming as a leisure activity. It also enables us to understand how the gender dynamics of different spaces create barriers to female participation, the reproduction or resistance to societal notions of gender appropriate interests, and how this changes with age and the adoption of other feminine roles throughout the life cycle.

● Gendering technology and domestic access to digital games

The mundane, local and everyday contexts in which gaming occurs are often neglected. Recognition of these everyday contexts allows a movement away from the relatively rare but spectacular examples of gender work in digital gaming (such as the creation of ultra-feminine or new gendered avatars, or mob attacks against female dwarfs in *Lineage*) towards an examination of more representative and everyday gendered experiences, and ways in which females are marginalized or excluded as part of the ordinary practices of digital gaming.

Paying attention to these mundane, routine and taken for granted modes of digital gaming allows us to do what Garfinkel described as 'making commonplace scenes visible' (Garfinkel, 1967: 36). This enables us to recognize that many of the 'properties of social life which seem objective, factual and transsituational, are actually managed accomplishments or achievements of local processes,' (West and Fenstermaker, 1993: 152). In short, we can understand that social relationships, ordinary practices, access to technology and gendering of space have a profound effect on digital gaming and female involvement at a point which proceeds engagement with the game itself.

Developing the notion that gender is constructed through everyday actions, Eileen Green has argued that to understand technology we need to address 'the interaction between technology, personal consumption and the construction of identity. We need to know more about the way in which "ordinary people" appropriate "ordinary technologies" ', (2001: 174).

In such a vein, Livingstone and Bovill (2001) have highlighted increasing mediation of children's leisure by technology as greater numbers of children have televisions, games consoles and computers in their bedrooms. However, within the home, access to technologies and leisure is not gender neutral. Having gaming equipment in the home has not meant that access to it has been equal for both male and female children, or that the growing number of homes with games consoles and broadband Internet access has meant that growth in online gaming has been equal across the sexes. Indeed, research on female access to leisure-related technologies suggests that internet use and its associated cultures are often experienced as highly masculine and potentially hostile to females (Schumacher and Morahan, 2001; Sullivan and Bryce, 2001).

To explore this gendered asymmetry in relation to digital games it is useful to examine the way in which gaming is positioned within ordinary domestic contexts, rather than primarily the spectacular context of online interactions.

Space as leisure constraint ●

The fact that digital games are situated and experienced within specific and local spaces is often overlooked in writing on gaming. Much of the research on online gaming is utopian and spectacular in its conceptualization of its constituent communities. Commentators have enthusiastically pointed towards 'grrl gamers' and female *Quake* or *Counter-Strike* clans in order to demonstrate that females can be interested in competition and masculine game themes of war and aggression. While this may appear to be contrary to expectations of feminine behaviour and interests, it is clear that such enthusiasts, while representing a powerful vanguard, do not represent the experiences of the majority of female gamers.

Michel Foucault has described our age as 'above all the epoch of space'. He argues, 'we are in the epoch of simultaneity: we are in the epoch of juxtaposition, the epoch of the near and far, of the side-by-side, of the dispersed' (1986: 22). For Foucault, as inhabitants in the modern world, we divide up and name the spaces we use. We appropriate them, move between them and define the relationships between them. As such we have domestic space, private space, office space, leisure space, family space, religious space and so forth.

Gender theory has examined the way in which spaces are involved in the construction of gendered identities and the relationship between spaces and social roles (Ahrentzen, 1992; Gunnarsson, 1997; Sullivan and Bryce, 2001). Given the variety of diverse locations in which gaming occurs, an examination of the gendering of gaming spaces and how these influence female access and participation can further contribute to understanding the gender dynamics of gaming. There is a body of research which has examined the changing ways in which female leisure is often focused around the home rather than public spaces in contrast to the leisure of males.

Private, domestic spaces have been traditionally conceptualized as the main site of female leisure through their relationship with domestic and family labour and the notion of 'bedroom culture'. This concept was originally used in the UK during the 1970s to describe the use of domestic spaces for leisure by young females and highlight the restrictions on their full access to many social and leisure spaces. As such, their leisure was largely home-based and profoundly linked to the development of friendships and identity (Frith, 1978; McRobbie, 1991; McRobbie and Garber, 1976). Drawing on American research from a similar period, Henry Jenkins (1998) highlights how significantly more of girls' play has often been centred in or near the home when compared to boys:

> Children's access to spaces are structured around gender differences. Observing the use of space within 1970s suburban America, Hart (1979) found that boys enjoyed far greater mobility and range than girls of the same age and class background. In the course of an afternoon's play, a typical 10–12 year old boy might travel a distance of 2,452 yards, while the average 10–12 year old girl might only travel 959 yards. For the most part, girls expanded their geographic range only to take on responsibilities and perform chores for the family, while parents often turned a blind eye to a boy's movements into prohibited spaces. (1998: 267)

This is an example of what has been referred to in theoretical and empirical work as 'leisure constraints'. This concept has been used to examine structural and psychological factors which prevent individuals from participating in desired leisure activities (Jackson and Henderson, 1995).

Time as leisure constraint ●

We can see that the manner in which leisure space is available to children is gendered but it is also possible to explore more broadly the way in which time available for leisure tends also to be demarcated along gender lines. There is a well established body of data that suggest that availability of time is a leisure constraint for women with women literally having less time for leisure.

For example, in 1974 Joann Vanek argued that the time American females spent doing housework had not changed in the previous 50 years despite the fact that much less food was prepared at home, the average family size had dropped, more females were in paid employment outside the home and that electrification and plumbing in homes had allowed adoption of a range of 'labour saving' devices. Although these findings have been much debated, recent data from Australia (Bittman et al., 2003) indicates that adoption of technologies such as microwaves, dishwashers, tumble driers and freezers has not reduced the amount of female domestic labour (although they do for males), and in some cases it actually increased time devoted to domestic work. The implication is that as domestic labour has been increasingly mechanized the amount of labour expected has increased as has the socially accepted level at which these tasks are performed. As such, tasks which have been traditionally associated with female unpaid labour such as laundry, cleaning carpets or bathing children have tended towards becoming daily activities rather than less regular ones.

The UK Time Use Survey 2000 indicates that females spend over an hour and a half per day more than males on housework (http://www.statistics.gov.uk/TimeUse/). Similarly, in the USA, employed females spent about an hour per day more than males doing household activities and caring for household members (http://www.bls.gov/tus/).

Of course, where work and leisure are considered separated activities, increased labour time means less time for leisure and other activities. As such, it is not surprising to see that just as females spend more time on domestic labour, they tend to have less time to enjoy leisure activities in the home. In the UK, males spend more time watching television and engaged in sport than females, and in Japan, husbands spend approximately 8 per cent more time a week watching television and reading newspapers or magazines than their wives www.stat.go.jp/english/data/shakai/). This gender difference is also seen in the US Department of Labor's 2003 figures which show that males spend, on average, 5.4 hours a day doing leisure activities compared with 4.8 hours for females. From these figures it is apparent that the level of time available to females to engage in leisure, including digital games, is notably less than that for males in a wide range of societies. As there is no clear biological explanation for this difference we must instead look at the social constraints that limit female access to leisure and how this influences experiences of digital gaming as a routine activity.

● Gender roles as leisure constraint

Recent ethnographic and qualitative research demonstrates evidence of the continuing control of domestic gaming by males and the marginal-ization of female gaming within the home. Schott and Horrell's (2000) study of digital gaming within families demonstrated that males often assume the role of 'expert' and undermine female skills and knowledge within domestic gaming spaces. This is consistent with Crawford and Gosling's (2005) suggestion that, even in their own home, potential girl gamers are not given the same rights to access game technologies as their male counterparts. They argue:

> Digital gaming still appears primarily a male domain into which women frequently have to be granted access by men. For instance, Green (2001) suggests that within many households leisure technolo-gies (such as computer and games consoles) continue to be primarily located within 'male' spaces (such as male sibling's bedrooms, and studies). … Even when games machines are located in shared 'family' spaces, conflict often arises as these continue to be seen as symbolically belonging to male household members. … Hence, digital gaming con-tinues to be viewed by many (both men and women) as culturally not 'belonging' to women, but rather something they are (sometimes) allowed access to in their family home. (2005: 46)

This is consistent with the increasing encroachment of masculine leisure activities into, what we saw above as, traditionally feminine and domestic leisure spaces. This is particularly the case with those activities which occur in the living room and use the family television, technology which has been claimed to fall under the control of the male members of the household (Gray, 1992; Morley, 1986). This suggests that despite the increased presence of gaming technologies within domestic spaces, traditional gendered patterns of access and control which have little direct relationship with digital gaming are reproduced and act to constrain female participation.

Gendering gaming spaces outside the home ●

Contemporary gaming spaces include not only the home but those which are public (as in arcades, public houses and service stations) and virtual (such as online game servers, Xbox Live, or massively multi-player online games). Public leisure spaces have traditionally been claimed to be highly gendered as masculine, placing constraints on female access to them. For example, Hey (1984) has looked at the way in which traditional British pub culture has excluded women from full participation and created distinct and limited roles for women's involvement – such as that of barmaid.

Such distinctions are also practiced within digital gaming environments. For example, in digital gaming tournaments and other competitions, as well as at many LAN parties (see Hand and Moore, Chapter 10), participants are still predominantly male, and those females that do participate too often are fitted into acceptable non-gamer roles such as mothers and girlfriends offering support and encouragement, rather than being active participants (Bryce and Rutter, 2003). Where women do compete in such spaces their participation is still framed in a number of ways not applied to male gamers. First, they are presented as 'exotic', unusual or the exception to the rule that digital gaming is properly performed as a male activity. Second, they are sexualized in a manner in which male gamers are not. Media coverage of female gamers tends to feature pictures of female gamers who conform to standard western notions of attractiveness, wearing makeup and facing directly to the camera, while men tend to be presented engaging with technology or visually absent, with images drawn from the games themselves replacing them. It is useful to compare gendered representations of gamers in online coverage of professional gamers by the BBC in the UK in their articles, 'Girl gamers strike at the boys' (Hermida, 2004) and of male gamers 'UK gamers aim to take Korea' (BBC, 2004). In this second article, references to gender are notably absent from the reporting suggesting that the male gamer is considered to be the 'natural' type of competitive gamer.

● Game content

Of course, just as media coverage of gaming shows differences in the way the different sexes are represented, so too there is apparent encoding of gender in digital games themselves. Issues of gendered representation within game content are also an important aspect of the relationship between digital gaming and gender. This chapter so far has focused on the way in which female gamers are excluded from, and constrained in, their engagement with digital games. These are factors which have an effect prior to engagement with game content and are not specific to individual games or gaming platforms. However, it is clear that the content, themes and style of digital games, in general, are strongly gendered as masculine.

It is widely claimed that there are a relatively low number of female characters in computer games, and that representations of females within computer games are consistently stereotypical. This has been the dominant focus of previous research examining the gendered dimensions of digital gaming, and content analyses of digital games at various times over the past decade appear to support this conclusion (Dietz, 1998; Greenfield, 1994; Kafai, 1996; Kinder, 1996). It has been claimed that the general themes of games are masculine (including war, crime, sport) and characterized by high levels of game aggression and violence, making them unappealing to females.

BREAKOUT BOX 11.2 ● ● ●

Common polarizations of male and female game preferences and playing styles

A number of differences are routinely offered to describe differences in digital gaming practices and preferences between male and female players. Some of these are listed below, but are these fact or assumption; natural or cultural; are the oppositions always so neat or do many games and gamers fit inbetween these polar opposites?

Female/feminine

Cooperative games
Puzzle-based games
Strategy and narrative

Male/masculine

Competitive games
Combat-based games
Action and scoring

(Continued)

(Continued)

Exploration and free movement	Repetition and completing levels
Creating	Destroying
Identifying with characters	Objectifying characters
Social interaction	Individual play
Mini games	Expansive games
Real world themes	Fantasy world themes
Learning to care and mother	Learning violence and confrontation

How do these oppositions apply to current digital games and are there any games which might combine these feminine and masculine aspects?

The analysis of 33 Nintendo and SEGA games (including *Super Mario 3*, *NBA Jam* and *Mortal Kombat 2*) conducted by Tracy Dietz (1998) demonstrated the ways in which digital games reproduced gender and sex stereotypes and how these were linked with violence. She suggests that it is not only important how women are represented in digital games, but that the 'most common portrayal of women was actually the complete absence of women', with this applying to 41 per cent of the games analysed (1998: 433). In addition, in 21 per cent of the games, female characters were proverbial 'Damsels in Distress' (1998: 433). However, the representativeness of the games analysed in these studies and the criteria by which gendered content was classified are unclear.

During the 1990s, game developers attempted to encourage more females to play computer games by developing games with a recognizably 'feminine' theme. In 1991 the Nintendo GameGirl was released and in November 1996 Mattel released *Barbie Fashion Designer*, which sold more than 200,000 units in the first month of release (Gorriz and Medina, 2000). However, the success of such attempts to expand gaming into the female market have not been sustained and were located within traditional conceptualizations of feminine interests and skills. As such they tended to reinforce the essentialist notion that females are not interested in 'masculine' activities and themes, and the binary opposition between gender categories which has been increasingly critiqued in contemporary gender theory.

Many of the games which are popular today continue to represent females in sexualized and stereotypical ways, as objects of voyeuristic spectacle or as narrative devices whose role continues to be a reward or object to be rescued (as in the cases of *Dead or Alive, Extreme Beach Volleyball, Project Rub* or *Fable*). This is consistent with a more recent analysis of 27 of the most popular PlayStation, Dreamcast and Nintendo 64 games in October 2000 which suggested that:

- Of games, 92 per cent had male lead characters, whereas 54 per cent had female lead characters.
- Of the games that contained female characters, almost half of them portrayed women in an unhealthy or stereotypical way.
- Of games, 38 per cent displayed female characters with significant body exposure; 23 per cent showed exposed breasts or cleavage; 31 per cent showed exposed thighs; 15 per cent displayed exposed behinds and 31 per cent showed exposed stomachs or midriffs.
- Of female, 38 per cent of characters had 'disproportionately large' breasts and 46 per cent had 'disproportionately small' waists.
- Of the characters, 85 per cent had large breasts, unusually small waists or very thin bodies.
- Over half, 54 per cent, of the female characters in the top-selling games took part in violent activities, such as fighting or shooting. (Children Now, 2000: 3)

There is a prevailing understanding that such representations make digital games unattractive to many potential female gamers. However, one little addressed issue is the way in which gender representation within games, gameplay and gaming contexts is separated in analysis rather than examining their interaction. Citing previous research of one of the authors, Yates and Littleton give some indication as to how these separate elements might be varied to different effect. They explored how successful children were at using two different versions of an adventure game:

> Two structurally isomorphic versions of a problem solving 'adventure game' were produced. The first, named 'King and Crown', consisted of a quest to recover a king's missing crown without encountering pirates and other obstacles. The second, called 'Honeybears', consisted of a quest to recover the bears' missing honey whilst trying to avoid honey monsters. Both games required the same solution strategy. Each game had characters with specific roles such as Pilot, Driver and Captain in the King and Crown; Airbear, Ponybear and Waterbear in the Honeybears. The representation of the bears in 'Honeybears' was as gender neutral as possible whereas the King and Crown contained more overtly male characters. (1999: 572–3)

Measuring performance by the number of 'successful moves', they found that girls' performance was 'substantially affected by the version of software in use' (1999: 573) despite the tasks being identical in both games. Performance of the boys, however, was not notably affected. Similarly, they report another experiment where the key activity was moving an onscreen hoop along a wavy line (in a manner similar to 'Electric Eels' found in fairgrounds). In this apparent test of hand–eye coordination, boys performed notably better when the activity was presented as a game rather than a task.

The importance of this work from Yates and Littleton is that it highlights that gendered representation has an apparent effect not only on whether females are likely to enjoy a game or be more disposed to playing it, but that it is apparently related to how well players are likely to perform. It demonstrates some of the ways in which digital games can be understood not just as representations of gender but cultural texts which are subject to having symbolic meaning read onto them (see Crawford and Rutter, Chapter 8). It is not necessarily digital games which are unappealing to certain females, but the way in which the game aesthetics are designed primarily to cater for male interests.

However, despite the breadth of highly gendered content in digital games, there are also a growing number of strong and capable female lead game characters. While many of these are still designed to fit masculine expectations of female sexuality (for example, Lara Croft in *Tomb Raider*, Jen in *Primal*), there are lead characters, such as Samus Arran in *Metroid Prime*, for whom being the object of male gaze is not the defining aspect of their representation. Such developments create possibilities for negotiating gender in digital gaming for both male and female players.

Other games also provide the opportunity to choose between playing as male or female characters (*Crazy Taxi*, *EverQuest*), alternate between playing as male and female characters during the game (*Gabriel Knight 3*), or create female skins for game characters (the *Quake* series). Further, the development of games such as *The Sims* and the increasing popularity of online gaming provide much more flexibility in the gendering of game characters as character creation and development is controlled to a large extent by gamers themselves. Similarly, MMORPGs, such as *Everquest*, *Star Wars Galaxies* or *Lineage* are built around communities of gamers who are able to choose their own characters' gender and behaviour, and play more than one avatar simultaneously. As such this places the potential for gendered and stereotypical or resistive character construction within the control of the individual consumer, consistent with performative theories of gender.

The increased inclusion of female characters who are presented in non-stereotypical feminine roles are consistent with changing understandings of what constitutes contemporary femininity. As such, they are consistent with changing female representations in the media in general, resistance to the traditional gendering of leisure interests and activities. In addition, they represent the continuing attempts of the games industry to appeal to a wider market of female gamers.

● Conclusion

This chapter has examined the gender dynamics of digital gaming and the proposed lack of female participation in this leisure activity. It has examined the spaces and content which constitute digital gaming, and demonstrated that gender is an important factor in the management of access to, and participation in, this activity. While female gaming in public spaces is relatively infrequent, survey data suggests that casual and domestic gaming is almost as popular among females as males in younger age groups. However, access and participation within this traditional feminine leisure space is still subject to the gender dynamics of technological access and the stereotyping of associated skills and interests in important ways.

The changing nature of female representation within contemporary game content, the increasing number of strong female characters, gamer controlled character development and female gaming clans are all evidence of a change in the gender dynamics of digital gaming. However, this must be considered within the context of the continuing strong identification of gaming culture as masculine. With development of these apparently contradictory trends it is, we argue, most useful to explore the ways in which these changes are consistent with changes in female participation in other activities considered to be 'masculine' (sports including rugby and football [soccer]). These activities can provide spaces in which the traditional conceptualizations of masculinity, femininity and their associated classifications of acceptable behaviour and interests can be challenged.

In addition, there has been a notable lack of analysis of representations of masculinity within games. The potential influence of engagement with these representations by both male and female gamers, and their relationship with the development of gendered identities, is another important area for future study.

However, it is important to consider gendered representations within games as consistent with that of other media such as film and television. These media reflect societal conceptualizations of masculinity and femininity, and are an important influence on the development of the gendered identities through which individuals learn gender-appropriate interests and behaviours. Alteration or reduction of stereotypical female representations within games cannot be entirely effective if conducted in isolation from the wider societal gender stereotypes present in all forms of media. Digital games are cultural products and, as such, sit within a rich menu of available leisure and consumption options. Changing the way in which gender is represented within games specifically, or in wider media representations will not necessarily lead to a change in gender role stereotypes within society, such change is required at a more fundamental social and cultural level. This is why an understanding of gender and digital games must incorporate a recognition of the role of societal gender stereotypes and role expectations, and the spatial and technological dynamics of gaming, in addition to analysis of game content alone.

Relevant web sites ● ● ●

'Call for radical rethink of games' news.bbc.co.uk/1/hi/technology/4561771.stm
Center for Digital Discourse and Culture's Various Fields Within Feminism www.cddc.vt.edu/feminism/fields.html
Game Girl Advance www.gamegirladvance.com
Game Girlz www.gamegirlz.com
Grrlgamer www.grrlgamer.com
IDGA's Women in Game Development Special Interest Group www.igda.org/women
WomenGamers.Com www.womengamers.com

Note ●

1 For reviews of the literature in this areas see Ferree (1990) and Korabik (1999).

References

Ahrentzen, S.B. (1992) 'Home as a workplace in the lives of women', in I. Altman and S. Low (eds), *Place Attachment*. London: Plenum Press. pp. 279–304.

Ashmore, R.D. (1993) 'Sex, gender and the individual', in L.A. Pervin (ed.), *Handbook of Personality Theory and Research*. New York: Guilford, pp. 486–526.

BBC (2004) 'UK gamers aim to take Korea', *BBC News*, retrieved 15 March 2005 from: http://news.bbc.co.uk/1/hi/technology/3577570.stm.

Bittman, M., Rice, J.M. and Wajcman, J. (2003) 'Appliances and their impact: the ownership of domestic technology and time spent on household work', SPRC discussion paper no. 129, The Social Policy Research Centre, University of New South Wales, retrieved 15 March 2005 from: http://www.sprc.unsw.edu.au/dp/DP129.pdf

Brannon, L. (2002) *Gender: Psychological Perspectives*, 3rd edn. Boston, MA: Allyn and Bacon.

Bryce, J. and Rutter, J. (2003) 'Gender dynamics and the social and spatial organisation of computer gaming', *Leisure Studies*, 22: 1–15.

Butler, J. (1990) *Gender Trouble: Feminism and the Subversion of Identity*. London: Routledge.

Children Now (2000) *Girls and Gaming: A Console Video Game Content Analysis*. Oakland, CA: Children Now.

Cockburn, C. (1991) *In the Way of Women: Men's Resistance to Sex Equality in Organisations*. London: Macmillan.

Colwell, J. and Payne, J. (2000) 'Negative correlates of computer game play in adolescents', *British Journal of Psychology*, 91: 295–310.

Crawford, G. and Gosling, V. (2005) 'Toys for boys? Women's marginalization and participation as digital gamers', *Sociological Research Online*, 10 (1), retrieved 31 March 2005 from: http://www.socresonline.org.uk/10/1/crawford.html

Dietz, T.L. (1998) 'An examination of violence and gender role portrayals in video games: implications for gender socialization and aggressive behavior', *Sex Roles*, 38 (5–6): 425–42.

Entertainment Software Association (2004) 'Essential facts about the computer and video game industry', retrieved 15 March 2005 from: www.theesa.com/files/EFBrochure.pdf

Ferree, M.M. (1990) 'Beyond separate spheres: feminism and family research', *Journal of Marriage and the Family,* 52: 866–84.

Foucault, M. (1986). 'Of other spaces', *Diacritics*, 16: 22–7.

Frith, S. (1978) *Sociology of Rock*. London: Constable.

Funk, J.B. (1993) 'Reevaluating the impact of computer games', *Clinical Paediatrics*, 32: 86–90.

Garfinkel, H. (1967) *Studies in Ethnomethodology*. Upper Saddle River, NJ: Prentice Hall.

Gorriz, V.M. and Medina, C. (2000) 'Engaging girls with computers through software games', *Communication of the ACM*, 43 (1): 42–9.

Gray, Ann (1992) *Video Playtime: The Gendering of a Leisure Technology*. London: Routledge.

Green, E. (2001) 'Technology, leisure and everyday practices', in E. Green and A. Adam (eds), *Virtual Gender: Technology, Consumption and Identity*. London: Routledge. pp. 173–88.

Greenfield, P.M. (1994) 'Video games as cultural artifacts', *Journal of Applied Developmental Psychology*, 15: 3–12.

Gunnarsson, E. (1997) 'Gendered faces? Teleworking from a Swedish perspective', in E. Gunnarsson and U. Huws (eds), *Virtually Free? Gender, Work and Spatial Choice*. Stockholm: Nutek. pp. 57–78.

Hart, R. (1979) *Children's Experience of Place*. New York: John Wiley and Sons.

Hermida, A. (2004) 'Girl gamers strike at the boys', *BBC News*, retrieved 15 March 2005 from: http://news.bbc.co.uk/1/hi/technology/3496963.stm

Hey, V. (1984) *Pubs and Patriarchy*. London: Tavistock.

Jackson, E.L. and Henderson, K. (1995) 'Gender-based analysis of leisure constraints', *Leisure Sciences*, 17: 31–54.

Jenkins, Henry (1998) '"Complete freedom of movement": video games as gendered play spaces' in J. Cassel and H. Jenkins (eds), *From Barbie to Mortal Kombat: Gender and Computer Games*. Cambridge, MA: MIT Press, retrieved 15 March 2005 from: http://web.mit.edu/21fms/www/faculty/henry3/complete.html

Kafai, Y.B. (1996) 'Electronic play worlds: gender differences in children's construction of video games', in Y.B. Kafai, and M. Resnick (eds), *Constructionism in Practice: Designing, Thinking, and Learning in a Digital World*. Mahwah, NJ: Lawrence Erlbaum Associates. pp. 25–38.

Korabik, K. (1999) 'Sex and gender in the new Millennium', in G N. Powell (ed.), *Handbook of Gender and Work*. London: Sage. pp. 3–16.

Kinder, M. (1996) 'Contextualizing video game violence: from Teenage Mutant Ninja Turtles 1 to Mortal Kombat 2', in P.M. Greenfield and R.R. Cocking *Interacting with Video*. Norwood, NJ: Ablex. pp. 25–38.

Krotoski, Aleks (2004) 'Chicks and joysticks: an exploration of women and gaming', ELSPA white paper, retrieved 15 March 2005 from: http://www.elspa.com/about/pr/elspawhitepaper3.pdf

Livingstone, S. and Bovill, M. (eds) (2001) *Children and Their Changing Media Environment: A European Comparative Study*. Mahwah, NJ: Lawrence Erlbaum Associates.

Maccoby, E.E. (1998) *The Two Sexes: Growing Up Apart, Coming Together*. London: Harvard University Press.

McRobbie, A. (1991) *Feminism and Youth Culture: From Jackie to Just Seventeen*. London: Macmillan.

McRobbie, A. and Garber, J. (1976) 'Girls and subcultures', in S. Hall and T. Jefferson (eds), *Resistance through Rituals: Youth Subcultures in Post-War Britain*. London: Hutchinson. pp. 209–22.

Morley, D. (1986) *Family Television: Cultural Power and Domestic Leisure*. London: Routledge.

Schott, G.R. and Horrel, K.R. (2000) 'Girl gamers and their relationship with the gaming culture', *Convergence*, 6: 36–53.

Schumacher, P. and Morahan, M. (2001) 'Gender, Internet and computer attitudes and experiences', *Computers in Human Behaviour*, 17: 95–110.

Sullivan, C. and Bryce, J. (2001) 'The Internet and masculinity: gender, technology and identity', paper presented to the British Psychological Society Wessex & Wight Branch Psychology and the Internet Conference, Farnborough, 7–9 November 2001.

West, C. and Fenstermaker, S. (1993) 'Power, inequality, and the accomplishment of gender: an ethnomethodological view', in P. England (ed.), *Theory on Gender/Feminism on Theory*. New York: Aldine. pp. 151–74.

West, C. and Zimmerman, D.H. (1991) 'Doing gender', in J. Lorber and S.A. Farrell (eds), *The Social Construction of Gender*. London: Sage. pp. 13–36.

Vanek, J. (1974) 'Time spent in housework', *Scientific American*, 231 (5): 116–20.

Yates, S.J. and Littleton, K. (1999) 'Understanding computer game cultures: a situated approach', *Information, Communication & Society*, 2: 566–83.

12 Digital games and the violence debate ● ● ●

Jo Bryce and Jason Rutter

To seek for evidence of 'the effects of media violence' is to persist in
asking simplistic questions about complicated social issues. (Buckingham
1997: 67)

Introduction ●

On 20 April 1999, two American high school students wearing trench
coats and armed with semi-automatic guns, rifles, knives and home-
made bombs went into Columbine High School in Littleton, Colorado.
By 12.30 that afternoon, the students, Eric Harris (18) and Dylan
Klebold (17), had killed 13 people and left over 20 injured in a 47
minute siege. Almost exactly two years later a group of families of
Columbine victims filed a lawsuit against 25 companies, including
Nintendo, SEGA, Sony, id Software, Acclaim, Activision, Capcom,
Interplay, Eidos, and GT Interactive, seeking damages of US $5 billion.
They argued that films and digital games, *Doom* in particular, had
directly influenced Harris and Klebold to kill their schoolmates.

Can digital games actually cause this type of behaviour? Is there
really a way of linking the routine playing of digital games to spectacular and extreme events such as those of the Columbine killings?

Concerns over the negative social and psychological consequences
of digital games, such as those claimed in litigation following the
Columbine tragedy, have been voiced by academics, parents and
governments for almost the entire history of the medium. This chapter
provides a critical overview of the theoretical and empirical literature in
this area. It specifically details the research exploring the hypothesis that

playing computer games, particularly those which contain high levels of violence, can increase aggressive attitudes and behaviours. A number of proposed effects of exposure to game violence and the methodologies used in such research are critically examined.

After reading this chapter, the reader should have a clear understanding of the proposed relationship between digital gaming and aggressive behaviour, the research that has examined these effects and the theoretical and methodological criticisms that potentially explain inconsistencies across research findings. This will provide the reader with the knowledge to approach research findings with analytical caution and the ability to contextualize their claims.

BREAKOUT BOX 12.1 ● ● ●

'Violence' and 'aggression'?

What is actually meant by the terms 'violence' and 'aggression'? These two concepts are commonly used in this research area but are notably different. While the terms 'game violence' and 'violent behaviour' are often used in the media and the research literature, the majority of research studies actually examine the development of aggressive attitudes and behaviour. However, as aggression is a social concept, observable actions are used as indicators or proxy measures. For example, aggressive behaviours can include attacking a doll, spreading rumours, play aggression, completing ambiguous scenarios with aggressive endings, self-reporting of behaviour, as well as time taken to recognize aggressive target words after priming through exposure to game violence. The definitional differences between the two concepts are outlined below.

Aggression

'Human aggression is any behaviour directed towards another individual that is carried out with the proximate (immediate) intent to cause harm. In addition, the perpetrator must believe that the behaviour will harm the target, and that the target is motivated to avoid the behaviour' (Anderson and Bushman, 2002: 28).

Violence

'Violence is aggression that has extreme harm as its goal. All violence is aggression, but many instances of aggression are not violent. For example, one child pushing another off a tricycle is an act of aggression but is not an act of violence' (Anderson and Bushman 2002: 29).

A number of negative consequences of the exposure to game violence have been proposed. These include claims that exposure to the media can cause individuals to believe that violence is a justified response to provocation, become less shocked by violence and aggression, and increase violent and aggressive behaviour in everyday life. However, attempts to link new media (and their uncontrolled availability) to the corruption of youth, women, ethnic minorities and the working class has a long history. From popular books known as 'Dime Novels' in the USA and 'Penny Dreadfuls' in the UK, to films of the home video generation including Sam Raimi's *The Evil Dead* and Stanley Kubrik's *A Clockwork Orange*, there have been fears that susceptible people will be made violent or otherwise corrupted through exposure to these media. These fears have influenced the research agenda for a large proportion of research on digital games, and much of this research has been based upon the theoretical and methodological frameworks of 'media effects' research.

Interestingly, authors such as Dill and Dill (1998) and Anderson and Bushman (2002) have argued that the consequences of exposure to game violence are actually more harmful than that of other media due to the interactive nature of games, schedules of reward and punishment, and active engagement with the game environment. The difference in the relationship between the gamer and game character has also been claimed to differ to that of the spectator/viewer of film and television violence (Anderson et al., 2004; Dill and Dill, 1998). As Emes argues:

> Television viewing is a passive experience; the viewer participates only as an observer. Playing video games, by contrast, is active, requiring more concentration and physical action. Video games involve the abstract simulation of aggression, whereas the violence depicted on television often imitates reality. (1997: 411)

The viewer of film/television violence has been conceptualized as a passive spectator, whereas the digital gamer is interactively engaged in controlling a game character and influencing the development of the game (see, Giddings and Kennedy, Chapter 8; Küchlich, Chapter 6). This interactivity has been claimed to increase identification with the character and their behaviour, leading to stronger reinforcement and modelling of such behaviour (Anderson et al., 2003). The media effects literature suggests that identification with the aggressor increases the amount of violence directed towards a victim (Leyens and Picus, 1973) and this argues that identification with violent game characters may increase aggressive and violent behaviour in everyday life.

These are serious issues for anyone engaged in researching digital games and given the quantity and methodological design of this research, it is important to develop an awareness and understanding of the key issues involved, the claims made by researchers, and criticisms of their research and analysis. The central issue in this area is not the violent nature of some digital games per se, but that engagement with them might encourage aggressive attitudes and behaviour in everyday life.

● Violent game content

A number of researchers have examined the characters, actions and themes of digital games in order to quantify the amount of violence contained within popular games at particular times. For example, a content analysis by Provenzo (1991) estimated that 40 of the 47 most popular computer games he surveyed contained high levels of violence. A more recent analysis, conducted by a panel of parents, rated the violent content of 78 of the most popular computer games in 1999. This study found that 25 per cent of the games contained intense representations of violence and 30 per cent contained some representations of violence (Walsh, 1999). Another study suggested that 89 per cent of games contain some level of violent content (Children Now, 2001).

It is hypothesized that frequent exposure to such violent game content increases aggressive attitudes and behaviour (Anderson and Dill, 2000; Anderson et al., 2004; Dominick, 1984). Studies examining this hypothesis have used self-report questionnaires to examine whether there is a relationship between the amount of time spent playing computer games and aggressive behaviour have had largely contradictory results. Lin and Lepper (1987) and Dominick (1984) found a correlation between frequency of gaming and aggressive attitudes and behaviours in male schoolchildren. However, this raises the question of causality – whether aggressive children prefer playing violent video games or whether video games make children violent. Other researchers have found that playing digital games had a calming effect on children (Kestenbaum and Weinstein, 1985), leading them to hypothesize that games help channel aggression, manage conflict and competition. They also found that regular gamers used play as a method of relaxation whereas infrequent gamers were more interested in competition and winning at all costs (Kestenbaum and Weinstein, 1985). This contradiction in research results is common and a critical examination of why this might be the case is provided in a later section of the chapter.

Priming and desensitization ●

Exposure to violent game content has been hypothesized to cause individuals to think more aggressively through the priming and elaboration of aggressive thought networks (Anderson and Morrow, 1995; Anderson et al., 1998, 2004). It is argued that digital games offer 'scripts' or models for appropriate behaviour in various circumstances. Scripts are cognitive plans which guide expectations, perceptions and behaviours in specific situations (such as how to respond to interpersonal conflict or how to behave appropriately in restaurants). These may then be retrieved or activated in the future to guide behaviour in a similar situation (Anderson and Bushman, 2002). The linkage between aggressive thoughts, emotions and behaviours has been claimed to be reinforced by repeated exposure to game violence, increasing their accessibility to activation in the presence of aggressive cues and situations, and subsequent aggressive behaviour (Anderson and Morrow, 1995; Anderson et al., 1998, 2004; Berkowitz, 1984, 1993).

Evidence for these effects have been demonstrated by research investigating the consequences of exposure to television and film violence, in which the cues associated with violence, such as the presence of weapons, have been found to lead to increased aggressive thoughts and behaviours measured by faster recognition of aggressive target words in a word recognition task (Anderson et al., 1998; Bartholow et al., 2005). Other experimental research compared the reactions of a control group of participants exposed to non-violent game content and an experimental group exposed to violent game content in an ambiguous scenario. Those participants exposed to game violence reported increased expectations towards a violent outcome in response to potential conflict scenarios (Bushman and Anderson, 2002).

Exposure to violent game content may also lead to the weakening of inhibitions against behaving aggressively and increase acceptance of using aggression to resolve conflict (Berkowitz and Geen, 1967; Dill and Dill, 1998; Huesmann et al., 2003). In addition, it has been claimed that gamers may become desensitized to the violence depicted within games and demonstrate reduced physiological reactivity to observation of violence. This increasing normalization further reinforces aggressive scripts and increases the likelihood that they will respond in an aggressive manner when faced with a conflict situation (Anderson et al., 2004; Dill and Dill, 1998; Huesmann et al., 2003).

Experimental research suggests that participants with a more aggressive personality (compared with those classified as less aggressive) showed decreased physiological arousal[1] when repeatedly exposed to scenes of violence in an experimental study (Lynch, 1994). There is also evidence this leads to desensitization towards real life representations of violence, and increases unhelpful behaviour towards victims. However, there has been no research examining whether decreased arousal actually stimulates aggressive behaviour, so the role of desensitization in determining short-term effects of exposure to game violence in the investigation of aggression is unknown (Anderson et al., 2003).

● Play and arousal

Playing violent computer games has also been claimed to lead to negative changes in affect or mood and increased levels of arousal which may lead to increased aggression to provocation after exposure to game violence (Anderson and Ford, 1986; Anderson et al., 2004). The excitement provided by exposure to violent game content has been claimed to have a number of physiological effects, including increased heart rate, systolic and diastolic blood pressure, which are related to the arousal of aggression (Anderson et al., 2003; Emes, 1997; Geen and O'Neal, 1969). This may lead to the misattribution of arousal to provocation by others and aggressive behavioural responses (Zillman, 1971, 1982).

Experimental studies have examined whether there are changes in affective states and/or levels of arousal before and after playing a violent, compared with a non-violent, game. Participants are randomly assigned to either an experimental group in which measures of various affective states or arousal (for example, hostility, irritability, blood pressure) are taken before and after playing a violent computer game, or a control group in which the same measures are taken before and after playing a non-violent computer game. Some studies have found evidence of significantly greater changes in affective states and levels of arousal after playing violent computer games, compared with those of the participants in the control group (Anderson and Ford, 1986; Ballard and Weist, 1996), while other studies show no evidence of such an effect (Nelson and Carlson, 1985; Scott, 1995).

Exposure to game violence is also hypothesized to influence behaviour through the modelling and social reinforcement of the behaviours they contain (Anderson et al., 2004; Bandura, 1973, 1986, 1994). Children learn behaviours through processes of socialization and systems of social reward and punishment from the family, peer-group, education and the media (Bandura, 1973, 1986, 1994). It is argued that gamers will imitate behaviour observed within their family, peer-groups and computer games when the person engaged in that behaviour is similar or attractive to them, when they identify with them, when the context is realistic and when the behaviour is followed by rewards (Anderson et al., 2004; Bandura, 1986).

Within such a theoretical perspective, violent game content has been claimed to reinforce the idea that aggressive behaviour is acceptable, increasing the likelihood that individuals will imitate violent game content (Anderson and Dill, 2000; Dill and Dill, 1998). Successfully playing a violent game requires the effective use and reward of aggression within the game environment, and this has been argued to encourage further play and exposure to violent content, increasing the priming of aggressive scripts and modelling of game violence (Dill and Dill, 1998). The often justified, rewarded and fun nature of represented game violence may also lead to the development of positive attitudes towards the use of aggression (Funk et al., 2003).

Dominick (1984) argues that game narratives often frame the game character as using justified violence against an 'evil' opponent who is using violence in an unjust, immoral or illegal way. Research suggests that justified violence, particularly that which has positive consequences for the perpetrator, arouses greater levels of aggression in spectators; compared with that which is portrayed as unjustified (Anderson et al., 2004). Such effects increase aggressive behaviour and weaken inhibitions against behaving aggressively (Berkowitz and Geen, 1966; Geen, 1990; Geen and Stonner, 1973).

Research on processes of reinforcement and imitation combine experimental designs with observations of child/adolescent play. Participants are randomly assigned to either a control group in which they play a non-violent game, or an experimental group in which they play a violent game. Both groups play their respective games for the same amount of time and are then observed in a free-play situation. Such designs allow an examination of whether the play of the children in the experimental group (those who have played the violent game) is more aggressive than those in the control group (those who have played the non-violent game). As with the research examining the relationship between frequency of gaming and aggressive attitudes/behaviours, research results in this area are often conflicting or contradictory. Some studies have found evidence that children in the violent game condition are rated as behaving more aggressively after playing, compared with those in the non-violent game condition (Cooper and Mackie, 1986; Irwin and Gross, 1995), whereas other studies find no such relationship (Graybill et al., 1987; Winkel et al., 1987).

BREAKOUT BOX 12.2 ● ● ●

The general aggression model

A theoretical and empirical attempt to combine the suggested consequences of exposure to violent game content is the general aggression model or GAM (Anderson et al., 1996; Bushman and Anderson, 2002). This model integrates perspectives on the learning, development, instigation and expression of human aggression, focusing on the knowledge structures (scripts and schemas) created through processes of social learning (Anderson and Dill, 2000). It also builds on research examining the use of knowledge structures in perception, interpretation and decision-making (Anderson and Bushman, 2002). The model specifies that knowledge structures develop from experience and influence perception at multiple levels, including complex behavioural sequences. Such responses can become automatized with use and be linked to affective states, and beliefs, guiding interpretations and behavioural responses to the social environment of individuals within their everyday lives (Anderson and Bushman, 2002).

● Moderating variables

In the previous section of the chapter we examined the proposed consequences of exposure to violent game content and associated research. The issue of causality was identified as central but potentially controversial. The 'casual effects model' (Harris, 2000), which dominates much of the research in this area, is problematic because of the assumption that correlation equals causation. An alternative perspective reverses the relationship and incorporates a consideration of the role of moderator variables in the relationship between exposure to violent game content and subsequent attitudinal or behavioural effects (Anderson et al., 2004; Wilson et al., 1997). This recognizes that vulnerability to the proposed effects of exposure to game violence may not have an equally negative influence on all individuals.

Individual personality characteristics have been hypothesized to moderate the effects of exposure to media violence. For example, highly aggressive individuals may be attracted to the use of violent media as a means of reinforcing and justifying their attitudes and behaviours (Anderson et al., 2004; Bushman, 1995; Gunter, 1983; Huesmann et al., 2003). Research suggests that highly aggressive individuals show greater development of aggressive thoughts and behaviour in response to exposure to game violence (Anderson and Dill, 2000; Bushman 1995; Kiewitz and Weaver, 2001). From this perspective, it is unlikely that individuals with no predisposition towards agressive behaviour would respond aggressively to violent game content. Although the importance of this is frequently acknowledged by researchers, it has not received sustained theoretical or empirical attention and remains an important direction for future research.

Critiques of the research literature ●

The research outlined above has produced a range of apparently contradictory findings rather than producing a coherent understanding of the possible consequences of exposure to violent game content for the development of aggressive attitudes and behaviour. In order to understand the contradictions in research findings, it is useful to look at a number of important methodological and analytical critiques of the research literature.

Correlation and causation ●

In some of the research conducted in this area, and certainly in popular discourse, there is often confusion between 'correlation' and 'causation'. For example, self-report questionnaire designs use correlations to examine whether there is a statistically significant relationship between two measured variables. If a correlation is significant, it can be claimed that there is a relationship between the two variables, but it is incorrect to interpret this as a causal relationship.

This can be illustrated using a hypothetical study which found evidence of a significant relationship between frequency of playing violent computer games and aggressive behaviour. What does this result then actually mean? It suggests that as the frequency with which participants play violent computer games increases, so does the frequency of aggressive behaviour. The important point to remember is that this does not mean that playing violent games *causes* aggressive behaviour, only that there is evidence of a *relationship* between the two.

Similarly, experimental designs in which participants are randomly assigned to play a violent or non-violent game only allow a statistical examination of differences in the measured outcome variables (such as aggressive play, word recognition times) between the experimental and control groups. In a similar manner to correlation, finding significant differences in the outcome variable between these two groups can only suggest a relationship between the experimental variable (level of game violence) and the outcome variable (aggressive play). This does not provide evidence of a causal link between the measured variables, only the existence of a relationship. Determining causal relationships between measured variables requires the use of more sophisticated and powerful statistical data analyses.

● Cross-sectional research designs

The use of cross-sectional designs in the majority of research in this area is problematic because they only provide the opportunity to examine the short-term effects of exposure to game violence and provide a snapshot of relationships between measured variables. Speculating about the long-term effects of playing violent computer games based on the results of research using such designs is not statistically valid, and requires longitudinal research. There has been a lack of this type of research because longitudinal studies require participant involvement over a long period of time (such as testing every five years for 20 years). This type of research is expensive and often suffers from high dropout rates and difficulties in maintaining participant involvement. Therefore, the conclusions that can be drawn about the long-term effects of exposure to game violence based on the existing literature are limited. If exposure to game violence influences attitudes and behaviour, such effects are likely to develop over a long period of time.

Conclusions cannot be extrapolated from the results of cross-sectional research designs, though this has been increasingly recognized by researchers in this area (Anderson et al., 2004).

Inconsistencies in operationalization of variables

Many of the studies investigating the relationship between violent game content, aggressive attitudes and behaviours use a wide variety of definitions of the variables 'game violence', 'aggression', 'aggressive personality' and 'aggressive behaviour', as well as different methods of classifying games as 'violent' or 'non-violent'(Goldstein, 2001).

These inconsistencies are demonstrated when considering the equivalence of the computer games used in experimental research. The process by which specific games are selected and classified is generally only vaguely discussed in the design sections of individual studies. The need for equivalence of games in empirical designs is central to the objective of controlling all sources of experimental bias, or factors unrelated to the aims of the study which differ between the experimental condition and the control condition. Ideally, the games chosen should only differ on the level of violent content as differences on other dimensions (for example level of interactivity, pace, complexity or genre) restrict the possibility to isolate the influence of exposure to game violence on subsequent measures of aggressive affect or behaviour. The researcher cannot definitively claim it is exposure to violent content which accounts for changes in the outcome variables. For example, the games used by Anderson and Dill (2000) in their experimental study of the effect of exposure to game violence on behaviour were *Myst* (non-violent) and *Wolfenstein 3D* (violent). The nature of gameplay and the objectives of these games are very different, regardless of their violent content, and this restricts the conclusions which can be drawn from the research results. Though this limitation has been recognized by some researchers, including recently Anderson and Dill themselves (Anderson and Dill, 2002; Anderson and Morrow, 1995; Anderson et al., 2004; Nelson and Carlson, 1985), it is not a common practice. Standardized methods for classifying games as violent or non-violent are required to increase comparability of results across studies.

Empirical research also uses proxy measures of aggressive behaviour such as observations of free-play, competitive reaction times, word recognition tasks and administering shocks to an opponent. However, equating free or 'rough and tumble' play or the intensity of administering shocks to an alleged opponent with aggressive behaviour is problematic. For example, although children's play may appear to be aggressive, it is qualitatively different from truly aggressive behaviour (Goldstein, 2001).

Sample size and generalizability

Sample sizes are relatively small in the experimental and cross-sectional research designs reported in the literature. For example, Lin and Lepper (1987) had 210 participants in their cross-sectional self-report study, Lynch (1994) had 75 participants for their experimental study and Irwin and Gross (1995) had 60 participants for their observational study. While it is important to recognize that different research designs have different requirements for valid sample sizes (for example, experimental designs require less participants than self-report studies), the size of the sample obtained influences the results of statistical analysis and the generalizability of the results to the general population. Given the popularity of computer gaming, it is important to consider the extent to which the results of a study using 100–200 participants reflects the relationship between measured variables in all gamers or sub-groups of gamers. Gamers are not a homogenous group, factors such as frequency of play, commitment, gender, age and genre preference all create different sub-groups of gamers. Unfortunately, the tendency to equate violent games with all computer games, together with the notion of gamers as a homogenous group, further impedes the ability to draw general conclusions regarding causality in relation to the consequences of exposure to violent game content.

Extrapolating to the everyday

Another criticism of empirical research in this area relates to contextual differences between playing a computer game in an experimental, laboratory-based situation and everyday gaming practices (Goldstein, 2001). Participation in experimental designs and random assignment to an experimental or control group provides no choice for participants over the game they play. This introduces a source of bias into the study as participants may dislike or be unfamiliar with the game. This may frustrate participants and account for the changes in attitudes and behaviour reported in some studies. It is of greater theoretical value to examine how individuals play and experience violent game content in the context of their everyday lives and leisure practices. This would provide more naturalistic data and allow stronger conclusions regarding the consequences of exposure to game violence to be drawn. It would also allow a more detailed examination, and recognition of, the influence of other factors in the development of aggressive behaviour such as developmental stage, gender and individual differences. However, such research is also costly and time-consuming to conduct, another factor explaining the bias towards the use of cross-sectional designs. Understanding how games are played and experienced in the context of everyday life is an important initial step in examining the potential consequences of exposure to violent game content within the everyday lives of children and adolescents.

Conclusion ●

Research on the proposed consequences of exposure to game violence is inconclusive and often contradictory. Further, the current body of research continues to demonstrate a number of issues which restrict the validity of attempts to apply questionnaire, self-report and experimental research results to the understanding of the antecedents of violent and aggressive behaviour in everyday life. For example, research has strongly focused on young children and adolescents, making extrapolation to other age groups problematic. This focus contrasts with the broad demographic of the computer gaming public where the average US digital gamer is 30 and the average game buyer is 36 years old.

Also, as experimental methods are designed to demonstrate a relationship between a stimulus and an action, they must assume that the target stimulus, in this case digital games, is asocial. As is demonstrated in several chapters in this volume, digital games are profoundly social in content, technology and use. Due to this, any digital game is difficult to conceptualize as a single discrete variable. Style of gameplay, duration of play, sound, graphics, imagery, narrative, experience, enjoyment and familiarity with equipment are all gaming-related factors experienced by gamers which have not been effectively delineated and explored by media effects researchers. This further demonstrates the failure of experimental research on digital games to adequately consider the role of these factors and their everyday, naturalistic contexts of experience.

As with the natural sciences, experimental effects research can only measure theoretically specified variables and draw conclusions about their potential attitudinal and behavioural effects. It cannot account for interactions that take place outside the experimental environment. For digital games, this means that experimental results cannot neatly be applied to the potential consequences of playing digital games within leisure and social contexts. They cannot adequately elaborate the complex motivational and experiential processes which surround decisions about when and how to play games. Moreover, the fascination with digital games as a stimulus for aggressive behaviour succeeds in reducing the importance of broader social and cultural factors known to have a significant effect on aggressive attitudes and behaviour. Much of the research described above fails to incorporate an examination of the influence of factors such as exposure to domestic violence, poverty and peer group relationships, and isolates the influence of the media on childhood social and cognitive development from its social and developmental context.

It is, therefore, important to examine the way in which game violence is experienced and the meanings constructed in relation to it. Approaches within media studies which examine the reception of violent media content are important in the developing context of digital games research as it can provide greater understanding of the processes by which exposure may increase aggressive attitudes and behaviours within the context of play, leisure and everyday practice (Gauntlet, 1995).

Given such a framework, it is impossible to demonstrate – and difficult to believe – that playing *Doom* turned Eric Harris and Dylan Klebold into killers in the absence of other psychological, social and cultural factors. While the media reports that Harris spent time producing mods of the game, and that one of the boys called the sawn-off shotgun used in the attack 'Arlene' after Arlene Sanders – a character from the novel *Doom: Hell On Earth* rather than the game – such stories are not evidence or proof of a definitive causal link.

This also raises the question of why digital games should be viewed as a catalyst for violence rather than any of the other factors which characterized the boys' lives. Reporting of the event shows that Harris and Klebold were exposed to a range of factors which may, or may not, have influenced events. Singly or together they were victims of school bullying, had parents with military training, combined a part-time job with education, had a history of petty crime, were enrolled on a juvenile diversion programme, were taking medication for depression, had access to weapons and were in home environments where guns and bombs could be stored in a bedroom without being noticed.[2]

In March 2002, US District Court Judge Lewis Babcock dismissed the lawsuit filed by the families of the Columbine victims. He stated, not that there was no link between the games and films the killers had seen and their subsequent behaviour, but that it was unreasonable to hold the creators liable for unforeseen acts of others. He said that requiring anyone who creates artistic or media content to anticipate and prevent 'the idiosyncratic, violent reactions of unidentified, vulnerable individuals' in their audience was impossible. As the quotation from David Buckingham at the beginning of this chapter suggests, the causes of violent and aggressive behaviour in contemporary society are more complex than much of the media effects research would suggest and require a recognition of the wide range of other potential causal factors.

Relevant web sites ● ● ●

Brad Bushman www-personal.umich.edu/~bbushman
Coalition of Entertainment Retail Trade Association www.erlam.org
Craig A. Anderson www.psychology.iastate.edu/faculty/caa
Entertainment Software Rating Board www.esrb.org
ESA on Games and Violence www.theesa.com/facts/games_youth_violence.php
Media Awareness Network www.media-awareness.ca/english/issues/violence
National Institute on Media and the Family www.mediafamily.org/research
Pan European Game Information www.pegi.info
IGDA Anti-censorship Statement www.igda.org/censorship

Notes ●

1 A reduction in the physiological factors (for example, heart rate, blood pressure) is associated with affective states such as excitement.

2 Marilyn Manson was also singled out in media coverage as one of the factors that made Harris and Klebold act as they did. One of Manson's articulate responses can be found at http://www.gothcentral.com/gothcentral/QuickShop/textfiles/manson.asp (retrieved 15 March 2005).

● References

Anderson, C.A. and Bushman, B.J. (2002) 'Human aggression', *Annual Review of Psychology*, 53: 27–51.

Anderson, C.A. and Dill, K.E. (2000) 'Video games and aggressive thoughts, feelings, and behavior in the laboratory and in life', *Journal of Personality and Social Psychology*, 78: 772–90.

Anderson, C.A. and Ford, C.M. (1986) 'Affect of the game player: short term effects of highly and mildly aggressive video games', *Personality and Social Psychology Bulletin*, 12: 390–402.

Anderson, C.A. and Morrow, M. (1995) 'Competitive aggression without interaction effects of competitive versus cooperative instructions on aggressive behavior in video games', *Personality and Social Psychology Bulletin*, 21 (10) 1020–30.

Anderson, C.A., Anderson, K.B. and Deuser, W.E. (1996) 'Examining an affective aggression framework: weapon and temperature effects on aggressive thoughts, affect, and attitudes', *Personality and Social Psychology Bulletin*, 22: 366–76.

Anderson, C.A., Benjamin, A.J. and Bartholow, B.D. (1998) 'Does the gun pull the trigger? Automatic priming effects of weapon pictures and weapon names', *Psychological Science*, 9: 308–14.

Anderson, C.A., Carnagey, N.L., Flanagan, M., Benjamin, A.J., Eubanks, J. and Valentine, J.C. (2004). 'Violent video games: specific effects of violent content on aggressive thoughts and behavior', in M. Zanna (ed.), *Advances in Experimental Social Psychology, Vol. 36*. New York: Elsevier. pp. 199–249.

Ballard, M.E. and Weist, J.R. (1996) 'Mortal Kombat™: the effects of violent video game play on males' hostility and cardiovascular responding', *Journal of Applied Social Psychology*, 26: 717–30.

Bandura, A. (1973) *Aggression: A Social Learning Theory Analysis*. Englewood Cliffs, NJ: Prentice-Hall.

Bandura, A. (1986) *Social Foundations of Thought and Action: A Social Cognitive Theory*. Englewood Cliffs, NJ: Prentice Hall.

Bandura, A. (1994) 'Social cognitive theory of mass communication', in J. Bryant and D. Zillmann (eds), *Media Effects: Advances in Theory and Research* Hillsdale, NJ: Erlbaum. pp. 61–90.

Bartholow, B.D., Anderson, C.A., Benjamin, A.J. and Carnagey, N.L. (2005) 'Individual differences in knowledge structures and priming: the weapons priming effect in hunters and nonhunters', *Journal of Experimental Social Psychology*, 41: 48–60.

Berkowitz, L. (1984) 'Some effects of thoughts on anti- and prosocial influences of media events: a cognitive-neoassociation analysis', *Psychological Bulletin*, 95: 410–27.

Berkowitz, L. (1993) *Aggression: Its Causes, Consequences, and Control*. New York: McGraw-Hill.

Berkowitz, L. and Geen, R.G. (1967) 'Stimulus qualities of the target of aggression: a further study', *Journal of Personality and Social Psychology*, 5: 364–68.

Buckingham, D. (1997) 'Electronic child abuse? Rethinking the media's effects on children', in M. Barker and J. Petley (eds), *Ill Effects: The Media/Violence Debate*. London: Routledge. pp. 63–77.

Bushman, B.J. (1995) 'Moderating role of trait aggressiveness in the effects of violent media on aggression', *Journal of Personality and Social Psychology*, 69: 950–60.

Bushman, B.J. and Anderson, C.A. (2002) 'Violent video games and hostile expectations: a test of the general aggression model', *Personality and Social Psychology Bulletin*, 28: 1679–86.

Children Now (2001) *Fair play? Violence, Gender and Race in Video Games*. Los Angeles, CA: Children Now.

Cooper, J. and Mackie, D. (1986) 'Video games and aggression in children', *Journal of Applied Social Psychology*, 16: 726–44.

Dill, K.E. and Dill, J.C. (1998) 'Video game violence: a review of the empirical literature', *Aggression and Violent Behavior*, 3 (4) 407–28.

Dominick, J.R. (1984) 'Videogames, television violence, and aggression in teenagers', *Journal of Communication*, 34: 136–47.

Emes, C.E. (1997) 'Is Mr Pac Man eating our children? A review of the effects of video games on children', *The Canadian Journal of Psychiatry*, 42: 409–14.

Funk, J.B., Buchman, D.D., Jenks, J. and Bechtoldt, H. (2003) 'Playing violent video games, desensitization and moral evaluation in children', *Applied Developmental Psychology*, 24: 413–36.

Gauntlet, D. (1995) *Moving Experiences: Understanding Television's Influences and Effects*. London: John Libbey Media.

Geen, R.G. (1990) *Human Aggression*. Pacific Grove, CA: Brooks/Cole.

Geen, R.G. and O'Neal, E.C. (1969) 'Activation of cue-elicited aggression by general arousal', *Journal of Personality and Social Psychology*, 11: 289–92.

Geen, R.G. and Stonner, R. (1973) 'Context effects in observed violence', *Journal of Personality and Social Psychology*, 25: 145–50.

Goldstein, J.H. (2001) 'Does playing violent video games cause aggressive behaviour?', Playing by the Rules Cultural Policy Center, University of Chicago retrieved 15 March 2005 from: culturalpolicy.uchicago.edu/conf2001/papers/goldstein.html

Graybill, D., Kirsch, J.R. and Esselman, E.D. (1987) 'Effects of playing violent versus non-violent video games on the aggressive ideation of aggressive and nonaggressive children', *Child Study Journal*, 15: 199–205.

Gunter, B. (1983) 'Do aggressive people prefer violent television?', *Bulletin of the British Psychological Society*, 36: 166–8.

Harris, J (2001) 'The effects of computer games on young children – a review of the research', (No. 72). London: Research, Development and Statistics Directorate, Communications Development Unit, Home Office.

Huesmann, L.R., Moise-Titus, J., Podolski, C.L. and Eron, L. (2003) 'Longitudinal relations between children's exposure to TV violence and their aggressive and violent behavior in young adulthood: 1977–1992', *Developmental Psychology*, 39: 201–21.

Irwin, R.A. and Gross, A.M. (1995) 'Cognitive tempo, violent video games, and agressive behavior in young boys', *Journal of Family Violence*, 10 (3): 337–50.

Kestenbaum G.I. and Weinstein L. (1985) 'Personality, psychopathology, and developmental issues in male adolescent video game use', *Journal of the American Academy of Child Psychiatry*, 24: 329–37.

Kiewitz, C. and Weaver, J.B. (2001) 'Trait aggressiveness, media violence and perceptions of interpersonal conflict', *Personality and Individual Differences*, 31: 821–35.

Leyens, J.P. and Picus, S. (1973) 'Identification with the winner of a fight and name mediation: their differential effects upon subsequent aggressive behavior', *British Journal of Social and Clinical Psychology*, 12: 374–7.

Lin, S. and Lepper, M.R. (1987) 'Correlates of children's usage of videogames and computers', *Journal of Applied Social Psychology*, 17: 72–93.

Lynch, P.J. (1994) 'Type A behaviour, hostility and cardiovascular function at rest and after playing videogames in teenagers', *Psychosomatic Medicine*, 56: 152.

Nelson, T.M. and Carlson, D.R. (1985) 'Determining factors in choice of arcade games and their consequences upon young male players', *Journal of Applied Social Psychology*, 15: 124–39.

Provenzo, E. (1991) *Video Kids*. Cambridge, MA: Harvard University Press.

Scott, D. (1995) 'The effect of video games on feelings of aggression', *Journal of Psychology*, 129: 121–32.

Thomas, M.H. and Drabman, R.S. (1975) 'Toleration of real life aggression as a function of exposure to televised violence and age of subject', *Merrill-Palmer Quarterly*, 21: 227–32.

Walsh, D. (1999) 1999 Video and computer game report card, National Institute on Media and the Family retrieved 20 December 1999 from: http://www.mediaandthefamily.org/1999vgrc2.html

Wilson, B.J., Kunkel, D., Linz, D., Potter, J., Donnerstein, E., Smith, S.L., Blumenthal, E. and Gray, T. (1997) 'Violence in television programming overall: University of California, Santa Barbara study', in M. Seawall (ed.), *National Television Violence Study,* Vol. 1. Thousand Oaks, CA: Sage. pp. 3–184.

Winkel, M., Novak, D.M. and Hopson, H. (1987) 'Personality factors, subject gender and the effect of aggressive videogames on aggression in adolescents', *Journal of Research into Personality*, 21: 211–23.

Zillmann, D. (1971) 'Excitation transfer in communication-mediated aggressive behavior', *Journal of Experimental Social Psychology*, 7: 419–34.

Zillmann, D. (1982) 'Television viewing and arousal', in D. Pearl, L. Bouthilet and J. Lazar (eds), *Television and Behavior: Ten Years of Scientific Progress and Implications for the Eighties: Vol. 2. Technical Reviews* (DHHS Publication No. ADM 82–1196). Washington, DC: US Government Printing Office. pp. 53–67.

13   Digital games and education ● ● ●

Tim Dumbleton and John Kirriemuir

ICT in the classroom ●

The increase in access to digital media is having a profound effect on policy and practice in education in the USA and the UK. Educational technology, or information and communications technology (ICT), is providing opportunities for teachers and pupils to engage with learning in different and new ways. For example, with easy access to enormous amounts of information via the Internet, teaching practice is moving away from a model where the teacher is the source of information, to a position where there is more emphasis on teachers enabling children to investigate, evaluate and interpret the resources available to them.

Pupils, in most cases, have grown up with digital technology around them and as a normal part of their environment. However, for most teachers, digital technology in the classroom presents new challenges and skills to learn. In the book *Digital Game-based Learning*, Prensky describes this relationship as follows:

> The Games Generations ... are *native speakers* of the digital language of computers, video games and the Internet. Those of us who were *not* born into this world but have, at some later point in our lives, become fascinated by and adopted many or most aspects of the new technology are, and will always be, compared to them 'digital immigrants'. (2000: 46)

This presents a unique position for many teachers, who are using technology in their lessons with pupils who will be more comfortable, and in some cases, more practised with that technology. At home, children are more likely to use digital technology, especially games technology, and bring to school very different expectations and interpretations of technology from their teachers.

In terms of structure, USA and English education are similar with an elementary or primary phase (USA: K-Grade 6; England: Foundation to Key Stage 2) and a secondary phase (USA: Grades 7–12; England: Key Stages 3 and 4). Also, both systems use a broad curriculum of subjects and topics to underpin children's learning and provide a common framework for teachers. The other countries in the UK (Scotland, Wales and Northern Ireland) have devolved but comparable education systems.

Publicly funded schools in both the USA and England have seen an enormous increase in access to hardware for teaching and learning. A key measurement used has been Internet access in schools. The USA has seen an increase from 3 per cent in 1994 of publicly funded schools with Internet access to an instructional room to 87 per cent in 2001. Similarly, in England, there has been an increase of Internet access to schools from 24 per cent in 1998 to over 99 per cent in 2002.

The introduction of technology as a key component in education (although it has been a strand for well over a decade) has meant that the majority of teachers may have found themselves being required to use something that is unfamiliar to them. Even where a teacher may use a computer domestically, this experience can be a stark contrast to combining learning objectives and knowledge of appropriate hardware and software, and delivering this in a classroom setting. This takes knowledge, support, and vitally, confidence. In attempting to provide the knowledge and support to help develop confidence, there are US and English schemes to collate or clearly 'badge' software and web resources as being suitable for use at a certain Grade or Key Stage (such as the Federal Resources for Educational Excellence website [USA www.ed.gov/free/index.html] or Curriculum Online [UK www.curriculumonline.gov.uk]).

Along with this are publicly funded sources of guidance on the use of technology and educational software publishers normally ensure that their products are marketed with teachers' notes and clear indications of curriculum relevance. This is not to say that educational technology and software is a closed shop; as any technology is only as valuable as the context it is used in, and there is no bar on what teachers can use, as long as it clearly supports learning objectives.

However, given that knowledge, support and confidence are key in an educational framework, most teachers will focus on what they have knowledge and experience of and what is clearly relevant to their situation. Willingness to experiment with software that has a poor public image, has not been designed for use in education and will not necessarily have any curriculum relevance is a very different proposition. Therefore, clear examples of effective games use in classroom situations and a good evidential base are needed if the links between games and educational objectives are to be considered.

Using digital games to educate ●

It is important to consider that education is not an activity confined to schools. Learning occurs at the home, in work, and more implicitly, in activities such as those of a social nature. Digital games and simulations are increasingly used as a facilitation, training or content exploration device in a number of fields.

Types of educational digital games ●

The current spectrum of educational digital games can be categorized as appearing in, or on, the following forms and platforms:

- **Edutainment** These are games explicitly designed to be educational in nature. Edutainment software has predominantly appeared on PCs, this being the IT platform of choice in the classroom.
- **Console games** These are 'pure' games developed for video games consoles, such as the Nintendo GameCube, Sony PlayStation 2 and Microsoft Xbox.
- **PC (and Apple) games** These are 'pure' games developed for use predominantly on a PC (though, increasingly, multi-platform games are developed for the PC and consoles).
- **Internet-based games** These are constructed in application languages such as Flash, and are typically much simpler than PC and console-based games.

Content and information is transmitted from the game to the user in one of two ways:

- **Textual** Here, the user is explained a particular situation in a straightforward written manner. For example, in the historical simulation game *Waterloo: Napoleon's Last Stand*, there is a section that explains the background history, and the historical scenario, prior to the battle of Waterloo.

- **Non-textual** Here, information is given to the user graphically, in picture, sound or animation form. For example, in medieval strategy simulations, the attire, urban environment and weaponry of tribes and nations is often displayed statistically or in animated form.

However, the real usefulness of digital games in education comes not of their use as 'dumb' transmitters of information, but as tools which the player (or learner) can use to create, manipulate, experiment and explore not just raw data, but scenarios, experiments and strategies.

For example, the simulation game from Maxis, *SimCity*, invites the player to take on the role of mayor of a city. The player allocates funds to building infrastructure such as schools, roads, hospitals and power utilities. Computer-controlled 'people' decide whether to move into a neighbourhood (or move out) depending on the facilities and infra-structure available. A lack of schools, if the player has allocated funds for other developments, will lessen the attractiveness of the neigh-bourhood to families.

In military simulations, similar 'cause-and-effect' simulations can be rendered. In the aforementioned *Waterloo* game, the player can alter the variables such as the weather conditions (which played a signifi-cant effect on the battle) in order not only to engage with the games but allow exploration of how these variables might have affected the move of Napoleon's troops towards Wellington's positions.

These cause and effect scenarios within games are of great potential to the educational, business and training sectors as:

- results (the 'effect') can be obtained quickly, therefore providing feedback on the outcome of a particular strategy;
- they can be re-run, often quickly, with various factor changes to view alternative outcomes;
- with some games, scenarios could be developed by a facilitator with a view to repeated use;
- in scientific simulations, such as mixing of chemicals to view reactions, there is no cost, mess, or (in these litigious times) danger involved.

However, there are significant drawbacks with such approaches, including:

- Scenarios are limited to the complexity of the games. The number of variables that the player can alter are, in most cases, limited. Real life contains an almost limitless number of elements, of varying degrees of likelihood, that can influence even mundane scenarios.

- Chance and luck, elements that occur in many scenarios, are infrequently programmed into games, or are provided in an explicit, limited manner. For example, elements such as a lucky shot or a friendly-fire accident killing a significant commander are rarely available in a battle simulation.

A computer-based simulation is not a replacement for real-life learning. For example, the student of chemistry may learn about reactions through the use of simulations, but he or she would still have to practice in the use of real laboratory equipment in order to support working or employment in a real laboratory.

However, firms in many industries use digital games or digital game-based technologies in order to train their staff, create better products or provide some kind of knowledge-based edge over their competitors. Four such industries conclude this section.

Vehicle design

Vehicle designers increasingly use simulations as a cost-effective and relatively quick method of modelling engine activity, before committing funding and resources to developing prototypes. There is a significant degree of collaboration, in both directions, between the video game and vehicle development sectors. The end product of this, for many people, are the street, racing and rally car simulation games.

Business and economics

There is a long history of simulations being used for teaching and training purposes within this particular sector. This is partially due to the relative ease of building such simulations, due to the base component being a discrete variable (a particular currency) and the mechanics being based on previously researched mathematical models. Complex economic simulation games are a core tool used in the training of staff who will be involved in macro fiscal work such as trading on stock exchanges.

Military simulations

Military games are, and have been, a popular category or multi-genre of entertainment games since the advent of home and arcade-based digital gaming. However, it is only in the last few years that digital games have been developed for widespread use by military forces. This is due to:

- the overriding need for accuracy in training as the soldier is learning about elements on which her or his life will depend;
- the need for realistic artificial intelligence, which can simulate things such as how opposing troops might respond in a counter-attack;
- the need for graphical and environmental realism as the soldier may require training in a variety of weather conditions; for example, opposing troops using the cover of a sandstorm to launch a surprise attack.

Medical simulations

The medical industry, like the military industry, has substantially more funding resource than the public educational sector. This has led to funding of increasingly realistic bio-medical simulations for use by doctors and medical students as well as more hardware-oriented technologies that can assist in remote surgery and medical assistance. However, the medical industry is highly protective of intellectual and other kinds of property rights. This, and an absence of gaming genres with a strong medical component, has meant that, so far, relatively little medical simulation technology has filtered through to the games industry for inclusion in commercial games.

Digital games in the classroom

Although there is a growing body of research and published papers which highlight desirable educational effects games may have (Jones, 1997; Mumtaz, 2000; Turkle, 1984) or how aspects of games may be repurposed in educational software, there are few explicit examples of the use of pure games to support a formal curriculum in the classroom.

In England, both the British Educational Communications and Technology Agency (Becta, 2001) and Teachers Evaluating Educational Multimedia (TEEM, 2002) have produced evaluation reports about the use of games in the classroom. The evaluations involved the use of a range of games, such as *The Sims*, and Microsoft's *Age of Empires*. Both reports offer broadly similar conclusions about the potential of games suggesting that where games are used in the classroom environment it is notable that:

- Pupil engagement is notably increased.
- Teamwork and thinking skills can be well supported by certain types of games.

However, less enthusiastically, they reported that:

- It can be difficult to maintain pupils' focus on learning objectives.
- Factual content relevant to the curriculum is minimal.

One specific example of attempts to understand the implementation of digital games in the classroom is the action research project 'Using a simulation game to aid understanding of Number' supported by The Learning Circuit. The project involved Key Stage 2 (8–11-year-old) pupils from four English schools. It focused on the use of *SimCity 2000* to support teaching and learning relevant to the ICT and Mathematics Curriculum and the Numeracy Strategy in the English National Curriculum. The key learning objectives addressed included understanding of simulations, making predictions based on the consequences of previous actions, analysing data and presenting findings, and responding to a given problem along with predicting and hypothesizing about possible answers.

Only one of the schools used the game directly in the weekly ICT lessons while other schools opted to use it during a weekly lunchtime club. The pupils used *SimCity* to support a number of activities such as exploring a simulation of an existing sim city, changing variables in the games and predicting consequences; identifying, extracting and interpreting data from the many charts and graphs used in *SimCity* and working in teams to develop strategies to improve a city. The teachers were positive about the effects of the game and its relevance to the teaching objectives. However, the critical factor limiting further effects of using *SimCity* was the difficulty in fully exploiting the game in the time available. All the teachers commented that if they were to repeat the work more time would be needed to use the games and discuss related topics in order to draw out the full educational benefits.

SimCity was introduced as a discrete case study project and so the report describes this rather than offering a snapshot of its ongoing use in the schools. The project involved the support of education advisors from the Local Education Authority in its instigation and implementation. The project gained legitimacy through the support of the advisors. The fact that three of the schools used the game during break times may suggest that using the game needed careful introduction and that due to that it could not be given priority over established resources in a lesson because it was 'unproven'. After the end of the project, the comments from the teachers were very positive with some either wishing they had had more time or expressing their intention to use the game again in extended work.

In terms of the actual value of the game itself the commentaries provided mainly emphasize the positive effect it had on helping pupils understand mathematics in a real-life situation and the effects of good for-ward planning. Comments from both pupils and teachers highlight increased engagement with the learning objectives. However, partly from the teacher's perspectives and the questions asked, there was a greater focus on the details of the learning objectives it helped address. Importantly, the game was not used in isolation and many of the activities it was used for also involved cutting and pasting data from graphs and interpreting the data in other media. The children were undertaking many of the actions that are part of the normal game play experience of *SimCity* (building up towns into cities, maintaining the mayor's popularity and so forth). But in the educational context, the value was produced by drawing out certain aspects of the game activity, or using the game in a limited way to simulate how mathematics impacts on the 'real world'. There is no doubt from the evidence provided through the project that engagement and enjoyment were important, but it was the recontextualizing of actions that already exist in the gameplay that provided the educational validity.

Another possible reason for the success of *SimCity* in the classroom con-text may also be the type of game that it is. It is open-ended and not goal-based, its pace and style favours a reflective and investigative approach to play (for example, where one must analyse data to work out why a city is not developing). It is not a 'twitch' game (Jones, 1997) where immediate reaction and feedback are central elements. Instead, *SimCity* requires the player to plan, test, analyse and plan again. This perhaps lends itself more obviously to many teaching and learning styles used for formal curricula. Twitch games may have their place in learning, but may be more difficult to integrate with existing educational practices in the first place.

There has been significant work in the USA to repurpose both games and games technology for classroom use; rather than evaluating the use of pure games. The Lightspan initiative provides PS One games consoles and compatible educational software to schools and families. Other examples, such as the Electronic Games for Education in Math and Science (EGEMS) project in Canada and the MIT Games to Teach programme, took aspects of games and integrated them into curricu-lum specific software.

Assessment through digital games ●

One of the crucial elements in any application of technology in education is that information relevant to the external assessment of learning is made available. It is vital for a pupil's achievement to be recognized for the accountability of schools. This does not mean that the technology has to be explicitly designed to record data for educational assessment purposes, but it must provide some kind of output that demonstrates learning.

For example, digital video is becoming more popular in schools as an engaging and flexible use of technology. The outputs of digital video activities can form part of a larger work (such as digital photos in a report) or may itself 'prove' a learning achievement as would a short film requiring script writing, media literacy and collaboration. Games, as argued in the TEEM report, seem to offer much potential for providing information about attainment (in this case within the game world itself) yet so far have not appeared to be able to provide clear information or exemplars relevant to formal educational assessment; for example, see the TEEM report (2002).

This seems odd given the importance of gameplay achievements that underpin most games – whether it is through player statistics on an *Unreal Tournament* server or completing *Metal Gear Solid* (*MGS*) once and being awarded the infinite ammo and bandana. In addition, the interest of some games is the way in which they capture and reinterpret data about a player's actions (as in the nurturing of the creature in *Black & White*). However, it is difficult to see how achievements such as getting the *MGS* bandana could be integrated in formal education assessment for two main reasons:

(1) The achievement only exists in that game and the game does not encourage the player to re-interpret their actions for other contexts. The bandana is a token of achievement rather than a demonstration of the learning that may have taken place. For the bandana to have external relevance, it would have to be generally, and formally, accepted what getting the bandana means.

(2) Educational assessment measures a combination of skills and knowledge that is recognized as culturally and economically valuable. Whereas there may certainly be skills expressed by completing *MGS*, there is little or no knowledge gained that is directly relevant to a curriculum subject: the storyline and subject matter of *MGS* is not 'normal'.

MGS is only one example, and does not represent the full range of game types, styles and subject matter. There are games, such as *Europa Universalis 1* and *2*, which do combine educationally useful facts with gameplay. However, even this example brings up another problem with educational use: the gameplay itself may detract from the facts contained within the game's subject matter (Europe between 1500 and 1800). Unless key areas of knowledge (such as the Spanish Armada) can be isolated, explored further and combined with other learning activities, then the game (in educational terms) can become a rapid passage through historical facts.

More potential for educational assessment and games has been found in turning games around so that the very process of creating a game can demonstrate relevant skills and knowledge. For example, the Playground project and lesson plans provided through the *Game On* exhibition in the UK have capitalized on the range of skills and knowledge that the creation of games involves. In addition, this can mean that the purpose of the game could be based on a topic contained in a curriculum. In effect, games in this context become a portfolio of skills and knowledge, which can effectively be combined with evidence of learning (including materials from the planning stages, storyboards and so forth.).

This may seem to diverge from commercial games but instead it may be a path of convergence. Game modding kits and the availability of scenario builders or mission editors are now commonplace. They provide access to tools that allow players to change the goals of missions, the pace and even the imagery in games but retain the quality of the graphics or AI engines and other important elements for producing professional games. Although there can be variable levels of technical knowledge required, this is certainly an area of potential. This reversal enables the player to use the game as a platform for demonstrating planning, communication of ideas, expression and creativity.

● Games in the classroom: stakeholders

Though the individual child, playing or using a digital game, is the focus for most research literature, it is important to consider the influence and views of other people connected with this child–game scenario.

Teachers, parents and governors ●

A significant barrier to the broader adoption of games in the classroom is the perception by many teachers and parents that games – even educational games – have little to offer in a learning context. This can manifest itself implicitly, in the assumption that because it is a 'game' it is a use of funding that can be spent on better things (Malkin, 1999). Typically, concerns among parents, teachers and school governors about games include worries that

- they are violent or have improper content;
- they are a corrupting influence;
- they are a commercial, and not an educational, product, and have been developed not by teachers, but by commercial organizations;
- they are an inferior replacement for a teacher;
- games are a 'boys thing' and girls will not be interested;
- they are playthings …
- … and therefore are not learning.

Some of these perceptions are based on limited experience of games. For example, many parents would see their children playing video games that involve fighting or sports on their home-based computers or consoles and identify games as a whole with these specific genres. The same parents may not be aware of more educational games, or games with strong educational components, if their children do not typically play these at home.

Some of these concerns do have valid foundations. Many games are indeed blatantly designed and marketed for males in their teens and 20s and do focus specifically on sports simulations and certain fighting games. The issue of how much a pupil is learning while they are playing is also one in which, until the last few years, little relevant research had been undertaken. Emerging research does not paint a clear picture, in large due to the fragmentary nature of education and ICT research, but also due to problems surrounding the accurate measurement of 'learning'.

Pupils ●

For many pupils, playing digital games is a normal part of their social environment. One survey by Johannes Fromme (2003) on games and their place in children's lives in Germany provides a view of children's engagement with digital games which is a very different picture from that of anti-social children compulsively playing the latest game. When compared to other activities such as listening to music, reading or playing outside, Fromme found that digital gaming was shown to be not as popular, or regularly engaged in. Further, he highlighted the manner in which digital gaming is not an anti-social activity but provides children a basis for sharing tips, demonstrating mastery and having a common reference point with their peers.

However, games and games technology do promote very different experiences in terms of graphics, engagement and pace compared to pupils' experiences of educational software. Research into pupils' perceptions of software in the home and school carried out by Mumtaz (2000) clearly found that pupils often felt bored and unchallenged by educational software and related activities in school.

One indication of the difference between pupils and teachers in their approaches to games is in the use of cheat codes. These codes, which can provide the player with additional health or resources within a game, are simply seen as cheating by non-gamers. However, in their actual use, cheats provide the player with an opportunity to explore the game environment fully. This allows the game to take on a different form, in some cases becoming an opportunity to express creativity.

The games industry

Much of the industry that creates these products does itself present barriers to use in education. Apart from formal issues, such as single user licensing and pricing, there is not a culture of sharing ideas or collaborating on development projects. Financial pressures and the importance of maintaining unique selling points and intellectual property integrity leave little room for speculative projects or forays into untested markets. This financial pressure also manifests itself in often producing games based around tried and tested formulas which, as outlined above, may be in conflict with the content and format requirements of the classroom. This situation, however, has been recognized by some companies and is being addressed by the industry itself. A combined need to ensure that skilled workers are attracted to the industry and the drive to improve the image of the industry in general is being expressed by engagement with education systems at different levels in the UK.

Barriers ●

We have explored a number of scenarios where digital games could be used in education. However, especially in younger school-based education, such facilitation is not universal, or even widespread in some developed countries. There are a number of inhibitory factors, three of which are discussed here.

The cost of hardware ●

Commercial games development is driven partially by a need to provide the most realistic and spectacular graphics, sound and animation. This gives the product an edge over their competitors, and increases the 'must have' factor for the game. Unfortunately, such games also require state-of-the-art hardware, such as PCs containing a substantial amount of memory, hard drive space and powerful graphics cards. The need for a machine specification greatly in advance of the minimum specified by the game is often paramount to avoid an unacceptable portion of the lesson time being spent getting the game to a state where the pupil is able to commence interaction. Most public schools cannot afford to replace or significantly upgrade their PC equipment on an annual or six monthly basis, creating significant problems in using those games which require the latest PC capabilities.

The cost of games ●

Computer and video games retail at US $20–50 per unit. However, these are never sold in bulk, or licensed for a multiple number of users. Therefore, the cost of providing such games for a classroom of pupils can become expensive and difficult to justify. One solution to this problem may assist both the games development industry and the educational sector. Many games have a very limited shelf-life, as players typically want the newest or most up to date versions; it is rare that a game is still sold at full launch price even just 6 months after its release. Therefore, the game developers and publishers only have a limited window of time in which to realize their investment and make a profit (see Alvisi, Chapter 4).

This matters less with games used in the classroom, where considerations of graphical splendour and in-game features have a lesser priority to that of the relevance of the content. Therefore, older versions of games which are no longer commercially available could be made available on a discount/bulk basis to schools. One body of thought within the academic gaming research community considers that games companies should develop 'lite' versions of games which have some curriculum-relevant components. The package containing this game would include:

- teacher learning materials;
- pupil learning materials;
- a cut-down version of the game, containing the curriculum-relevant components only;
- removal of inaccurate components of the game as in the use of 'magic' inside medieval strategy simulations; and
- teacher verified documentation showing how the game is relevant to explicit components of the curriculum for the benefit of teachers, governors, parents and school funders.

This is starting to happen on a limited basis with explicitly educational titles such as the *SimCity* range of urban resource management simulations.

Classroom time and curriculum requirements

The pressures of classroom time (especially in heavily curriculum and test-oriented countries such as the UK and the USA) result in teachers being under pressure to ensure that the pupils are learning immediately. Even games that contain an obvious amount of educational components, such as a strategy simulation set realistically and accurately in a historical period, can present several time-consuming logistical problems. A series of non-gaming issues are routinely encountered by teachers wishing to use relevant games in the classroom:

- the game needs to be loaded or pre-installed;
- introductory sections, especially if repeating, need to be skipped over to save wasting time …
- … but instructions on using the game effectively cannot be missed, as these need to be learnt by the pupil;
- the teacher needs to know how to use the game immediately for educational effect, and therefore requires pre-lesson training in its use;
- the pupil needs to keep focus on the task in hand and not wander off into non-educational parts of the game.

Emerging trends ●

Increases in graphic and processor power within hardware platforms will result in more complex and impressive games being developed over time for conventional platforms, especially the stand-alone computer. However, there are two emerging areas in particular that offer, as yet largely untapped, educational gaming potential.

Mobile games ●

Mobile digital gaming is a rapidly evolving field, being primarily driven by advances and convergence in a range of technologies. Platforms for mobile games can roughly be divided into three, increasingly overlapping, groups:

- **Mobile phones** Mobile phone games from 1999–2002, which resembled those of the first console games in simplicity and graphical crudeness, have been superseded by more involving and complex games. Many mobile phone games allow local play such as the playing of a game of snooker with other people in the same room, using Bluetooth wireless connectivity.
- **PDA or handheld computers** As these platforms merge with mobile phone technology, so downloadable games are becoming more popular. There is already interest in educational uses of these devices, although not involving mobile gaming (see Becta, 2003).
- **Gaming consoles** The Nintendo handheld GameBoy series has been recently joined by the Sony PSP handheld console. Newer Nintendo consoles and the Sony device contain facilities for both local wireless play (where games designers have incorporated such a feature), or for wireless-to-Internet play.

Online gaming ●

Networked games have been in existence on PCs since the 1980s. Whereas many early games were heavily based around gaming scenarios such as role-playing and fantasy simulations, a take-up of such gaming by a more mainstream audience has led to a more diverse portfolio of online game genres. As an example of this diversification we can note that one of the largest demographics of online gamers involves middle aged and elderly people playing card games against friends and relatives.

However, the nature of online games means that their use in educational settings introduces complications involving security and online costs. Another significant complication is that of communicating with other players, especially in collaborative games, and with players who do not speak the same first language. Many online games offer varieties of in-game communication, such as limited vocabularies and microphone based speech.

There is an emerging school of thought that such communication-based games can help to counter the perception of games as being solitary, unsociable experiences, and also to assist students in developing speech, language, communications and social skills. Significantly more rigorously academic research is needed in this, and the whole genre of online games, in order to establish their educational relevance and potential. However, many schools and regional education authorities do have access to local area networks (LANs) or wide area networks (WLANs) which could potentially support educationally relevant aspects of online games.

● Conclusion: unmeasured potential?

As digital games continue to outpace most other media in terms of their complexity, content, usability and desirability, so their potential for education becomes more attractive. Advances in mobile gaming, and online gaming, and a widening of gameplaying demographics to cover all age groups and social classes, make the case for using such technologies in education increasingly compelling. Indeed, it is increasingly paradoxical that an interactive media that is used so much, by so many people, worldwide, is not already in widespread use as a vehicle for education.

Central to any significant expansion of the use of digital games in formal education, is the relationship between the digital games industry and the teaching community. The former has largely ignored the potential for using digital games technology to educate and teach; the examples described in this chapter are some of the exceptions, as opposed to the rule. The latter needs to look objectively and dispassionately at what digital games can offer and specify (in terminology both camps understand) what is required to make digital games a useful tool for public learning, education and teaching.

Underpinning this expansion is a need for a substantial increase in relevant, unbiased and robust research into the use of digital games in education. It is only through validated examples of where digital games can prove to have been a benefit to education, that widespread confidence in using these technologies will facilitate such an expansion. Much research in this area is reactionary and short term, addressing contemporary or media-oriented concerns (as funding is more easily available), rather than examining more detailed, or longer (in terms of timespan) effects of using digital games for education. It is here, and in unlocking the educational potential of this mainstream technology, that private, public and commercial funders can resolve this educational paradox.

Relevant web sites ● ● ●

Becta, Computer Games in Education www.becta.org.uk/research/research.cfm?section=1&id=519
Centre for the Study of Children, Youth and Media www.ccsonline.org.uk/mediacentre/main.html
Curriculum Online www.curriculumonline.gov.uk
Electronic Games for Education in Math and Science www.cs.ubc.ca/nest/egems/index.html
Federal Resources for Educational Excellence (FREE) www.ed.gov/free/index.html
Games and Education Research Network (GERN) www.bris.ac.uk/education/research/networks/gern
Game-to-teach Project www.educationarcade.org/gtt
Marc Prensky www.marcprensky.com
NESTA Futurelab www.nestafuturelab.org
Room 130 labweb.education.wisc.edu/room130
Serious Games Initiative www.seriousgames.org
Social Impact Games www.socialimpactgames.com

References ●

Becta (2001) 'Computer games in education project', Coventry, BECTA, retrieved 15 March 2005 from: www.becta.org.uk/page_documents/research/cge/report.pdf

Becta (2003) 'Portable ICT devices: handheld computers in schools', retrieved 15 March 2005 from: www.becta.org.uk/research/research.cfm?section=1&id=541

Fromme, J. (2003) 'Computer games as part of children's culture', *Game Studies*, 3 (1), retrieved 15 March 2005 from: www.gamestudies.org/ 0301/fromme/

Jones, M.G. (1997) 'Learning to play; playing to learn: lessons learned from computer games', paper presented at the Association for Educational Communications and Technology, Albuquerque, NM, February, 1997, retrieved 15 March 2005 from: www.gsu.edu/~wwwitr/docs/mjgames/

Malkin, M. (1999) 'Reading, writing, PlayStation?' *Jewish World Review*, 27 December 1999, retrieved 15 March 2005 from: www.jewishworldreview. com/michelle/malkin122799.asp

Mumtaz, S. (2000) 'Using ICT in schools: a review of the literature on learning, teaching and software evaluation', Coventry: Centre for New Technologies Research in Education, University of Warwick.

Prensky, M. (2000) *Digital Game-based Learning*. New York: McGraw-Hill.

TEEM (2002) 'Report on the educational use of games', retrieved 15 March 2005 from: www.teem.org.uk/publications/teem_gamesined_full.pdf

Turkle, S. (1984) *The Second Self: Computers and the Human Spirit*. New York: Simon & Schuster.

Index